BOOKS BY DAVID R. EYLER

Job Interviews That Mean Business

More Than Friends, Less Than Lovers: Managing Sexual Attraction in the Workplace (written with Andrea Baridon)

Sexual Harassment Awareness Training (written with Andrea Baridon)

Starting and Operating a Home-Based Business

The Executive Moonlighter: Building Your Next Career Without Leaving Your Present Job

The Home Business Bible

Working Together: The New Rules and Realities for Managing Men and Women at Work (written with Andrea Baridon)

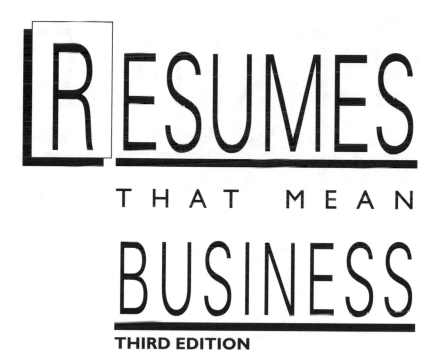

RESUMES

THAT MEAN

BUSINESS

THIRD EDITION

RESUMES

RANDOM HOUSE
NEW YORK

T H A T   M E A N
BUSINESS

THIRD EDITION

DAVID R. EYLER

To the divine discontent
that keeps us seeking more
—in our work and in our lives.

PREFACE

Whether you are an entry-level applicant or a mid-career executive approaching a six-figure salary, your chances of successfully applying for a new position depend largely on your power to communicate such vital information as your:

- Ability to do the job
- Appreciation for what the hiring company does
- Aspirations that are compatible with the position
- Awareness of job requirements
- Motivation to succeed
- Relevant preparation for the position
- Potential value to your new employer

All employers want assurance that you can meet these tests. Further, they want to know that you can establish this on paper clearly, succinctly, and in a convincing manner—preferably in one or two pages. That calls for top-flight resume writing skills and appreciation for what the hiring official wants to know.

Resumes that Mean Business is a highly pragmatic guide to the preparation of winning resumes. Eighty actual model resumes give you gut-level insights into what you should emphasize and what you should leave unsaid. Each resume is graphically critiqued to show you ideal resume length, format, and weighting of detail—what is *really* needed to bring your resume out of the stack. Example after example will show you how to convey meaningful knowledge—of what the employer *does, needs to have done,* and *why you are the person to do it.*

Supporting chapters provide you with essential information on:

- The role of your resume within the hiring process
- The employer's perspective—how your resume rates compared to others
- Your resume's role in getting you job interviews
- Word-processing, videotape, and other cutting-edge resume-preparation technology
- Electronic resumes
- Using the Internet
- Job-seeking advice for individuals with special needs
- Trends in the job market
- Protecting your employee benefits when you change jobs
- Accommodating forced career changes

The objective is to present you with examples of a wide range of the very best resumes. All of them represent approaches to jobs from the fastest-growing employment sectors of our economy. Traditional job seekers will glean both resume skills and useful career-potential information. Special-needs readers will gain fresh perspectives on directing successful searches with their particular purposes in mind.

David R. Eyler
deyler@worldnet.att.net

Arlington, Virginia
September, 1998

CONTENTS

INTRODUCTION

The preparation of a compelling resume is a practical art—a delicate balance of things said and left unsaid, detail provided and information meaningfully summarized, the efficient use of space and the power of pleasing graphic effect—or the deliberate lack of it in electronic resumes. You can learn by example and comparison. The purpose of this book is to give you the benefit of many examples and much comparison. From it emerge rules and suggestions for the right and wrong ways of composing a resume, but in the final analysis you are the judge of what makes the best case for your unique talents. The only arbiter that counts is the employer who concludes that what you have put on paper bodes well for what you will contribute to the organization's success.

Using This Book

This is a book that you will probably not read in order from cover to cover. It is arranged to let you choose the help you need and spend your time to best advantage. Still, *most* of the information will be useful to *many* people, so read this section carefully as you begin your task of building a great resume—it will guide you to the specific help you need.

RESUME FIRST AID

Set the stage for analyzing your own resume by examining five samples that are critically reviewed in before-and-after formats. This depth of comparison is not possible on the 75 Model Resumes that follow so use these introductory examples to see quickly how the same information can yield both failed and successful resumes.

75 MODEL RESUMES

The unrivaled core of this book is Chapter 3, "75 Model Resumes." Here each resume is analyzed to show you the general strategy behind the resume with 10 key points noted about the resume's content and composition. Paging through this section you will find the ideas and the inspiration to craft your own special and highly unique resume. The many examples, techniques, and formatting tips will help you pull it all together into something characteristically "you."

If you do not find your job title listed among the examples, that is no cause for concern. They were selected as a diverse group of employment categories that were both classic and contemporary—easy to extrapolate from—the kinds of situations that generalize comfortably to other fields. The professional person seeking a senior management position may well find the suggestion she needs in the example for a paraprofessional or tradesperson—and *vice versa*. You should view Chapter 3 as a repository of ideas and examples to be mixed and blended freely to your own best advantage. More details on how to do this will be presented in Chapter 1, "Preparing a Winning Resume," and Chapter 2, "How to Use the Model Resumes." Also refer to my companion to this book, *Job Interviews That Mean Business* (Random House, 1999), for additional information on how to apply and interview successfully.

PROTOTYPE RESUMES

Three basic types of resumes serve as the prototypes for the models:

- **The Work History Resume**—sometimes referred to as a chronological resume because jobs and personal data are listed in the order they occurred;

- **The Focused Resume**—often discussed as a targeted resume because it presents capabilities and achievements in a manner that caters to a particular kind of job; and

- **The Competency Cluster Resume**—also known as a functional resume because it groups skills and qualities under headings that constitute important functions in a particular kind of job.

Chapter 2, "How to Use the Model Resumes," goes into each of these approaches to resume writing in more detail. Remember that the prototypes are offered to illustrate how you have the power to take your employment assets and, in all honesty, arrange them for their greatest impact for the situation at hand. It would not be wrong or unusual to see a successful resume incorporate the qualities of more than one prototype—or omit one or two of the prototype's expected characteristics. There is nothing exclusive or discrete in the art of resume writing—be eclectic, and comfortably use what you glean from many sources in a way that best describes you for a particular opportunity.

PRESENTING YOUR CREDENTIALS

The written resume is certainly a key element in a job search, but obviously not the only one. Chapter 4, "Cover Letters and Interviews," deals with the cover letter, the interview process, and all of the subtle things that can turn initial interest, generated by a great resume, into an offer of employment.

RESUME TECHNOLOGY

Resume writing is still basically a matter of putting words on paper in the correct and most persuasive way. Yet the influence of readily available technology is encroaching in a number of ways. Understanding it and how to use it to enhance everything from the production of your resume to your ability to prevail in the subsequent phases of the hiring cycle can mean the difference between getting the job or falling by the wayside. Chapters 5, "Computers, Fax, and Videotape," 6, "Electronic Resumes," and 7, "Using the Internet," provide the advice you need to make your case most effectively. Internet tips are inserted throughout the book, suggesting relevant Web pages that can help you make the most of the latest resume and job search technology.

SPECIAL SITUATIONS

If you are among those *not* making a lock-step progression to the next logical rung on a career ladder, review Chapter 8, "Special Situations." There is timely counsel for everyone in the following circumstances:

- Individuals who have lost their jobs
- Individuals returning to the organizational world after a period of family-raising or self-employment
- Executive partners (spouses) returning to work after death or divorce ends a period of being in the midst of—but not an employee in—a successful professional career

- Students seeking part-time employment that will lead to full-time positions
- Early retirees from the military or other careers looking for new jobs
- People interested in nontraditional working arrangements that offer greater flexibility
- New citizens and foreign workers uncertain about communicating their skills in the American workplace

TRENDS

In this chapter there is a look at the job market and the work force as it shifts to meet the realities of another century. It can aid you in setting a course for a solid, successful work life. No one knows the future, but there are definite trends you should consider when planning a career. Chapter 9, "Trends in the Work Force," alerts you to what U.S. Department of Labor economists have to recommend in their most recent projections.

PROTECTING YOUR EMPLOYEE BENEFITS WHEN YOU CHANGE JOBS

When you leave your job, you will not want to sacrifice important pension and health care benefits that you may have a right to continue. In this chapter you will learn how to determine your entitlements and to invoke the laws meant to protect them if necessary. Complete summaries of **ERISA** (pension) and **COBRA** (health care) regulations are included, along with specific contacts within the agencies that administer them.

ACCOMMODATING FORCED CAREER CHANGES

You need to begin viewing career changes as something to anticipate in the normal course of your working life and plan for them. In this chapter you will learn: (1) to make the best of a job dismissal, (2) to plan future career changes as controlled growth experiences instead of a series of unpleasant surprises, and (3) to take a lesser job, if necessary, to renew your climb on the career ladder.

RESUMES

THAT MEAN

BUSINESS

THIRD EDITION

1 PREPARING A WINNING RESUME

Your resume has a purpose. It must impress potential employers sufficiently to consider you further in the hiring process. It is the document that—in one or two pages—represents everything you have done to become desirable in the employment marketplace. Salary, security, and career satisfaction all depend on the job you hold. Your resume shows where you have been professionally and where you are qualified to go next.

The preparation and presentation of a resume is part of the standard job-application process. It is at once a challenge and a great opportunity to make a favorable impression. Before hands are shaken or voices heard, images and expectations are formed in the minds of those who will judge your worthiness. Your resume makes those first impressions.

Why Your Resume Is Important

The hiring official is probably considering dozens, even hundreds, of applications along with yours. Equal opportunity regulations, modern communications, and highly mobile life-styles are but a few of the most obvious factors contributing to the large number of applicants for desirable positions.

Serious contenders will know the rules of the resume game and see to it that their resumes receive serious consideration. The hiring process often begins on a negative note—reducing the number of candidates to a manageable level. Here are candidates who are not contenders:

1. The sloppy resume senders. They could be perfectly qualified or even applicants whose qualifications make them standouts in the crowd. There are often a few such people in every hiring cycle. They are fine until someone just as good comes out of the stack who took the trouble to make a professional presentation.

2. The resistibles. Here are applicants who have dropped a stitch in the procedural quilt—they missed the "received by" date, failed to include the three references required, a college transcript, or whatever. They have given cause to be eliminated.

3. The underqualified. They lack the required master's degree or some other clearly advertised prerequisite, but thought that would be okay. Objective turndowns.

4. The negative standouts. They sent a mimeographed, unpersonalized cover letter; spilled something on their resume and sent it anyway; crossed out entries from their last try and scribbled in your key words or people; and so on. Subjective turndowns.

5. The poor communicators. Applicants who are apparently qualified, but whose resumes just don't communicate in some important regard—too much obvious fluff, too long (more than two pages, except in rare cases), sentences and paragraphs that go on and on, and so forth. They just don't come across as being capable of making their point—they are not the ones hired, if there are other choices. Largely a subjective judgment.

6. The overqualified candidates. They have held vastly superior positions or salaries, have degrees or work histories that are inconsistent with the position, etc. They fall by the wayside for inability to read the situation realistically, although they are not apt to be given that reason for the turndown. More than likely they will just find that someone else was judged to be "more appropriate" for the position.

7. The technologically–challenged candidate. Applicants today are expected to present at least minimal evidence of comfort with workplace technology. Ineptly sent e-mail, inability to check the company's Web page, a dot–matrix printed resume in an era of high resolution lasers and ink–jets all can flag applicants with unacceptably steep technological learning curves.

An executive in an East Coast human resources firm wrote in a *National Business Employment Weekly* reprint (Richardson, undated):

> I keep seeing resumes that are little more than buckets into which a lot of data has been dumped in the apparent belief that I will fill in the gaps, synthesize diverse information, connect the dots, and tell you what kind of product you are. I have no incentive to do this, given the number of knights eager to enter the lists. *It is not my job to make sense out of your life.* [Italics added.]

This man reflects the plight and the attitude of many potential employers who face large stacks of resumes. It is important to recognize that you have the power to present him with what he considers material worth reading as he moves rapidly through the pile cutting it down to size.

Communicating Technological Awareness

Candidates for most jobs, technical and otherwise, face the challenge of presenting themselves as being a good fit for the employer's technology environment. How they handle it depends on the position for which they are applying, their place on the technology continuum, and the actual situation.

If you are a non-technical person your objective is to come across as someone familiar with workplace technology as a user. Whatever your field, technology surely serves it and you should know the role technology plays, be conversant in the jargon associated with it, and be able to demonstrate at least minimal skills in using it.

As you go up the management chain, the ratio of hands-on technological expertise to simple awareness changes. The manager may not be expected to be a programmer, but it could be awkward if he were unable to perform routine operations on spreadsheet and word processing software. It might also raise eyebrows if she couldn't find her way around the Internet or use presentation software. Management candidates have to instill confidence in the hiring committee that they are aware of technology, can function intelligently with it, and know enough about it to hire and manage technical staff.

Technical people applying for positions on predominantly non-technical staffs have other problems to overcome. They need to come across as communicators who can relate to both worlds. People understand that they have to acquire someone with unique skills, but hiring committees react poorly to people who cannot relate to them on their own terms. They fear the Data Nazi, the technical staffer who some-how threatens to restrict and control the way they do business.

Your challenge as a technical-expert applicant is to show reasonable under-standing of the business in which you will function. Convey an appreciation for your understanding that technology is just one more way to accomplish the overall mission of the organization. Lead with the caveat that you would have to be there awhile before determining how appropriate such ideas might be, but generally re-late how you see technology making the organization more productive.

Resume First Aid

Before we discuss the rules for writing a great resume, let's look at some examples of what can be done. Following are a series of before and after versions of actual re-sumes that have been improved using the recommendations in this book. Start by just comparing the visual impact of the before and after versions. Then read the point-by-point descriptions of how and why they were changed.

The first aid section contains five resumes not found among the 75 Model Re-sumes. If you are later looking for an occupational example, return to this section for the following resumes:

- College Counselor
- English-as-a-Second-Language Teacher
- Investment Officer
- Senior Executive Assistant
- Senior Manager

It is also worth noting that these before and after resumes illustrate three of the Special Situations described in Chapter 8:

- *A person from another culture adapting to the American job application process* is illustrated by the English-as-a-Second-Language Teacher example;
- *A spouse returning to the job market following the loss of a life partner* is illustrated by the Senior Executive Assistant example; and
- *The transition from a military career to a position in the civilian sector* is illustrated by the Senior Manager example.

College Counselor

General Problems

Ms. Brewster's resume shows a profound lack of focus—both visually and substantively. The information is there, but she ignores the fact that resume readers will not take the time to make sense out of her life. She has to do that for them. On resumes, both the format and content must be logically presented to make the information readily understandable to readers.

Specific Points

❶ If the **Objective** is going to be a simple job title, don't add qualifiers that only say the obvious—"Counselor/advisor in an academic setting" unnecessarily complicates the presentation from the outset.

❷ The chronology hops and skips all over the place—if you cannot present a set of logically connecting dates, don't emphasize the irregularity by using this kind of listing. It is only recommended when one position leads neatly to the next.

❸ **Experience** needs to be sorted out—as presented, the reviewer faces an interpretation task that distracts from judging overall strengths. Their job is to evaluate, not organize, your information.

❹ Many of the experiences are very thin—that weakness is only made more clear by listing and describing each one separately this way.

❺ With little variety in formatting, the different parts of the resume blend together. Even with just the ability to use boldface and underline, it is possible to separate the different sections.

❻ **Education** is a checkoff item (you have it or you don't) for the kind of job being sought and belongs at the bottom.

❼ Never offer information that might label you eccentric or different. While there is nothing at all wrong with being a dream interpretation enthusiast, it is not something to feature prominently.

❽ Mention relevant skills, but play down the business aspect for this job.

❾ References are obviously available upon request—no need to say so.

❿ Musician information is harmless, but superfluous—she needs white space more.

BEFORE

Erika M. Brewster
2365 Northwest Avenue, Apartment 38
Washington, DC 20017
202-912-7666

OBJECTIVE: Counselor/advisor in an academic setting

EXPERIENCE:

1989 - Present   **Administrative Assistant: Association of Colleges Serving the Military (American Colleges and Universities), Washington, DC** Provide administrative assistance, including revising handbooks and other training materials used internationally.

1988 - 1989   **Conference Coordinator. American Education Association, Washington, DC** Managed logistics of national conference including: registration, travel and on-site arrangements, post-conference follow-up.

1988   **Advisor. Honors Program, The International University, Washington, DC** Advised and counseled students in large honors program; liaison between director and students; planned special cultural events.

1987 - 1988   **Counselor. Internship at The International University, Washington, DC** Led two small groups in addition to one-on-one counseling. Focus on unconscious processes as related to academic and social issues.

1984 - 1988   **Project Coordinator. The New Agenda, Projects JKSS, NETWORK, The International University, College of Education, Washington, DC** Managed the daily operations of an educational research office. Research duties included conducting preliminary research searches, report writing and analysis of data. Publicity duties included liaison between national media and project and dissemination of research findings. Managed logistics of training and dissemination conferences. Drafted and wordprocessed correspondence, reports and other materials. Fiscal duties included accounting, procurement and reconciliation. Supervised support staff.

1985 - 1986   **Housing Director. Shenandoah Musical Academy, Delton, VA** Administered all phases of resident housing. Duties included conflict resolution, informal counseling, supervision of student managers.

1982 - 1983   **Secretary. The International University Security Department, Washington, DC** Performed administrative personnel functions for part-time employees, including general payroll tasks, statistics, and projections. Duties included answering telephone calls, wordprocessing, typing and filing.

EDUCATION: **Master of Science in Education** (Counseling emphasis), The International University, Washington, DC, June 1988.
Bachelor of Science in Business Administration (Personnel), The International University, Washington, DC, June, 1983.

PUBLISHED WORKS: Three test-bank chapters in <u>Learning Theory Models</u>, Teachers Guide, Wilson & Wilson, Newhouse Press, 1987.
Articles in <u>The Finder</u>, Winter 1982, Summer and Fall 1984.
<u>Dreaming for Success</u>, Starlight Press, 1985.
Help From Dreamers," paper presented to the Dreamers Association, Fall, 1988.

OTHER: Owner of Typing, Inc. - a wordprocessing business, contract researcher and wordprocessor for special projects and dissertations; contributing writer/editor for <u>The Finder</u>; freelance musician; dream counselor.

REFERENCES: Available upon request.

College Counselor

AFTER: FOCUSED RESUME

General Solutions

Ms. Brewster's resume now shows unambiguously what she wants to do and lists, in order of importance, the experiences that will be of interest to the hiring official. Visually, the resume has been given several points of focus and white space separates one section from another.

Specific Points

❶ The **Objective** has been simplified to communicate clearly and remove unnecessary wording that might require interpretation.

❷ Since the dates of her jobs were overlapping and left gaps, they have been relegated to secondary status—provided, but not stressed.

❸ Experience has been grouped in its strongest possible clusters—first that which is directly related, next the more generally related, and finally the supporting information.

❹ Since the lack of primary experience in counseling will be apparent to someone in the field, the positions are related positively, but credibly, as student experiences.

❺ Type size and face were changed using a computer word-processing program. Variety tends to separate the sections more clearly and gives each section greater impact.

❻ Wording of her present position title was changed just enough to add an academic twist to an otherwise purely administrative job description.

❼ Dream analysis is mentioned, but more matter-of-factly. The comment linking it to counseling was eliminated since the avocation may taint the professionalism of the primary field. The resume is no place to assert rights, stand on principle, or advocate special interests with any potential for raising eyebrows.

❽ Word processing and research are treated more as skills, less as a business.

❾ Reference availability is omitted and nothing lost.

❿ Education is listed to confirm formal qualifications—no elaboration needed.

AFTER: FOCUSED RESUME

Erika M. Brewster
2365 Northwest Avenue, Apartment 30
Washington, DC 20017
202-912-7666

(1) Objective: COLLEGE COUNSELOR

(3) COUNSELING EXPERIENCE

- <u>Counseling Internship</u>: Completed a supervised practicum that was a part of my master's degree program. Consisted of leading two small groups and additional one-to-one counseling. Emphasis was on academic and social adjustment issues. The International University, Washington, DC, 1987-88. ← **(2)**

(4)
- <u>Honors Program Advisor</u>: Advised and counseled students in a large honors program. Served as liaison between students and the director. Planned cultural events. The International University, Washington, DC, 1988.

- <u>Housing Director</u>: Counseled students as a part of my overall duties administering a college resident housing program. Shenandoah Musical Academy, Delton, VA 1985-86.

(5) GENERAL HIGHER EDUCATION EXPERIENCE **(6)**

- <u>Academic Program Administrative Assistant</u>: Provide curriculum database management for college degree programs, including revising handbooks and other training materials used in the advisement of military students internationally. Association of Colleges Serving the Military (American Colleges and Universities), Washington, DC, 1989 - present.

- <u>Conference Coordinator</u>: Managed the registration, travel, on-site services, and post-conference follow-up for a major national conference. American Education Association, Washington, DC, 1988-89.

- <u>Educational Research Project Coordinator</u>: Managed operational aspects of an educational research office, including preliminary searches, report writing, analysis of data, liaison between national media and the project, dissemination of findings, logistics of conferences, preparation of publications, fiscal management, and staff supervision. The New Agenda, Projects JKSS, NETWORK, The International University, Washington, DC, 1984-88.

- <u>Secretary</u>: Performed administrative personnel functions including payroll, statistics, and projections, clerical and telephone duties. The International University Security Department, Washington, DC, 1982–83.

OTHER EXPERIENCE

(7)
- <u>Writing</u>: Authored three chapters in *Learning Theory Models,* Instructors Guide, Wilson & Wilson, Newhouse Press, 1987. Articles published in *The Finder,* 1987-88. Published *Dreaming for Success,* Starlight Press, 1985, and presented "Help From Dreamers" paper at Dreamers Association, Fall, 1988.

(8)
- <u>Wordprocessing and Research</u>: Owner of a private wordprocessing and contract research business.

EDUCATION **(10)**

- Master of Science in Education (Counseling Emphasis), The International University, Washington, DC, June 1988.

- Bachelor of Science in Business Administration (Personnel), The International University, Washington, DC, June, 1983.

(9)

English as a Second Language Teacher

BEFORE

General Problems

Ms. Wang is a foreign student. Most of her experience and education are from China. While her resume does a good job of listing the facts of her situation, it does little to explain what she is trying to accomplish and why that is a plausible goal. Equal formatting strength is given to important and far less important items of information. The reader has to struggle to package her attributes in a way that shows her potential.

Specific Points

1. Her name would be unfamiliar to most American employers—they need to know at least whether they are addressing a woman or man, if for no other reason than corresponding with her comfortably.

2. None of the **Work Experience** entries describe duties, beyond job titles.

3. American and foreign experience is combined and, while not difficult to distinguish, the two should be shown more clearly.

4. **Education** lists specialized foreign certificates on a par with degrees and offers no explanation of their content or relative value.

5. Translation experience is useful, but the listing does nothing to enhance it.

6. The interpreter experience is also useful, but lacks any focus.

7. Office skills are worth mentioning, but need a professional context.

8. Typing speed is inappropriate in a resume for a professional position.

9. Visa status needs further elaboration.

10. A specific reference would be more helpful in this situation.

BEFORE

LAN WANG
717 Belmont Place, SE, Apartment 1122
Washington, DC 20004
(H) 202-339-1725
(W) 202-667-4612

Work Experience:

- **Senior Administrative Assistant, April 1989   Present, Association of North American Colleges,** 3 Circle of the Associations, Washington, DC 20007
- **Full-Time Graduate Teaching Fellow, 1988-89** (Teaching English to foreign students - TOEFL) English Language Department, Chadwick University, CA
- **Instructor of English, 1982-87,** Foreign Language Department, Shenyi Teachers College, Shenyi, Linhai, China PRC
- **Instructor of English, 1987 Spring Semester,** English Training Program for Managers, Administrative Bureau of New Industry, Shenyi, Linhai, China PRC
- **Instructor of English, Grade 9, 1985 Fall Semester,** Experimental Secondary School of Linhai Province, Shenyi, Linhai, China PRC
- **Video Tape Announcer and Translator, 1982-89,** Audio-Visual Center, Shenyi Teachers College, Shenyi, Linhai, China PRC
- **Mandarin Chinese Radio Announcer, 1974-78,** Town of Mengenh, District of Shenyi, Linhai, China, PRC

Education:

- **M.S - Education, Curriculum and Instruction, May 1989** (Included extensive work in TESOL and Linguistics) Grade Point Average 3.89 on 4.00 scale. Chadwick University, CA
- **Certificate, Graduate Program in English Linguistics and Literature, 1986,** Shenyi Teachers College, Shenyi, Linhai, China PRC
- **Certificate, English for College Teachers, 1983,** Dayan Institute of Technology, Dayan, Linhai, China PRC
- **B.A.- English Linguistics and Literature, 1982,** Foreign Language Department, Shenyi Teachers College, Shenyi, Linhai, China PRC

Translation Experience:

- **"Final Sayings"** - Short Story Journal of Shenyi Teachers College, January 1985.
- **History of American Literature, Section IV, Walt Whitman.**
- **Comparative Literature: Preface to the First Edition.**

Experience as an Interpreter:

- **Interpreter for Joann Williams,** Visiting English Teacher, 1985-86, Shenyi Teachers College, Shenyi, Linhai, China PRC

Membership in Professional Organizations:

- Washington Area Teachers of English as a Second Language (WATESOL)
- Association of Foreign Language Translation, PRC
- Association of International Linguistics and Literature, PRC

Office Skills:

- Experienced in IBM, Macintosh, and Apple Computers (WordPerfect, Microsoft Word, dBase, Lotus 1-2-3)
- Typing speed - 50 WPM

Visa Status: F-1, Practical Training (9/89 - 7/90)
Date of Birth: 7/30/56
References available upon request

English as a Second Language Teacher

AFTER: FOCUSED RESUME

General Solutions

Ms. Wang's resume has been given an introductory statement that prepares the reader for the unique combination of experiences that follows. The list of information has been broken into groups more readily grasped by the reader and brief elaborations are provided at appropriate places.

Specific Points

❶ The **Overview** lets the reader know that the writer is a woman, and clarifies her situation and what she is trying to accomplish. Gender would normally not be stressed, but when a foreign name does not convey enough to select a proper term for addressing the applicant, such elaboration is appropriate.

❷ Degrees are singled out for prominence under the **education** heading and not confused with other training, which is shown later in the resume.

❸ **Experience** is broken into subheadings, and listed in order of importance.

❹ The most important experience is teaching in America, so it leads the list. A modest job description adds to clarity.

❺ The Chinese teaching experience is separated from other work done there and left to stand on the strength of the job titles.

❻ Interpreter and translator skills are combined for simplicity—similar skills.

❼ Current position is listed as professional, but clearly not teaching. A brief statement of duties gives the position as much professional status as possible.

❽ Office skills sound better as something related to her professional skills.

❾ Visa status is explained enough to show an intended progression.

❿ An approachable reference is provided to give the reader an efficient way to clarify anything at issue without getting involved in complex correspondence or awkwardly contacting the applicant before being comfortable in doing so.

AFTER

LAN WANG
717 Belmont Place, SE. Apartment 4122
Washington, DC 20004

202-339-1725 Residence
202-667-4612 Office

① **Overview:** Chinese woman fluent in English, with recently completed American graduate degree, seeks opportunity to teach English as a second language to students of any language background. Also receptive to other opportunities that would capitalize on language and cultural knowledge.

Education

Master of Science - Education	Bachelor of Arts
Curriculum and Instruction	English Linguistics and Literature
(TESOL/Linguistics Concentration)	Shenyi Teachers College
Chadwick University, CA	Shenyi, Linhai, China PRC
1989	1982

Experience

TEACHING

USA

④ • *Teacher of English as a Foreign Language*, English Language Institute, Chadwick University, CA, 1988-89. As a full time graduate teaching fellow, taught English as a second language to foreign students.

CHINA

⑤ • *Instructor of English*, Foreign Language Department, Shenyi Teachers College, China, 1982-87.
• *Instructor of English*, English Training Program for Managers, Administrative Bureau of New Industry, Shenyi, China, 1987.
• *Instructor of English*, Grade 9, Experimental Secondary School of Linhai Province, Shenyi, China, 1985.

TRANSLATION **⑥**

• *Interpreter* in China for visiting American teacher of English, 1985-86.
• *Scholarly translation* of several works from English to Chinese.

OTHER PROFESSIONAL

⑦ • *Senior Administrative Assistant,* Association of North American Colleges, Washington, DC, April 1989 - Present. Duties include assisting in the coordination of college level academic programs for members seeking college degrees throughout the world. Various roles aiding in response to user inquiries by telephone and writing. Assist in the preparation of organizational publications.
• *Video Tape Announcer/Translator,* Shenyi Teachers College, 1982-89.
• *Radio Announcer*, Mandarin Chinese language, China, 1974-70.

Related Skills

Experienced in operating IBM and Apple Macintosh personal computers.
Software proficiency: Microsoft Word, WordPerfect, dBase, and Lotus 1-2-3.

Additional Training

Certificate	Certificate
Graduate Program in English Linguistics and Literature	English for College Teachers
Shenyi Teachers College	Dayan Institute of Technology
1986	Dayan, Linhai, China
	1983

Professional Affiliations	**References** **⑩**
Washington Area Teachers of English as a Second Language (WATESOL)	Dawson Weber, Ph.D.
Association of Foreign Language Translation	Associate Director
Association of International Linguistics and Literature	Association of North American Colleges
	202-667-4612

Personal	
	Immediate reference • Contact freely
	• Others provided upon request.

⑨ F-1 Student Visa currently working under the Practical Training provision.
H-1 Work Visa upon attaining permanent professional employment.
Born September 21, 1955

Investment Officer

BEFORE

General Problems

Mr. Ames has smothered perfectly good qualifications in a sea of overstatment, misplaced emphasis, and disorganization. Adding a paragraph that gives some specifics about performance as an investment manager and deleting—or relegating to a proper place—things no one in his present career field wants to hear about his teaching days can salvage the resume.

Specific Points

❶ A telephone number is essential in an age when your first contact from an interested employer is apt to be a call—he failed to list one.

❷ The **Objective** leads off with rambling hyperbole that only vaguely relates to managing investments.

❸ Claims of being articulate, an excellent communicator, respected leader, etc. are lost in too many words—the paragraph is actually harmful to his image and needs to be removed.

❹ **Experience** is presented too broadly—there needs to be a clear division between what supports the current professional goal and that which is background.

❺ Description of the investment duties is fine as far as it goes, but it lacks the performance specifics expected in such a readily quantified field.

❻ The educator background is largely irrelevant to the objective of getting a better investment management position—set it apart and reduce it in size and detail.

❼ Minor speeches, coaching roles, etc. have no place in this resume.

❽ The securities examination is a test passed, not education gained—show it as a professional credential under the relevant job description.

❾ The **Personal** information contributes nothing—delete it.

❿ **Education** listings should not be vague about whether a degree has been completed or merely pursued.

BEFORE

BRUCE D. AMES

454 Hermosa Beach Drive Los Angeles, CA 90254

OBJECTIVE

To utilize my repertoire of professional and interpersonal expertise through a dynamic position which requires exceptional communicative skills and extensive contact with the community. Special interests include investments management and marketing.

Recognized as an action-oriented individual who possesses leadership skills and administrative ability integral to the successful implementation of projects. Welcome the challenge of working with new people and changing situations. Articulate . . . communicate proficiently with people at all levels. Respected for unique ability to assess needs, formulate goals and devise strategies to effectively achieve managerial objectives. Demonstrate excellent speaking, writing and research capabilities. Capable of influencing others to perform tasks efficiently.

PROFESSIONAL EXPERIENCE

Since 1979, Assistant Vice President and Trust Investment Officer, The Bank of West Orange County. Establish investment policy, directly supervise investment administration, manage individual and comingled portfolios, evaluate accounts, securities, research and comparative performances. Monitor operations, supervise clerical functions, meet with customers and clients, represent the department.

Co-designed curriculum, taught college preparatory Math (grades 10-12) during tenure as Faculty Member at The Monument School. Developed and co-wrote <u>New Theories in Teaching Mathematics</u> and <u>Mathematics Instruction in the Private Academy</u> (1974). Directed preparation and publication of these textbooks currently used as units of instruction. Presented National 4-H Club speech (1975). As Assistant Volleyball Coach, was responsible for conditioning both boys' and girls' teams. Analyzed performance, instructed team members in game strategies and techniques to prepare for athletic competition.

At Pacific Military and Girls Academy, taught Mathematics, geometry and junior algebra. Participated in faculty and professional meetings, education conferences and teacher training workshops. Cultivated interpersonal skills while a Resident Adviser in a closed dormitory environment. Provided individual and group counseling services relative to problems of personal, social and scholastic nature. Assisted pupils in selecting course of study, counseled students with adjustment and academic problems. Directed dormitory orientation programs, supervised recreational and social activities.

Conducted college-level courses in Basic Mathematics and Arithmetic Theory at the Community College of the North Woods, MN, instructed prospective teachers in teaching mathematics to high school students. As Graduate Teaching Assistant at the University of Minnesota, instructed prospective teachers in Secondary Schools Teaching Methodology. Created and compiled book of formulas, presented classroom orientation lectures.

EDUCATION

Registered Securities Representative, 1979, The Bank of West Orange County.
Post-baccalaureate study (Master of Business Administration), Long Beach College, 1976-79.
Post-baccalaureate study (Master of Education Fellow), University of Minnesota, 1971-75.
Bachelor of Arts in Mathematics (emphasis, Boolean Logic Theory), University of Michigan, 1971.

PERSONAL

Strive to promote highest degree of success in fulfilling potential for self and others. Pleasures include all sports (particularly sailing, cross-country skiing, tennis and swimming) and extensive reading. Interested in developing growth-oriented programs which foster creativity in achieving objectives.

Investment Officer

AFTER: FOCUSED RESUME

General Solutions

Mr. Ames's resume has been purged of excessive words. It now defines clearly the primary and secondary information, although the format has remained essentially unchanged. A few more headings and a lot less words have transformed a weak effort into a great resume.

Specific Points

❶ Telephone numbers have been added without the addition of a single line.

❷ The **Objective** is now much shorter and to the point. It includes his interest in people skills and marketing, but is phrased to fit the business environment instead of a graduate school class.

❸ **Experience** has been divided and reordered to place the emphasis on the business at hand—investment management.

❹ A brief paragraph was added to describe his actual investment activities and performance, using a recognized standard.

❺ The professional credential has been inserted at a more meaningful point.

❻ Teaching is presented in the context of its current importance—proof that there was a responsible use of his time before coming to the investment world.

❼ For the purposes of this resume, the teaching positions can be treated as generic events that share a common, brief description.

❽ Teaching part-time while a graduate student shows some initiative, but little more relevant to the investment job; account for the periods of time and move on.

❾ **Personal** was removed and left for interview small talk—if that.

❿ **Education** has been clarified to list the bachelor's degree and relegate the others to their proper place as study toward degrees not completed.

AFTER

BRUCE D. AMES

454 Hermosa Beach Drive • Los Angeles, CA 90254 • 213-324-0078 (O), 213-445-0988 (R)

OBJECTIVE

To obtain an opportunity for further growth as a Bank Trust Investment Officer, with an emphasis on marketing investment products to groups and individuals.

EXPERIENCE

Trust Investments

1979 - Present: Assistant Vice President and Trust Investment Officer, The Bank of West Orange County.

- Establish investment policy, directly supervise investment administration, manage individual and comingled portfolios, evaluate accounts, securities, research and comparative performances. Monitor operations, supervise clerical functions, meet with customers and clients, represent the department.

- Perform as an investment generalist working with both fixed and equity funds. Use major outside contract research firm in an advisory capacity. Sit on the Trust Investment Committee. Currently responsible for the management of $150 million of personal and $276 million of institutional funds. Aggregate investment performance according to CDA has been 25th percentile nationally for the past 5 years. Regularly accompany officers from employee benefits and other divisions to assist in developing new business.

- Registered Securities Representative.

Teaching

Prior to beginning my investment career, I served as a teacher at two institutions:

1971 - 1973 The Monument School, Orange, CA.

1974 - 1976 Pacific Military and Girls Academy, Laguna, CA.

In both situations, I taught Mathematics, geometry and junior algebra. Participated in faculty and professional meetings, education conferences and teacher training workshops. Cultivated interpersonal skills while a Resident Adviser in a closed dormitory environment. Provided individual and group counseling services relative to problems of personal, social and scholastic nature. Assisted pupils in selecting courses of study, counseled students with adjustment and academic problems. Directed dormitory orientation programs, supervised recreational and social activities.

Part-time Teaching During Periods of Graduate Study

Conducted college-level courses in Basic Mathematics and Arithmetic Theory at the Community College of the North Woods, MN, instructed prospective teachers in teaching mathematics to high school students. As Graduate Teaching Assistant at the University of Minnesota, instructed prospective teachers in Secondary Schools Teaching Methodology. Created and compiled book of formulas, presented classroom orientation lectures.

EDUCATION

- Bachelor of Arts in Mathematics, University of Michigan, 1971.
- Additional graduate study toward the following degrees:
  Master of Business Administration, Long Beach College, 1976-79.
  Master of Education Fellow, University of Minnesota, 1971-75 (Summers).

Senior Executive Assistant

BEFORE

General Problems

Ms. O'Conner fails to set the context for her experiences. She portrays herself too objectively as an older divorced woman with spotty training and an irregular work history when, in reality, she has done common things in an uncommon setting—as an executive's spouse. Her resume doesn't present her as a woman of multiple talents who can operate comfortably with executives, and that is her greatest asset.

Specific Points

❶ Her actual work experience is not as much of an asset in her job search as is her experience functioning comfortably in management circles.

❷ She unwisely leads her list of accomplishments with an unexplained temporary position.

❸ Since her work history is not a clear progression up a particular career ladder, it should be de-emphasized.

❹ The education entries do little to enhance her professional image, so they should be generalized, not featured prominently.

❺ Detailed high school and secretarial school information only draw attention to her nonprofessional education and her age.

❻ Phrased as it is, the college entry emphasizes her lack of a degree.

❼ These sound like things of secondary importance that an executive's spouse might do when, in fact, they can be broken out into valuable competencies.

❽ It is unnecessary to give personal information.

❾ Marital status and family size are neither required nor should they be volunteered.

❿ The availability of references is a given and should be omitted.

BEFORE

BERNADETTE J. O'CONNER
1455 CORYELL COURT SOUTH
SEATTLE, WA 98112
206-448-0992 RESIDENCE

① EXPERIENCE

② July 1995-Present: Office temporary, Kelly Personnel Services, Bellview, WA. Typing, filing, receptionist, and as-needed office work as an on-call gal Friday.

September 1982-May 1987: Substitute teacher, Salmon Run Elementary School, King County Public Schools. Taught young children in the absence of their regular teachers.

May 1976-June 1977: Administrative assistant, Bishop Walsh Catholic Church, Renton, WA.

August 1971-January 1974: Secretary, Chief, Computing Services & LAN Branch, Aircraft Manufacturers Association, Washington, DC

③ April 1969-November 1970: Receptionist and administrative aide, Inland Aerial Port Authority, Arlington, VA.

④ EDUCATION

Canton Kansas Senior High School, General Diploma, 1962 ◀—— **⑤**

Kathryn Cummings Business School, Kansas City, KS, Certificate in Office Administration, 1966

Kansas City University, 1962-1965, various college courses **⑥**

⑦ ACTIVITIES

President of the Corporate Officers Wives Club. Organized an informal training program for new spouses to familiarize them with their obligations under the company's social protocols. Sponsored youth activities and initiated the neighborhood crime watch.

⑧ PERSONAL

Divorced; 2 adult children **⑨**

REFERENCES UPON REQUEST **⑩**

Senior Executive Assistant

AFTER: FOCUSED RESUME

General Solutions

Ms. O'Conner's resume was recast to place less emphasis on her actual work experiences and educational accomplishments and more on her ability to function comfortably in the executive environment. Instead of listing specific jobs and educational experiences, her resume was designed to emphasize competencies that would be valued in the job market. Where they were acquired is relegated to a secondary position.

Specific Points

❶ An overview was added to set the context lacking in her original resume. The reader immediately knows he or she is evaluating someone whose professional refinement exceeds her actual credentials.

❷ A list of her competencies is the first thing encountered by an evaluator. Its headings telegraph her strengths, and it isn't necessary to search for them in the understated credits of her original resume.

❸ The key to getting her a job at the level she is used to occupying is experience interacting with executive-level people, so that is stressed.

❹ Her resume next establishes that she has tangible workplace skills drawn from both formal work experiences and quasi-personal activities.

❺ Her language capability may be used directly; if not, it denotes refinement, helps her image, and compensates for weak formal education credentials.

❻ Teaching becomes instructional experience—more easily related to needs of the working world outside educational institutions.

❼ A connection was made between her teaching children and applying similar skills in the company environment as her activities are tied into her job competencies.

❽ Work history is honestly presented, but de-emphasized.

❾ Education remains a category, but it is generalized and interpreted to mean something in the job market; also, it reflects less formal experiences like using a personal computer and attending company training sessions.

❿ Her incomplete college experience is stated more favorably.

AFTER

BERNADETTE J. O'CONNER
1455 CORYELL COURT SOUTH
SEATTLE, WA 98112

206-448-0992 RESIDENCE

OVERVIEW AND OBJECTIVE

1 Mature executive career partner with cultivated social and organizational skills wishes to combine that background and personal bearing with tangible professional administrative talents to support achieving the objectives of a challenging organization.

COMPETENCIES **2**

3 **Executive Interpersonal**—As the career partner of a senior international corporate officer, became an accomplished participant in, and facilitator of, executive social functions. These strengths were developed in an environment of foreign and domestic, military and civilian, senior professional people.

4 **Organizational, Managerial and Clerical**—As the senior person among a professional social hierarchy of other executive career partners, organized and managed a variety of social services related to company families and personnel. As an administrative specialist supporting the secretarial and clerical needs of large organizations, developed an ability to organize and accomplish administrative tasks.

Foreign Language—Written and spoken French **5**

6 **Instructional**—As a substitute teacher, managed a classroom and accomplished learning objectives. Similar results were achieved outside the educational setting by imparting the skills of an executive career partner to younger associates.

7

8 EMPLOYMENT HISTORY

- 1962-1994: Spouse of a senior corporate officer supporting the development of his professional financial management career internationally.
- 1993-1994: Substitute teacher and aide, Salmon Run Elementary School, King County Public Schools. Temporary administrative work for Kelly Personnel Services as a device for re-entering career employment.
- 1961-1989: Various administrative positions including Secretary to the Chief of Computing & the Local Area Network Branch, Aircraft Manufacturers Association and support positions in such organizations as the Inland Aerial Port Authority, Memphis, TN.

9 EDUCATION

- Liberal arts college preparation ← **10**
- Attended a variety of career partner professional courses associated with such institutions as the International Business Association
- Secretarial and clerical training
- Basic computer literacy

23

Senior Manager

BEFORE

General Problems

Mr. Woodland's resume is written in the language and format of the military service of which he is no longer a part. His task now is to communicate to the broader world of work what he has done that they might value. This requires evaluating his terminology, determining its relevance in a civilian hiring situation, and making it understood by those not familiar with the military.

Specific Points

❶ Unless the application is directed to someone known to understand and value military rank, remove it from the address. The value of rank should be obvious and, if relevant, it can be integrated into the work history.

❷ He should help the resume reviewer quickly classify him by offering an introductory line suggesting how he fits into the civilian job market.

❸ Move education to the end of the resume. A college education is assumed for the kinds of positions for which he will apply, so it becomes something to verify at the end rather than a leading item.

❹ Listing a series of normal professional development courses is unnecessary. A resume from industry would not likely list comparable ones.

❺ Accomplishments are worded too much like a military personnel evaluation. More natural, less inflated-sounding statements would serve him better, especially if they are related to the civilian workplace.

❻ Career positions show too much detail. Simplify and group them.

❼ Career positions' terminology is stilted, military-oriented, and not apt to be understood. They need to be roughly translated into civilian equivalencies.

❽ The chronology is muddled and too detailed.

❾ Sort the military assignments into clusters that portray a logical work history that accounts for time and shows expected career progression.

❿ For most hiring situations, awards and decorations are best left as unlisted assets to acknowledge as appropriate. Work history statements can sometimes properly mention combat leadership with honors or service with distinction, but understatement is the rule.

BEFORE

Thomas A. Woodland, Colonel, USA (Retired)
2933 Crepe Myrtle Lane
Gaithersburg, MD 20879
301-562-6403

Education

University of Maryland - Bachelor of Science in Business Administration
Park University, Missouri - Master of Arts in Management
Basic Armor Officer's Course, Military Personnel Officer's Course, Adjutant General's Corps
Officers Advanced Course, Armed Forces Staff College, and Command and General Staff
College

Accomplishments

Significant roles in the planning and execution of every Department of the Army program through Desert Storm. Supervised and lead offices of as many as 108 goal oriented team members. Twenty-eight years of direct office management experience. Recruiting, hired, trained, evaluated, and fired personnel. Coordinated, led, supervised, monitored, and assigned work within eight major divisions of the Department of the Army.

Career Positions

United States Armor Center at Fort Knox, Kentucky, 1969, Training Battalion Executive Officer; United States Army Aviation Center & School, Fort Rucker, Alabama, 1970, rotary wing flight training; 23rd Aviation Brigade, Da Nang, South Vietnam, 1971, Scout Helicopter Platoon Leader; 81st Aviation Squadron, Fort Knox, Kentucky, 1972, Platoon Leader and Operations Officer; Personnel Office, Fort Knox, Kentucky, 1972-74, Personnel officer; Hanau, West Germany, 1975-78, 75th Signal Battalion, Battalion Adjutant, HQ Detachment Commander; Fort Lewis, Washington, 1978-81, Reserve Component Advisor for the Northwest Army Readiness Group; Yongsan, South Korea, 1982-85, Plans Officer for the Combined Forces Command; Fort Sill, Oklahoma, 1986-89, Post Adjutant General; Carlisle Barracks, Pennsylvania, 1990-93, Chief of Plans & Operations Division, Directorate of Academic Operations, United States Army Staff College; Fort Jackson, South Carolina, 1994-97, Senior Army Advisor at the Army Reserve Complex, Columbia, South Carolina.

Awards and Decorations

Bronze Star, Defense Meritorious Service Medal with one Oak Leaf Cluster, Meritorious Service Medal with three Oak Leaf Clusters, Army Commendation Medal with one Oak Leaf Cluster, Vietnam Service Medal with Star, Armed Forces Reserve Medal, Republic of Vietnam Gallantry Cross with Palm, the Army Aviation Badge, and the Air Assault Badge.

Senior Manager

AFTER: COMPETENCY CLUSTER RESUME

General Solutions

Mr. Woodland's resume now a competency cluster resume. Since his market value is in the specifics of what he did rather than in which organizations he served, the objective is to reveal his competencies. Work history and education are relegated to the important but secondary roles of verifying assumed levels of performance and training.

Specific Points

❶ Military rank is removed from the address element since in most situations it will no longer be part of his professional identity. Exceptions exist where rank is beneficial, but they are apt to be known at the time of application. An e-mail address conveys technology awareness.

❷ An overview is added to telegraph that a senior manager's credentials are being examined and that his experience includes administrative, personnel, and financial responsibilities.

❸ Competencies are extracted from the maze of military job titles and summarized in ways that give context and scope to the responsibilities.

❹ Civilian occupational parallels are drawn—budget, training, recruitment.

❺ Technical literacy is highlighted, not as a technician but as a senior manager literate in and comfortable with modern technology.

❻ Career positions that were formerly a litany of military posts held are brought together into meaningful clusters of functional experience.

❼ His work history highlights and verifies a successful progression from entry-level to senior management.

❽ The job chronology is simple, clear, and accurate. It shows the evaluator what he or she wants most to see—his career progression and no periods unaccounted for.

❾ At the bottom of the work history is a summary that relates military training, combat experience, and a discreet mention of honors.

❿ Education is listed at the end of the resume verifying degrees in business and management. A summary statement covers in-service training.

AFTER

① THOMAS A. WOODLAND
2933 Crepe Myrtle Lane
Gaithersburg, MD 20879
301-562-6403
tawoodland@worldnet.att.net

OVERVIEW

② After a successful career as a senior officer managing the administrative, personnel, and financial aspects of large, complex organizations in the United States, Asia, and Europe, interested in applying my talents and experience to meeting the challenges of a new organization.

③ COMPETENCIES

⑥ Management—oversaw the operation of offices of more than 100 people serving organizations consisting of thousands of individuals. Experienced and trained in modern management practices. Recruited, trained, evaluated, and mentored people ranging from entry level to senior managers. **④**

Financial—planned, executed, and was accountable for budgets of tens of millions of dollars.

Training—senior administrative management of major training organizations.

Technology—responsible for the evaluation, acquisition, and use of state-of-the-art computer systems and software. Conversant in the terminology and competent in the use of modern office and instructional technologies.

⑤

⑦ WORK HISTORY

⑧ 1994-1997—Senior Management and Technical Consultant at the Army Reserve Complex, Fort Jackson, SC. The active duty army's oversight person for a large organization of civilian reservists relating their civilian and military skills. Policy making, motivation, program quality control, and mentoring.

1990-93—Chief Academic Planning and Operations Officer, the United States Army Staff College, Carlisle, PA. Planned and implemented a national level program for managers. Duties included budgeting and program development.

1972-89—Middle management positions of increasing responsibility. Duties included personnel, operations, and planning in major units located in Germany, Korea, and the United States.

1969-71—Training as a military officer and aviator, with periods of combat leadership with honors. **⑨**

EDUCATION

⑩ Park University, Missouri—Master of Arts in Management, 1987
University of Maryland—Bachelor of Science in Business Administration, 1969
A wide range of in-service leadership and management courses.

Do's and Don'ts of Resume Writing

There is a large body of wisdom about what you should and should not do in preparing a resume. The following is a collection of the considerations that warrant your attention. They also demand your *good judgment*—every rule does not apply to all situations and you will have to determine when to depart from the conventional approach enough to give your resume the little something extra that is appropriate in your circumstances.

Use this summary as a checklist when it comes time to plan and critique your resume.

Do	Don't
View yourself as a product to be sold to the reader of your resume.	Assume the reader has time to absorb more than the essentials.
Make your resume believable.	Stretch small or incomplete things into more than they will be if scrutinized.
Start with something that the reviewer can identify with and attach value to easily.	Bore the resume's reader.
Use only the words needed to convey your message.	Try to impress anyone with big words or philosophical statements.
Leave white space.	Fill every inch of paper with type.
Lead the reviewer through your points with headings, bullets, bold type, underlining, etc.	Get too carried away with different type faces or graphic effects that can distract instead of lead and separate.
Ignore the traditional rules of formatting (other than logical arrangement) if you are submitting a text-only electronic resume.	Waste effort prettying-up an electronic resume that you will likely send as plain text.
Include keywords, especially in electronic resumes or those apt to be scanned for electronic evaluation and filing.	Use elaborate explanations at the expense of crucial keywords needed to pass the electronic screening process.
Avoid opening up problem areas that were not required items or things clearly to your advantage.	Volunteer a photograph or similar unexpected extras—attractive, average, or too good-looking can all pose problems in the wrong situations.

Do	Don't
Limit your resume to a page or two unless there is a compelling reason to make it more.	Use white space and formatting gimmicks to the extent that they make your resume too long.
Keep relevant content at the center of your thinking as you present your information.	Drift into listing more than the reviewer for this particular job wants to know.
Make your goals and objectives fit the job under consideration.	List your broader life goals and values in your resume.
Show that you know something about the job and the company.	Mention skills or interests that the job would never demand.
Be clear about the level of authority or responsibility for both your objective and in describing past duties.	Leave it to the reviewer to guess where you fit into the organization—theirs or the ones in your past.
Let your achievements speak for themselves—state them clearly, quantify and define where desirable.	Embellish your accomplishments—their substance has to be strong enough to convey their value.
Go easy on the adjectives.	Don't try to show action or importance with modifiers whose purpose is obvious to the reader.
Give specifics where there isn't a compelling reason not to—names and numbers let the reader judge the significance of the things you mention.	Expect the reviewer to attach importance to things that you haven't demonstrated as being significant.
Include a clear qualifications statement in your resume.	Leave it to the reviewer to figure out how your preparation might satisfy his requirement.
Use a brief summary statement that embraces your overall qualifications.	Make your summary a second resume.
Determine that the position has the potential to meet your realistic salary requirements before applying.	State a salary requirement in your resume.
Prepare a list of relevant references and make them aware of your job-hunting activity—get their permission to use their names.	List references in your resume or state the obvious—that they are available on request. Don't let an employer surprise a reference by contacting them before you do.

(cont'd)

Do	Don't
Resist the urge to include personal data not directly relevant to the job.	Tell the reviewer about your hobbies, number of children, excellent health, love of boating, other than professional memberships, etc.
Let your accomplishments and preparation speak for themselves.	Appraise your own worth.
List dates even in the modified resumes that are not chronological lists of past positions.	Make the dates the main feature of any resume that deserves a different focus.
Avoid qualifying statements such as "had exposure to."	Stretch your experience beyond that which can be directly claimed as yours.
State an honest reason for leaving if other than just looking for a better opportunity.	Make negative statements about the job or people you are leaving behind.
Show evidence of hard work and dedication.	Merely state that you are hard-working and dedicated—if it has to be separately claimed, you didn't communicate it substantively.
Prepare your resume professionally—that doesn't necessarily mean go out and hire someone. It does mean, at the very least, using a good typewriter and paper—try to gain access to a quality word processor.	Settle for a mechanically weak resume that looks like something out of a beginning high school typing class.
Eliminate unnecessarily long words, sentences, and paragraphs.	Overstate your case.
Say enough to market fairly what you have to offer.	Be so sparse as to show disinterest or less substance than you actually have.
Proofread carefully—better yet, use a word-processing program that checks spelling, perhaps grammar too.	Commit to final copy without aging your early drafts for a few days and subjecting them to some editing.
Use a good quality paper and an interesting type style that suits your circumstances.	Choose an unusual size or color paper—same for ink, type face, etc.
Determine who should receive your resume and address it accordingly.	Send your resume to some broad entity like the personnel department unless specifically directed to do so.

(cont'd)

Do	Don't
Provide telephone numbers that will respond with a businesslike answer.	List a telephone number that will elicit a "she no longer works here" response, is disconnected, or otherwise fails to leave a favorable impression.
List your most recent job first.	Give the same attention to old jobs as those of recent years—condense them if necessary and make a collective statement.
List military service if it represents important employment or training—and do it in that way.	Dwell on past military experience, honors, etc. unless they relate to the job at hand.
Mention civic clubs and community service only if such activity is an expectation for the job—college president, etc.	Fill the end of the resume with a summary of everything you ever belonged to or achieved privately—Eagle Scout, pilot's license, etc.

2 HOW TO USE THE MODEL RESUMES

The resumes of Chapter 3 serve as illustrations—examples of how a resume can sell the talents of a job applicant. Their best use is as a pool of stimulating ideas, rather than as specific models to emulate with precision. To give you a framework for using this resource, the resumes have been labeled as belonging to one of three general types. In some you will clearly see the qualities of the other two—a Work History chronology may be the perfect way to end a Competency Cluster Resume, for example. The Work History Resume may be most effective if the individual job descriptions becomes miniature Focused or Competency Cluster Resumes. You are advised to see the broad potential and select the most powerful combination with which to portray your unique talents.

Resume Prototypes

THE WORK HISTORY RESUME is sometimes referred to as a Chronological Resume because jobs and personal data are listed in the order they occurred. It is the traditional resume and the one most commonly used when pursuing a regular career progression that has one position logically and continuously leading to the next.

Strengths	Weaknesses
Shows ideal job progression.	Exposes spotty career pattern.
Showcases strong employers and positions held.	Highlights inconsistencies in levels and types of employment.

(cont'd)

Strengths	Weaknesses
Sets the stage for next most logical growth move in your career.	Fails to support your aspirations if the building blocks are not there in terms of the right positions previously held. Not a career-changer's resume.
Stresses impressive job titles.	Reveals insignificant positions.
Everything easily accounted for.	Everything revealed.
Sets the stage for presenting strong references from prior positions.	Risks inviting reference checks where you would just as soon not have them.
Looks like a "real" resume—straightforward and traditional in both content and presentation.	Not particularly imaginative—relies on excellent content to give it value.
Clearly links dates of employment and verifies continuity.	Indicates breaks in employment as well as brief tenure in job.
Shows long experience.	Makes your age obvious; suggests you may have been stalled in a job too long; reveals periods of unemployment.

Work History Resume Template

> Name
> Address
> Telephone Number(s)

Overview or Summary, Goal or Objective. An appropriately brief and revelant statement of your main qualifications and goal. This is optional and can be omitted if it simply states the obvious.

Employment—A chronological list of the jobs you have held. Format can vary, but respect these rules:

- Most recent position is listed first.
- List dates continuously and consistently by month and year—or year only.
- Account for gaps in the sequence.
- Avoid showing each new position with the same employer as a new job.
  (Use a subheading approach to avoid repeating the same information.)
- State your job title.
  (Give some brief indication of what that means in the organization—the title of the person to whom you reported, for example.)
- Describe your duties and responsibilities in terms that mean something.
  (Number of people supervised and their status.)
  (Volume of business generated.)
  (Amount of change in indicators that measure what you do.)
- Mention several believable, verifiable accomplishments
  (Things that would be valued by the employers you are now seeking to impress.)
- Consolidate older and less relevant experience at the bottom of the resume.
- Respect the one-page limit—two at the most and only if justified.

Education—List your most important degree or certificate of training first in the section which, itself, will go either at the beginning or end of the resume, depending on the relative importance of your work and education. Provide name of school or college, major (if it adds to the value for the job in question), year of graduation, and state (possibly city) where college is located, depending on how well known it is.

Comments, professional affiliations, or other concluding statements can be added if kept brief and if they contribute to, rather than detract from, the main resume.

Examples of Work History Resumes

William K. Akrin

56 Tura Road
Bennington, CT 48009
860-222-9988 (Office)
860-333-9075 (Residence)

Overview

Technical Writer with formal training and experience in computer technology and technical writing seeks editorial opportunity with mass market user's magazine.

Experience

January 1991 - Present: Technical Writer
Brainware Computer Products, Inc., Bennington, CT.

Assist in the preparation of technical manuals that support the use of software products created at Brainware. Experience includes interviewing programmers and systems engineers to identify program features. Convey features and step-by-step instructions for use in lay language. Attend national workshops to receive feedback on manuals and products. Full range of mass market software including desktop publishing, graphic arts, and business packages featuring word processing, data bases, spread sheets, etc.

September 1987 - December 1990
Full-time study for bachelor's degree.

June 1985 - August 1987: Customer Service Technician
Matson Software, Ltd., Norwich, CT.

Telephone contact for users of Matson Software products including their complete line of word processing, spread sheet, graphic presentation, and data base programs. Assisted users in isolating their problems and guiding them to solutions. Maintained records on nature of questions addressed and assisted technical writing staff in the revision of manuals.

Education

Associate in Arts (AA)
Computer Studies
Asnutuck Junior College, CT, 1985

Bachelor of Technology (BT)
Technical Writing
West Connecticut College, CT, 1992

Darlene W. Robinette

96 Galveston Lane
Houston, TX 77271
281-222-9988 (Office)
281-333-9075 (Residence)

Education

Bachelor of Science
Business Administration
Smith University, 1970

Master of Business Administration
Finance
University of Texas, 1981

Chartered Financial Analyst (CFA)
1986

Experience

April 1988 - Present: **Vice President & Trust Investment Officer, National Bank & Trust of Eastern Texas, Houston, TX ($1.5 billion trust department).** Senior portfolio manager in a group of 6; managing both fixed and equity in collective and other funds (personal, pension, and endowment). Responsible for all fixed income funds (aprx $300 million personal/$100 million employee benefits); responsible for most equity funds (aprx $400 million personal/$20 million employee benefits); foundations and charities account for an additional $75 million. Involved in business development activities, including presentations to support new business and existing accounts — also cooperative development projects with other elements of the trust department. Handled installation of IBM-AT dedicated to investment function; computer literate and proficient with DOS, LOTUS, asset allocation programs, Microscan, LOTUS Financial, Norton Utilities, communications, and disk maintenance.

June 1987 - March 1988: **Vice President & Trust Investment Officer, United Bankshares Trust, Fort Worth, TX ($580 million trust department).** Chaired the investment committee. Lowered transaction costs 32 percent. Implemented standard investment procedures. Established a research capability and client newsletter. Brief tenure accrues to inability to adapt to the culture and lifestyle of the area.

July 1984 - May 1987: **Assistant Vice President and Trust Investment Officer, Chicago Retail Trust Bank, Chicago, IL ($250 million trust department).** Senior investment officer responsible for setting overall investment posture; conceived and implemented a new common trust fund, revised others. Organized and conducted investment conference for 200 members of the local professional community. Implemented formal procedures to control commission use and allocation. Established investment management goals, including performance measurement techniques. Wrote monthly economic/investment commentary for distribution to 300 regional bankers, government officials, corporate officers and selected clients.

Eight previous years: **Retail stock broker,** Scott & Delmonico, Inc., Milwaukee, WI.

Comments: Reason for leaving relates to the declining economy of the region where oil, gas, and space programs show little promise in the near future. Investment performance for the past five years: 14th percentile equities; 23rd percentile fixed income; 19th percentile combined.

THE FOCUSED RESUME is often discussed as a Targeted Resume because it presents capabilities and achievements in a manner that caters to a particular kind of job. The Focused Resume is somewhat like the Competency Cluster Resume and shares a number of its advantages and disadvantages. The emphasis in both is on extracting and highlighting selected characteristics of your work history, rather than listing it in a traditional way. The difference is that the Focused Resume aims at a particular job and is arranged in blocks of abilities and achievements, whereas the Competency Cluster Resume is more general and is centered around a series of functional areas under which your talents are grouped.

Strengths	Weaknesses
Makes a strong case for a specific type of job.	Is relatively narrow and can leave out some things that might have been valued by the reviewer.
Showcases abilities in a single light.	May have less impact than your overall experience.
Demonstrates that you know what is important to this particular employer.	You may misjudge what the emphasis should be.
Can be customized with a different focus for each of several situations.	Selectively limits your presentation.
Tends to deemphasize your employers and positions held—a strength if you are not strong in these areas.	Tends to deemphasize your employers and positions held—a weakness if it obscures outstanding entries in these categories.
Useful when you are applying for a job that does not logically flow from your last position or general work history.	Unnecessarily vague if you are building on a clear career ladder.
Useful for people with beginning or interrupted work histories—focuses on current skills, not prior jobs.	Fails to take advantage of job progression record, if it exists.
Useful where work history is scattered or has not moved at the expected pace.	Unclear for the employer who is interested in linking every statement you make to a past job.

Focused Resume Template

```
Name
Address
Telephone Number(s)
```

Overview or Summary, Goal or Objective. An appropriately brief and relevant statement of your main qualifications *and goal*—the focus of your resume must be developed clearly at this point.

Abilities or Strengths or Assets.

- A series of short (a line or two) bulleted statements that tell the employer exactly *what you can do* for his company. (It requires that you know what is vital in the job.)
- Your statements reflect on your past training and experience—in the form of current abilities.
- Your statements reflect on your awareness of what the employer needs—and how you can supply it.

Achievements or Accomplishments.

- A series of short (a line or two) bulleted statements that show *what you have accomplished*.
- The more related to the job you have in mind, the better.
- Give measures of the magnitude of your achievements.
- Put them into a context that is easily evaluated by this particular employer.

Work History—List your jobs in the order held, most recent first. Dates should be given, but how you do that will depend on how much emphasis you want to place on them. Just listing the years is acceptable. If there are breaks and you want to deemphasize them, list the dates on the ragged right of the paragraph showing your employment history and make the reader look for them.

Education—List your most important degree or certificate of training first in the section which, itself, will go either at the beginning or end of the resume, depending on the relative importance of your work and education. Provide name of school or college, major (if it adds to the value for the job in question), year of graduation, and state (possibly city) where college is located, depending on how well known it is.

Comments, professional affiliations, or other concluding statements can be added if kept brief and they contribute to, rather than detract from, the main resume.

Examples of Focused Resumes

Margaret A. Arnold
89 University Drive
Santa Marina, CA 93455
805-886-1903 (Office)
805-876-3921 (Residence)

Overview

Award winning Television Support Technician with national experience in multiple aspects of professional news, talk show, and drama productions seeks network or national cable opportunity.

Professional Abilities

- SET MANAGEMENT — 6 years of experience in the management of set activities supporting news, talk show, and dramatic television productions.

- LIGHTING — 4 years as associate lighting director for a producer of nationally syndicated television musical productions. Accomplished user of Kludge and special effects lighting in television applications.

- SET DESIGN — 3 years professional and 5 years amateur set design. Professional years included assistant background construction director for the Emmy Award winning docudrama *War and Space.*

Achievements

- Union cards held in the areas of television stage management, lighting, and set design.

- On the staff of 7 production companies that received national industry recognition for excellence during my tenure.

- 1988 Audience Appreciation Award winner for set design in the live audience participation Minnie Walker Talk Show series.

Experience

June 1988 - Present: Set Manager, Gordon Boxwood Studios, Hollywood, CA.

June 1987 - May 1988: Set Design Specialist, KNBB Santa Clarita, CA.

July 1984 - May 1987: Lighting Technician, Samuel Whitworth Production Company, Los Angeles, CA.

Education

Associate in Science (AS)
Electronics Technology

Allan Whetstone Junior College, CA 1984

Wadsworth T. Sandsome

35 North Island Drive
Haleiwa, HI 96740
808-675-8345 (Office)
808-776-9078 (Residence)

Position Sought

Director of Counseling Services

Abilities

- State Certified School Guidance Counselor.
- Specialized training in the recognition and treatment of adolescent substance abuse.
- In-depth familiarity with the use of computer databases designed to aid students in the selection of appropriate colleges and majors.
- Experienced group counseling leader.
- Knowledge of private as well as public sources of college bound student financial aid.
- Extensive work with private sector community work-study arrangements.

Achievements

- 80 percent of counselees admitted to college of their choice for the past five years.
- Awarded Parents' Club Award for Excellence 1989 in appreciation for efforts to establish private sector linkage between North Shore School and the burgeoning hospitality industry.
- Founder of Island Helpers Teen Substance Abuse Hotline that serves 3500 callers weekly.
- Summer Consulting Fellow to College Boardroom, a non-profit organization that designs career planning software for students.

Experience

June 1992 - Present: Guidance Counselor, North Shore High School, Kawela Bay, HI.
June 1988 - May 1992: Counselor, Kanehoe Intermediate School, Kanehoe, HI.
July 1984 - May 1988: History Teacher, Pearl Harbor High, Pearl City, HI.

Education

Bachelor of Science (BS)
Social Studies Education
University of Maryland, 1982

Master of Education (MEd)
Guidance and Counseling
University of Hawaii, 1988

THE COMPETENCY CLUSTER RESUME is also known as a Functional Resume because it groups skills and qualities under headings that constitute important functions in a particular kind of job. The Competency Cluster Resume is somewhat like the Focused Resume and shares a number of its advantages and disadvantages. The emphasis in both is on extracting and highlighting selected characteristics of your work history, rather than listing it in a traditional way. The difference is that the Competency Cluster Resume is more general and is centered around a series of functional areas under which your talents are grouped, whereas the Focused Resume aims at a particular job and is arranged in blocks of abilities and achievements.

Strengths	Weaknesses
Good for showing skills not apparent in recent job descriptions.	Unclear as to just which skills relate to which jobs.
Can place the emphasis on families of expertise not represented in your past work history.	Fails to support with specific sources the expertise presented.
Blurs the progress of your career in favor of concentrating on selected skills you choose to emphasize.	Represents no clear career path.
Makes the best of disjointed work experiences.	May not connect logically constructed career-building steps.
Shows a series of different skill areas.	Makes it obvious if you have only a few areas of expertise.
Can be arranged to stress current objectives rather than past history.	Lacks the support of past employment history related to current goals.
Highlights selected abilities rather than past job titles and employers.	Minimal support in the way of working experience in your current specialty.
Does not repeat similar job events.	Deemphasizes work experience.
Good for beginning or changing career directions.	May underemphasize the value of past positions held.
Able to show nonjob-related abilities such as those gained in hobbies or nonpaid employment.	You may have to explain at the interview that this experience has no base in paid employment.
An out-of-date, irregular, or irrelevant work history can be subordinated to skills you actually possess.	Expect to explain the nontraditional work history when asked.

The Competency Cluster Resume Template

> Name
> Address
> Telephone Number(s)

Overview or Summary, Goal or Objective. An appropriately brief and relevant statement of your main qualifications and goal— optional if it is obvious and adds nothing to the resume.

Competency Headings.
- Select several headings under which you can group the most valuable things you do.
- List these headings in order of importance.
- Develop under each heading a series of short statements that make it apparent that you can perform in that area of specialization.
- Use specific examples.
- Give measures of the magnitude of the skill—quantify the number of people involved, the amount of growth achieved, dollars saved, etc.
- Use names, company names, project designator, or anything that aids the reader in judging the significance of your claims.

Work History—List your jobs in the order held, most recent first. Dates should be given, but how you do that will depend on how much emphasis you want to place on them. Just listing the years is acceptable. If there are breaks and you want to deemphasize them, list the dates on the ragged right of the paragraph showing your employment history and make the reader look for them.

Education—List your most important degree or certificate of training first in this section, which will go either at the beginning or end of the resume, depending on the relative importance of your work and education. Provide name of school or college, major (if it adds to the value for the job in question), year of graduation, and state (possibly city) where college is located, depending on how well known it is.

Comments, professional affiliations, or other concluding statements can be added if kept brief and if they contribute to, rather than detract from, the main resume.

Examples of Competency Cluster Resumes

Lynn J. Andersen
973 Albacort Circle
Savannah, GA 31407
912-929-6479 (Office)
912-938-7783 (Residence)

Overview and Objective

Professional Secretary with six years of advanced office services experience seeks
Executive Secretary position with potential for assuming an administrative
management role.

Education

Associate in Science (AS)
Secretarial Science
Metropolitan Community College, GA, 1988

Professional Skills

OFFICE MANAGEMENT
- Coordination of office clerical routine.
- Schedule management.
- Vendor liaison with suppliers of services.

DOCUMENT PREPARATION
- 60 WPM using electronic typewriter or word processing equipment.
- Advanced user of principal word processing software packages.

EQUIPMENT OPERATION
- Personal computers and associated peripheral equipment.
- Fax and modems.

DICTATION/TRANSCRIPTION
- 60 WPM vocal dictation.
- Accomplished transcriber.

PERSONNEL
- Preparation and placement of advertising.
- Applicant response, appointment arrangements, EEO record keeping.

EXECUTIVE ASSISTING
- Planning of meetings and conferences, locally and at remote sites.
- Arranging business travel.
- Screening and appointment management.

Experience

November 1992 - Present: Secretary to the Director of Marketing, Rockaway
Manufacturing Company, Ltd., Savannah, GA.

May 1988 - October 1992: Secretary, Jensen & Jensen Management Consultants, Tyron, GA.

Patricia D. Lyle
51-C Mount Pleasant Drive
Providence, RI 02906
401-222-9988 (Office)
401-333-9075 (Residence)

◦ Competencies ◦

<u>Computer Graphics</u>	Color and B&W graphics capabilities using Aldus Freehand on the Macintosh II computer system. Experienced In using both text and graphic scanners. Preparation of products at 300 dpi and full professional quality formats. Expert at trace modification art and logo design.
<u>Desktop Publishing</u>	Oversized Radius screen used for layout of single illustration and multipage publications with desktop publishing software, principally PageMaker. Experienced in brochure, tabloid, magazine, and newspaper layout—expert integration of graphics, including photography.
<u>Drawing Board Artist</u>	Nine years of combined college and commercial experience. Began as illustrator and paste-up person for university publications. Followed by three years of newspaper and two years of national magazine advertising and story art.

◦ Awards ◦

- Computer Monthly Magazine, 1994 First Place Award for Commercial Graphics
- The New England Gazette Syndicate, 1990 Award for Excellence in Advertising Graphics
- Numerous collegiate graphic arts and journalism awards.

◦ Employment ◦

<u>1992 - Date</u>: Senior Graphic Artist, Rhode Island Weekends Magazine, Providence, RI
<u>1990 - 1992</u>: Paste-up and Insertion Technician, The Providence Daily, Providence, RI
<u>1988 - 1990</u>: Free-Lance Artist/Photographer

◦ Education ◦

Bachelor of Arts
Commercial Design
Rhode Island College of Design, 1988

◦ Comments ◦

Interested in taking combined artistic, journalistic, and commercial experience and applying them in a computer equipped graphic arts studio.

3 | 75 MODEL RESUMES

The resumes that follow are representative of how the standard formats can be applied effectively to a wide variety of situations. Do not be alarmed if your job title is not on the list. They are illustrations of suggested methods and styles and should not be viewed as the perfect format for a given kind of job. The job titles selected here include the categories projected to have the best employment growth rate for this decade. Page through them all and let the cumulative impact of a lot of good ideas work for you.

While the model resumes are based on real life situations, names of people, organizations, professional terminology, numbers, and the data in general are pure fiction. They have been deliberately altered to avoid any chance of conflict with personal or proprietary information. You will be able to look at the samples and determine what real life substitutions should be made to reflect your circumstances most appropriately.

With the first two chapters as background, you should now shop your way through the rich lode of resume technique that fills the following pages. To ease your access to what might appear to be an overwhelming array of material, use the index below as a starting point.

All 80 resumes from Resume First Aid and 75 Model Resumes are indexed below. (The five resumes introduced under Resume First Aid in Chapter 1 are marked with an asterisk.) They are listed alphabetically by job title under the following categories:

- Administrative Resumes
- Artistic Resumes

- Education and Institutional Resumes
- Financial Resumes
- Health Care Resumes
- Information Technology Resumes
- Law Enforcement and Security Resumes
- Marketing and Sales Resumes, and
- Scientific and Technical Resumes.

Index by Job Category and Title

ADMINISTRATIVE RESUMES

Note—Resumes marked * are found in Resume First Aid, Chapter 1.

ARTISTIC RESUMES

Job Title	Resume Type	Page
Graphic Designer	Competency Cluster	118
Interior Designer	Focused	128
Landscape Architect	Work History	132
Television Support Technician	Focused	192

EDUCATION AND INSTITUTIONAL RESUMES

Job Title	Resume Type	Page
Child-Care Worker	Focused	76
College Counselor*	Focused	10
College Professor	Work History	80
English as a Second Language Teacher*	Focused	12
Minister	Focused	142
School Administrator	Competency Cluster	174
School Guidance Counselor	Focused	176
Teacher Aide	Competency Cluster	186
Training-and-Development Specialist	Work History	194

FINANCIAL RESUMES

Job Title	Resume Title	Page
Bank Collector	Focused	62
Bank Officer	Work History	64
Bookkeeper	Competency Cluster	70
Credit Manager	Work History	94
Financial Analyst	Work History	112
Investment Officer*	Focused	16

Note—Resumes marked * are found in Resume First Aid, Chapter 1.

HEALTH CARE RESUMES

Job Title	Resume Type	Page
Dental Assistant and Hygienist	Work History	100
Emergency Medical Technician	Work History	106
Hospital Administrator	Work History	122
Medical Records Technician	Focused	140
Nurse	Competency Cluster	148
Pharmacist	Focused	152
Physician Assistant	Work History	154
Veterinary Technician	Competency Cluster	198

INFORMATION TECHNOLOGY RESUMES

Job Title	Resume Type	Page
Computer Maintenance Specialist	Focused	82
Computer Operator	Focused	84
Computer Programmer	Work History	86
Computer Systems Analyst	Focused	90
Database Administrator	Focused	98
Internet Security Engineer	Focused	130
Network Administrator	Focused	144
Supervisory Systems Analyst	Focused	184
Web Developer	Focused	200
Word Processing Operator	Competency Cluster	202

LAW ENFORCEMENT AND SECURITY RESUMES

Job Title	Resume Type	Page
Corrections Officer	Work History	92
Private Investigator	Competency Cluster	156
Security Manager	Focused	182

MARKETING AND SALES RESUMES

Job Title	Resume Type	Page
Advertising Account Executive	Competency Cluster	54
Advertising Copy Writer	Focused	56
Advertising Sales Manager	Competency Cluster	58
Computer Sales Representative	Focused	88
Fund Raiser	Focused	116
Insurance Agent/Financial Planner	Work History	126
Manufacturers' Sales Representative	Competency Cluster	138
Product Manager	Work History	158
Real Estate Broker	Focused	164
Retail Buyer	Focused	168
Retail Salesperson	Competency Cluster	170
Travel Agent	Focused	196

SCIENTIFIC AND TECHNICAL RESUMES

Job Title	Resume Type	Page
Biological Technician	Competency Cluster	66
Biomedical Engineer	Focused	68
Business-Machine Service Representative	Work History	72
Chemist	Competency Cluster	74
Civil Engineer	Work History	78
Electronic Engineer	Competency Cluster	104
Environmental Technician	Work History	110
Food Technologist	Focused	114
Heating, Air Conditioning, and Refrigeration Mechanic	Focused	120
Robotics Engineer	Work History	172
Technical Writer	Work History	188
Telecommunications Specialist	Competency Cluster	190

Administrative Assistant

WORK HISTORY RESUME

General Strategy

Ms. Williams chose the **Work History Resume** to quickly highlight her two blocks of highly relevant experience—

- four years as a military officer with leadership training, experience, and substantial responsibilities; and

- current employment in a dynamic business position that shows success in the demanding field of marketing.

A brief **Overview** section says what she has done and what she wants to do. **Comments** clarify that she wants to apply her skills assisting a senior manager with the clear implication that she views the position as a stepping stone to the executive ranks herself.

Her resume conveys the message that she has succeeded in two entry-level positions, but doesn't want to pursue either specialty as a career. Rather, she presents herself as a proven performer ready for higher-level, more general management duties. She builds her case on a foundation of clearly stated work experience that would instantly command the respect of a senior person looking for a sharp assistant who has already been in the trenches.

Specific Points

❶ What she has done and what she wants to do.

❷ Evidence of success in being persuasive with professional people.

❸ Proven ability to communicate aggressively.

❹ Industry knowledge that can be valuable assisting a senior executive.

❺ Tangible proof of effectiveness in setting and meeting business objectives.

❻ Relevant, applied leadership training.

❼ Ability to travel and function successfully away from home.

❽ Demonstrated success in taking on responsibility rapidly.

❾ Tangible proof of recognition by her supervisors.

❿ Relevant academic preparation for the role she seeks.

Carol J. Williams

1256 Kolorotura Drive
Washington, DC 20099
202-222-9988 (Office)
202-333-9075 (Residence)

1

Overview

Strong organizational and people skills. Proven leader with over 6 years of progressively successful experience in personnel, management, and sales. Seek to combine talents at senior management level as administrative assistant with potential for assuming broader responsibilities.

Experience

2

June 1997 - Present: *Account Executive,* Witherspoon & Company Investments, Washington, DC. Twice awarded outstanding salesperson of the quarter as a retail stockbroker catering to professional clients. Organize and conduct on-going business development activity including extensive telephone contact and mailings. Licensed broker with broad market knowledge in a variety of industries. Generated $2.5 million dollars in new business during the last year including 8 employee benefits accounts for professional corporations.

3

4

5

June 1993 - May 1997: *Administrative Officer,* U. S. Air Force, Ramstein AFB, Germany. Following 3 months of officer candidate school and 4 months of administrative officer training, assigned as Assistant Personnel Officer of 287 person reconnaissance squadron. Responsible for pay, benefits, and assignment processing of all new and departing staff. Promoted to Chief Administrative Officer after 13 months, responsible for personnel and operational administrative matters, reporting directly to the commander. Awarded commendation medal for outstanding performance that included exceptional ratings in 8 high level operational readiness inspections. Concluded active duty obligation as a Captain. In the active reserve as a Major.

7

8

6

9

July 1989 - May 1993: **Various part-time positions** while attending college including retail sales, secretarial positions in professional offices, and assisting my father in the operation of his consulting firm.

Education   **10**

BSc, Business Administration, Northwestern University, 1993

Comments

While I have succeeded in direct selling on the professional level, I prefer to combine that experience with my administrative talents and pursue a career in management. Combined leadership, sales, and administrative perspectives prepare me as a seasoned administrative assistant to a senior manager.

Advertising Account Executive

COMPETENCY CLUSTER RESUME

General Strategy

Mr. Kirk used the **Competency Cluster Resume** because his strong points center around two things that his potential employers care most about:

- He has managed large advertising accounts successfully and shown that he can generate new business.

- He can relate well to the creative side of the house in the advertising business because he has been there as an award-winning professional.

The college affiliation has been placed prominently because he knows his alma mater has a great reputation in the field and a lot of hiring officials are also graduates.

Work history is solid, but not exceptional. Better to lift the skills and present them as valued competencies than to try to paint a glowing picture within the context of pedestrian jobs. His **Overview** says as much—nine years of successful experience that covers both the creative and marketing sectors—strength is in making the clients happy by mustering the best efforts of his former peers in the creative part of the agency.

Specific Points

❶ **Overview** establishes his dual skills and identifies his industry specialty.

❷ **Education** is an important identity factor in his industry, so it is stressed.

❸ Quantification of what he does and what it's worth in dollars is important.

❹ Identifies the specific class of clients he is skilled at dealing with.

❺ Proven ability to take over an account and make it grow.

❻ A record for attracting new business that promises significant profits.

❼ Shows he can bridge the gap between clients and creative people.

❽ Experience in dealing successfully with a large, prominent client.

❾ Major regional award from national industry group—worth mentioning.

❿ Employment is self-descriptive to those who would evaluate him.

Hugh M. Kirk

2179 Beach Drive, Apartment 142
Jacksonville, FL
904-222-9988 (Office)
904-333-9075 (Residence)

Overview

❶ Advertising manager with nine years of successful experience in both the creative and marketing sectors of consumer electronics. Proven ability to develop existing and new business using thorough industry knowledge and creative persuasion within the firm's specialized divisions and the client's organization.

❷ Education

Bachelor of Science
Marketing Management
North Florida University, 1990

Account Development ❸

❹ Currently overseeing 6 accounts with annual agency revenues of $250,000 to $1.5 million each. Product families include consumer electronics directed toward the home-based professional and small consulting firms. Assumed management of 4 ◀❺ existing accounts each of which have been increased by over 20% in less than 18 months. Added two accounts in the same period, each with the potential for exceeding the annual fee volume of present largest client within 2 years.

Creative Experience ❻

❼ Acquired present position while serving as an independent consultant to the advertising layout department. Was employed full time to oversee the artistic ◀❽ development of print media advertising for the largest retail electronics chain in North Florida. Campaign won Southeast Region Style Award from the American Advertisers' Guild in 1997. ❾

Employment Summary

❿ Wilson & Johnson Agency, 39th Floor, Suite 300, Gulf Life Building, Jacksonville, FL. Account Executive. July 1995 to Present.

Creative Design Consultants, 15 Business Park Circle, Orlando, FL. Artistic Layout Consultant. June 1992 - July 1995.

Daytona Evening Press, 3500 Del Ray Avenue, Daytona Beach, FL. Advertising Department Apprentice. June 1990 - May 1992.

Advertising Copy Writer

FOCUSED RESUME

General Strategy

Ms. Baker is advised to use the **Focused Resume** because it is an efficient way to present her unique combination of talents, which would not stand out in separate job descriptions. She needs to communicate quickly to the employer—who is known to be in the business of high-fashion sportswear, since she is *focusing* on that job market—that she:

- grew up in the retail clothing business;
- has traveled to where her clients go (can identify with them as she writes copy designed to appeal to them); and
- is herself a former fashion model.

A few years as a clerk in the family store and a few more as a model turn into an attractive applicant when *focused* on the specific job she has in mind.

Specific Points

❶ Brief **Objective** tells the employer she has a special combination of skills for the particular position.

❷ A geographic preference is important to her, so she says so up front.

❸ Worked in the industry already—with a major retailer, even though it was family.

❹ Merger—a logical reason for not continuing in the family business.

❺ Evidence that she knows technological as well as fashion side of sportswear and has hands–on experience using the Internet to market sportswear.

❻ Model background adds both fashion credibility and glamour.

❼ Shows she has lived the lifestyle of those for whom she intends to write.

❽ A highly respected agency, known in the region, endorses her stature.

❾ Advantage to being in the family—saw all sides—more than a clerk.

❿ Respectable liberal arts degree is fine for what she is trying to achieve.

Kathryn C. Baker
38 Ohio Place, Apartment 403
Rapid City, SD 57709
605-222-9988

❶
❷

Objective: Copy writing position in an established mail order firm in the North Central region. Particularly interested in applying strong sense of style and knowledge of top market sportswear gained working in family retail clothing business and modeling career.

ASSETS

❸
❹

- **Overall perspective** on the national sports clothing market from a lifetime of participation in my family's store which was the 2nd largest retailer of sportswear in Minnesota prior to its acquisition by a national chain upon by father's retirement.

❺

- **Familiarity with the trends and technological features** associated with contemporary all-weather sports clothing.
- **Internet aware** creator of a personal Web page for direct–marketing several of my own design. Used Web–authoring tools provided by my Internet service provider.

❻

- **Fashion sensitivity** in the sports garment industry enhanced by over 2 years of successful modeling in Chicago market following college graduation.
- **Extensive travel** throughout the winter sports areas of the United States, Canada, and Europe.

❼

EMPLOYMENT

❽

The Wood Agency, 1000 Market Square, Mercantile Center, Chicago, IL. Model specializing in active sportswear. June 1997 - January 1999.

❾

Outdoor Classic Design, Wilmount Mall, Minneapolis, MN. Seasonal sales work in family business from age 16 through college. Observed and participated in buying and merchandising as well. December 1988 - June 1997.

EDUCATION

❿

Bachelor of Arts
Liberal Arts
National College, 1997

Advertising Sales Manager

COMPETENCY CLUSTER RESUME

General Strategy

Mr. Kearney decided to bracket his employment so boldly that it needed no heading, such as Objective. In six words he makes clear:

- what he wants to do—sell radio advertising;
- the level at which he wants to operate—management; and
- the market for his talents—top-ten radio.

With that taken care of, the best way to proceed is with the **Competency Cluster Resume** where he continues the powerfully simple message he has begun. The headings alone say he is competent in marketing, management, creative, and technical aspects of his specialty. He then goes on to say exactly how under each heading, briefly puts forth a career path that endorses his readiness for sales management, and concludes with a pair of degrees that complement what he is trying to do occupationally.

Specific Points

❶ Six introductory words can say a lot about what you want to do.

❷ Sidebar headings themselves serve as an outline of competencies.

❸ Identifies the specific market niche in which he is knowledgeable.

❹ Quantifies sales productivity with dollar figures and percentage of growth.

❺ Shows he can develop other salespersons—a key skill for a sales manager.

❻ Proves he is a creative ad man—major station/regional awards/bonuses which are only paid when efforts generate the profits to pay for them.

❼ Demonstrates early work ethic and shows valuable experience as a DJ.

❽ Even a simple electric typewriter will generally **bold** and <u>underline,</u> adding interest to the resume and distinguishing between levels of headings.

❾ Career path is shown clearly in this simple listing of positions held.

❿ Degrees listed vouch for general education and specific business preparation relevant to a career in sales management.

Alfred D. Kearney

289 Atlantic Boulevard
Alameda, CA 94502
510-722-9988 (Office)
510-443-9075 (Residence)

①

Advertising Sales Manager, Top-Ten Radio

② **Marketing**

③ Successful radio advertising sales experience for major market top-ten station. Established in the college and young adult market segments including physical conditioning, fast food, and sportswear. Servicing **④** 37 accounts with annual ad budgets in the $4000 to $175,000 range yielding combined yearly revenues of $3.2 million. Increased account dollar value base by average of 30% annually while adding new accounts at a rate of 2 monthly.

Management

⑤ Developed a team of six junior sales representatives from point of recruitment through field training and into independent operation. Retained 4 of the 6 after 2 years with 2 earning individual productivity awards and all substantially exceeding minimum production objectives.

Creative

⑥ Three years as advertising copywriter for lead station in the Western Radio Group. Twice earned regional awards for creative impact and client retention. Each involved substantial, documented, renewal bonus.

Technical

⑦ During 4 years of college, worked average of 20 hours weekly as combination disk jockey and station engineer for mid-size university town AM station serving a comprehensive rural market.

⑧ **Employment**

WQRA Alameda, Group Advertising Sales Manager. 1993-Present.
WLUX Phoenix, Advertising Copywriter. 1990-93.
WTBP Manhattan, KS, Disk jockey/engineer. 1988-93. **⑨**

Education

Associate in Science		Bachelor of Science
General Studies	**⑩**	Business Administration
West Kansas Junior College, 1980		Manhattan College, 1993

Apartment Manager

FOCUSED RESUME

General Strategy

Mr. Blakemore is making application within a specialized employment field and is advised to use the **Focused Resume** in order to:

- highlight his professional certification and minimize his lack of a college degree, which is not overly relevant here and easily compensated for; and

- stress the base of successful experience doing exactly what he is asking to do in yet a larger, higher-paying facility.

This resume format is ideal for placing the emphasis on the skills, experience, and training most immediately applicable to the position in question.

Specific Points

❶ **Overview** is used to categorize immediately the scope of his experience.

❷ It is also the place to establish the existence of his instantly credible professional certification, the Certified Building Manager (CBM) designation.

❸ Tells what kinds of projects he has managed and for how long.

❹ Says what the employer wants to hear—occupancy up, turnover down.

❺ Can supervise the sort of employees known to exist in the new setting.

❻ Experienced in dealing with a union work force.

❼ Gets along well with the project staff—an essential quality for a manager.

❽ Knows how to deal with tenant organizations.

❾ Has practical experience applying Internet marketing techniques in the rental real estate market.

❿ Work history shows responsible positions logically supporting aspirations.

Wilson W. Blakemore
3179 Clayton Place, NW
Washington, DC 20039
202-821-9988 (Office)
202-538-9075 (Residence)

Overview

❶ <u>**Residential property manager**</u> with 16 years of progressively more responsible positions in 250 to 500 unit up-scale apartment projects. Certified Building Manager (CBM) with highly successful combined operating and marketing experience. **❷**

Strengths

❸
- <u>**Managed 2 general population buildings**</u>, each for a period of approximately six years prior to assuming general management of present major senior retirement complex in 1995. Occupancy **❹** increased from mid-70% to 95% range in each situation with corresponding reductions in tenant turnover.

❺
- <u>**Oversaw building engineers, building and grounds maintenance staffs, contract marketing efforts, and lobby personnel**</u> in each facility. Twice in collective bargaining situations. **❻** Staff retention raised from average of 8.3 months to over 3 years in high attrition positions. Executive staff stabilized completely.

- <u>**Successfully dealt with tenant organizations**</u> in each situation. **❼** Established sufficient goodwill to reduce litigation to management **❽** companies involved by an average of 30% within 1 year of assuming duties. Led crucial tenant relations campaign resulting in voluntary condominium conversion of major inner city property following 8 years of costly opposition.

❾
- <u>**Collaborated with Web site developer**</u> on the preparation and maintenance of a corporate page displaying available properties.

Employment

❿
- Simonton Place Apartments, 487 unit seniors' rental facility, predominantly 2-bedroom, top-decile rent category. Washington, DC. General Manager. 1995-Present.
- Wilkins Gardens, 364 unit general population rental complex, mixed 1, 2-bedroom, and efficiency building with extensive grounds including golf course. Richmond, VA. Resident Manager. 1980-1995.
- Randal Place Apartments, 295 unit young professional building, 85% efficiencies, remainder 1 and 2-bedroom, mid-town location. Washington. DC. Resident Manager. 1983-1989.

Education

Diploma
Business Management
District Business College, 1993.

Bank Collector

FOCUSED RESUME

General Strategy

Mr. Rogers has completed a career in the navy with an outstanding record and a lot of highly relevant skills. He needs to showcase those talents without drawing undue attention to the fact that they were gained while working in a military environment and for a single employer. His best approach is to use the **Focused Resume,** with which he can establish that he:

- welcomes the challenge of public contact and problem solving;

- has comparable skills to someone in a personnel career in the civilian sector;

- has been successful in positions of considerable responsibility; and

- possesses the practical training necessary to do the job.

Specific Points

❶ An **Objective** statement makes it clear that he is willing to take on the challenge of solving problems with the general public—a general focus suited to many civilian jobs, including Bank Collector.

❷ Immediate verification of his experience in dealing with people.

❸ Qualification of the scope of his responsibilities and the fact that they dealt with financial matters.

❹ Notes that current technology was available to him in his environment.

❺ Experience in relating to all levels of clients—junior to very senior.

❻ Was an innovator in using the same kinds of technology called for in a bank conducting credit collection efforts over a large region.

❼ Verifiable success in handling sensitive issues to the satisfaction of the customer would be attractive to those reading his resume.

❽ Another specific illustration of initiative and successful results.

❾ A simple statement of work history that speaks for itself.

❿ A brief **Comments** statement can do a lot to meld experience with objective—bridges the gap between careers in divergent settings.

Charles L. Rogers
9075 Salem Place South
Augusta, GA 30901
706-662-9988

1 **Objective**: **To obtain a business position that involves problem solving and public contact.**

Strengths:

2 • Twenty year career as a Navy non-commissioned officer in the personnel specialty — customer service and problem solving.

3 • Managed a 9 person office adjudicating pay and benefits claims for a command (customer base) of 7,000 sailors.

4 • Conversant in telemarketing techniques and equipment as applied to financial applications.

• Mature, experienced manager accustomed to dealing successfully with diverse clients ranging from new enlistees to senior flag officers. **5**

Achievements:

6 • Established an 800 number service line for Navy pay and personnel problem resolution.

7 • Increased customer satisfaction rate by 42 percent while reducing staffing and support costs by one-half.

• Set record for Navy Fund (United Way-type organization) participation in the Pacific Command by using telephone solicitation techniques. **8**

Work Experience:

1979-1999: United States Navy **9**

Education:

Diploma
Office Management
Wilson Business School, 1979

10 **Comments**: Enlisted in the Navy following graduation from business school. During 20 years of service, attended an on-going series of professional development courses in the personnel and financial services specialties. While work experience has been limited to military, human relations and financial skills are essentially the same as among civilian clientele.

Bank Officer

WORK HISTORY RESUME

General Strategy

Ms. Anson chose the **Work History Resume** because she has a straightforward pattern of employment in her professional field. It is effectively described by listing each position in order and detailing her various responsibilities:

- starting with minor experience in the industry as a summer teller;
- beginning her professional lending career in the recognized entry-level position of credit analyst; and
- moving up to Assistant Loan Officer.

Her well-ordered, brief resume establishes that she is moving successfully through the progression expected for the next step in her career ladder—a lateral move to a better opportunity or larger institution or a promotion to full fledged Loan Officer status.

Specific Points

❶ The **Overview** effectively states level of experience in a single sentence.

❷ Continuity is shown by the dates of employment at each institution.

❸ Large employers like these are understood in their industry—no further description of them is necessary.

❹ The position title is sufficient to tell those in the business the kind of work she does—what is needed is enough quantification to describe exactly what level of responsibility she had in the position.

❺ When it can be safely verified by future reference checks, ranked performance is a strong way to demonstrate strength. Knowledge of how to apply Web page technology to a profit center in the industry is an invaluable point to illustrate when possible.

❻ Expected background experience is established by this entry-level position.

❼ Shows rapid, successful assumption of responsibility.

❽ Discreet, matter-of-fact explanation of reason for leaving first position.

❾ Career-oriented degree shows commitment to the profession.

❿ Professional affiliations are enhanced by noting a leadership role.

Sally N. Anson
8567 South Murray Lane
Columbia, SC 29205
803-222-9988 (Office)
803-333-9075 (Residence)

OVERVIEW

①

Commercial lender with four years of successful experience in regional bank lending to middle market accounts as a credit analyst and corporate calling officer.

EXPERIENCE

③

June 1997 - Present: *Assistant Loan Officer,* **Southland Banks,** Columbia, SC. Commercial loan officer with extensive business development responsibilities in the Carolinas, Georgia, and North Florida. Manage a $35 million portfolio which includes $27 million outstanding and $8 million committed. Generated $11 million in new deposits and $19 million in new loans in 2.5 years— **⑤** number 2 performer on a staff of 12 regional lenders. Using the text editor BBEdit, developed an on-line loan application section on the bank's Web page that pre-qualifies candidates and significantly reduces the number of lending officer calls on unqualified prospects.

②

④
⑥

June 1995 - May 1997: *Credit Analyst,* **Coastal National Bank,** Sea Pines, GA. Entry position upon college graduation. Credit review and analysis for middle market companies. Rapidly assumed full supporting activities for lenders prior to leaving and assuming an officer position in the interest of professional growth not available at Coastal National. **⑧**

⑦

July 1991 - May 1995: Various part-time positions while attending college including seasonal retail sales, clerical positions and **summer employment as a bank teller.**

EDUCATION

Bachelor of Business Administration
⑨ → Banking and Finance
University of West Georgia, 1995

⑩ ## PROFESSIONAL AFFILIATIONS & TRAINING

Professional Member, Robert Morris Associates,
Secretary of Carolinas' Chapter.
Currently pursuing the National Commercial Loan School,
Norman, Oklahoma.

Biological Technician

COMPETENCY CLUSTER RESUME

General Strategy

Mr. Woodward is just completing his college studies and, while he has some valuable experiences, they do not lend themselves to a traditional resume where dates must show continuity, one position follows another, etc. Because his experience is part-time and irregular, but important to potential employers, he was advised to use the **Competency Cluster Resume.** This allows him to say precisely what he did— and even where and when he did it—but without having to emphasize the mixed nature of his experiences.

With this approach, he can clearly highlight the fact that he:

- has laboratory work experience;
- has field experience;
- has contributed to formal research; and
- was educated for this speciality.

Specific Points

1 Combined and categorized, two summer jobs take on greater meaning.

2 Work ethic demonstrated by evening employment during college.

3 Classifying his and his supervisor's levels of responsibility defines the magnitude of the work done.

4 Field experience for a regionally known organization is worth noting.

5 Establishes a lifelong working knowledge of applied animal biology.

6 Cites applications that will be valued by the kinds of firms apt to hire him.

7 Associates himself in an appropriately limited way with known research.

8 The right degree for his career, earned from a respected local institution.

9 Notes a nationally recognized association's accreditation of his program.

10 An entry-level person, in particular, needs strong, relevant references.

Vernon D. Woodward

1279 Creek Valley Avenue
Pittsburgh, PA 15214
412-222-9988 (Office)
412-333-9075 (Residence)

LABORATORY EXPERIENCE

(1)
- Two summers of full-time experience assisting biochemists at University Associates, Inc. in the analysis of test-animal body fluids, drug reactions, and food assimilation studies.

(2)
- Evening employment with National Labs in the capacity of a biological ←**(3)** technician aide during final academic year. Assisted senior microbiological technician in immunological research.

FIELD EXPERIENCE

(4)
- Summer experience with Save The Lake Foundation assisting wildlife biologists in the collection of data on the effects of pollution on the ecosystems of Western Maryland.

(5)
- Grew up working on family poultry farm constantly involved in practical application of nutrition and disease management including assisting in **(6)** taking blood samples, mass vaccination drives, on-site analysis and data gathering by feed contractor's scientists.

RESEARCH CONTRIBUTIONS

(7)
- Acknowledged for supporting efforts in Wilson-Walker study of immunological parasitology in farm/college environments, 1997.

EDUCATION

Associate in Applied Science **(8)**
Laboratory Technology
Allegheny Junior College, 1999

COMMENTS

(9)
Formal clinical training in AJC's nationally accredited program in Laboratory Technology supplemented by significant periods of employment in the industry on a part-time basis. Life-long exposure to applied application of laboratory technology in field settings. High motivation and competency verifiable by references upon request.

Biomedical Engineer

FOCUSED RESUME

General Strategy

Ms. McNair has excellent credentials, but a history of short terms of employment. Her choice of the **Focused Resume** is a wise one because it tends to showcase her strong abilities and achievements without making the employer search for them in a string of positions that didn't last very long. All of her employers are important names to mention and the dates are not withheld, just not emphasized.

With this approach, the reviewer's attention is *focused* on:

- six powerful sets of professional skills;
- three clearly important professional achievements;
- six nationally recognized employers; and
- the right degrees and affilations.

Specific Points

❶ A headline-type **Objective** classifies the field and level of employment.

❷ Established abilities in the technical specialty.

❸ Indications of ability to lead other scientists and work within standards.

❹ Proof of being able not only to design, but to implement her achievements.

❺ Security clearances may be an attractive asset worth mentioning discreetly.

❻ National professional recognition establishes stature in her field.

❼ By moving the dates of employment to the right of the employer and not making them a separate column, they are deemphasized, but available.

❽ Rapid movement to more important job titles does much to compensate for relatively brief tenure with various employers.

❾ Excellent degrees and universities discreetly noted.

❿ The expected professional affiliations are confirmed.

Edith K. McNair

8236 Thurmont Street
Petersburg, VA 23805
304-333-9075 (Residence)

❶ OBJECTIVE: Biomedical Engineer—Research and Development

ABILITIES:

❷ • Apply computer aided design to advanced prosthesis testing
• Adapt artificial intelligence to mechanical applications
❸ • Direct design staff integrating digital/mechanical dimensions
• Liaison with civilian and military government scientists
• Conduct feasibility testing within established industry standards
• Coordinate with regulatory boards on operating approvals

ACHIEVEMENTS:

❹ • Designed and implemented advanced aerospace prosthesis applications for unmanned environments
• Applied CAD/CAM principles to previously unapproached design areas within the aeromedical arena (details classified) ◄— **❺**
• Woman Engineer of the Year Award winner in 1997 for work in articulating joint modification mechanics in AI theory
❻

WORK HISTORY:

• Woodruff Laboratories, 1998-99   Senior Scientist
• Digital Medical Corporation, 1995-98   Applications Developer
• Johnston Medical, Inc., 1994-95   Design Engineer
• NASA, 1992-94   **❼** Biomedical Researcher   **❽**
• Johns Hopkins University, 1990-92   Graduate Assistant
• United States Air Force, 1986-90   Engineering Instructor

EDUCATION:

Bachelor of Science   **❾**   Master of Science
Mechanical Engineering   Biomedical Engineering
Virginia Polytechnic Institute, 1986   Johns Hopkins University, 1992

PROFESSIONAL AFFILIATIONS:

• Society of Women Engineers
• Biomedical Engineering Society

Bookkeeper

COMPETENCY CLUSTER RESUME

General Strategy

Mr. Joseph has only held one position, but he has the kinds of abilities that would be very attractive to an accounting firm looking for a bookkeeping associate. The best way to display his strengths is with the **Competency Cluster Resume.** It allows him to relegate his single employer to the bottom of the page and draw attention to his most marketable qualities:

- an associate degree in accounting from a respectable local college;

- experience preparing taxes for small business clients;

- outstanding applied knowledge of accounting-related computer software; and

- a willingness and ability to work directly with clients.

Specific Points

❶ In the absence of a long work history, the academic credential is important.

❷ Practical, quantified experience with which the employer can identify.

❸ Bread-and-butter business for the kind of firm he seeks to join.

❹ Demonstrates software knowledge and proper role relative to professional staff—knows how to fit into the team.

❺ Ability to use an important class of software and an indication that he can figure out the use of others by using the manuals provided.

❻ Knowledge of relevant computer hardware and peripheral equipment.

❼ Valuable skills in using computer communications equipment and programs are alluded to in this point.

❽ Level of responsibility indicated by representing the firm to clients directly.

❾ Respect for professional strengths and limitations shown here—i.e., won't be getting the firm into trouble by making decisions better left to the CPAs.

❿ Solid, continuous employment history with an established firm.

Enrique E. Joseph

491 Baldwin Place, Apartment 29
Corpus Christi, TX 78404
512-261-9988 (Office)
512-443-9075 (Residence)

Education

(1) Associate in Science
Accounting
Bee County Junior College, 1996

SMALL BUSINESS TAXES

(2) • Maintain ledgers, statements, and running status forms for 36 small business clients.

• Prepare federal and state quarterly withholding forms for clients. **(3)**

COMPUTER USE **(4)**

• Enter tax data into TaxWise software under the direction of professional staff of CPA firm

• Data entry and routine analyses using the Primary Spreadsheet software package and related manuals. **(5)**

(6) • Data entry and reports generation using the Twin Ledger II system on the ProCal 37 computer and operating system.

• Operate modem data exchanges quarterly with 3 large client companies. **(7)**

CLIENT CONTACT **(8)**

• Serve as point of contact for 17 small business owners whose books are maintained by the firm.

• Explain reporting procedures and respond to client assistance requests not involving CPA advisories. **(9)**

Employment

(10) 1996 - Present: Bookkeeper
Bell & Weathers, CPAs, PC

Business-Machine Service Representative

WORK HISTORY RESUME

General Strategy

Ms. DuVall has held two positions that display her talents quite well. For that reason, she has chosen the **Work History Resume** format. It allows her to show:

- the right kind of formal technical education;
- inside technical service employment;
- field service employment; and
- an impressive array of manufacturers' specialized training schools.

Specific Points

1 The applied electronics degree is a valuable asset worth using as a lead item in this resume directed toward technical employment.

2 Current employment is both verified and described as relevant.

3 Position title is self-descriptive, but needs further qualification as to whether she was a generalist serving many lines or a specialist limited to one or two categories of equipment.

4 Competency as confirmed by a competitive award is worthy of mention.

5 Customer relations is very important in this field and her ability to cite strength in that area adds value to her credentials.

6 Demonstrated in-house competence speaks well for her ability to coordinate field troubleshooting with the main office staff—speaks their language—has "been there."

7 Good to specify the kinds of service work done—warranty, preventive maintenance, etc.

8 Current manufacturer-specific training is invaluable—stress it if you have it.

9 A subtle expression of willingness to travel and pursue opportunities for technical growth is also conveyed in this list of courses attended.

10 Progress in achieving formal professional certification should be noted.

Elaine P. DuVall

472 Ross Road, NE
Frederick, MD 21702
240-222-9988 (Office)
240-333-9075 (Residence)

Education

(1) Associate in Applied Science
Electronics Technology
Middletown Community College, 1993

Experience

June 1997 - Present: **(2)** **(3)** <u>Technical Representative,</u> Micro Copiers & Office Electronics, Inc., Frederick, MD. Install and service complete line of office copiers, mail processing, and personal computer equipment on site. Runner-up in Mid-Atlantic Region **(4)** Xeno Technical Trouble Shooting Contest last year. Customer satisfaction bonus this year. **(5)**

June 1993 - May 1997: **(6)** <u>Bench Technician</u>, Wilmont Office Systems, Rockville, MD. In-house service technician responsible for major repairs to all kinds of office electronics products. Testing, preventive maintenance, and component replacement on top lines under warranty of manufacturers. **(7)** Formally recognized for outstanding performance on six occasions.

(8) <u>Specialized Manufacturers' Training</u>

(9)

- October 1993—2 week resident course, Xeno Corporation Training Center, Portside, NC, Copier Repair Courses I & II.

- April 1994—1 week resident course, Mika Computers Technical Center, Palo Alto, CA, Office Computer Trouble Shooting Basics.

- July 1996—10 day seminar, Appricot Service Center, Taos, NM, Upgrading and Maintaining Appricot Computer Systems.

- September 1997—date: Computer Assisted Instruction courses by the Office Electronics Institute in preparation for certification tests. Passed Series I & II, completion of Series III & IV anticipated in 1999 for designation as a Certified Office Electronics Technician (COET). **(10)**

Chemist

COMPETENCY CLUSTER RESUME

General Strategy

Dr. Hasenworth has outstanding credentials, but her experience does not include full-time employment outside the academic community and related work-study positions. She is advised to stress her excellent abilities and all that she has achieved, without drawing undue attention to the fact that she has never held a job. The **Competency Cluster Resume** is the best format for accomplishing this. With it she can show that she:

- knows where her training can best be used in industry;

- has the industry-related skills and achievements to be attractive; and

- holds academic credentials appropriate to an advanced research position.

Specific Points

❶ In a brief introductory **Objective** sentence, she establishes that she is pursuing a position in industry, not the academic world.

❷ Practical, industry-related research is noted vs. the esoteric, academic variety that might be of less importance to the people who will read her resume.

❸ Computer literacy appropriate to her field is established authoritatively.

❹ Sensitivity to a possible role as an industry spokesperson to environmental and other community groups may make her a more attractive candidate in today's climate, which is filled with such concerns.

❺ Linkage with a respected industry group as credibility by association.

❻ Evidence of working with up-to-the-minute issues and technology.

❼ National stature confirmed by competitive award in her field.

❽ Respect of mentors implied by selection for key studies and publications.

❾ The correct academic credentials are in place for top-level research.

❿ References are key to confirming her qualities and potential in the absence of a traditional employment record.

Jill C. Hasenworth

367 Jamesway Avenue
Overland Park, KS 66211
913-333-9075 (Residence)

① **OBJECTIVE:** An advanced research position within the polymer coatings segment of the paint industry.

COMPETENCIES:

② • Designed polymer coating testing procedures based on computer modeling and mathematical weather effects simulation.

③ • Extensive computer programming capabilities in specialized scientific languages and servo linkages among non-complementary systems.

• Outstanding lay communication skills invaluable asset in articulation of scientific needs and achievements to broader scientific and business constituencies. ← **④**

• Broad industry exposure across the specialized polymer segment gained during work-study and research fellowships supported by the Polymer Council over five years of graduate work-study.

⑤

ACHIEVEMENTS:

⑥ • Applied attrition analysis assumptions successfully to the oblique abrasion theory permitting breakthrough advances in space age coating durabilities.

⑦ • Placed second in national competition sponsored by American Chemical Institute's Polymers Division in new research articulation.

• Selected as one of a team of three doctoral students to continue the grant-based work of Hans Bremmer in polymer isolation.

• Dissertation entitled "Assumptive Bremmerian Polymer Attitudes Beta Testing"
⑧ published as a monograph of the ACI Institute, Polymers Division.

EDUCATION

Doctor of Philosophy
⑨ Theoretical Polymer Chemistry
University of Chicago, 1989

Master of Science
Chemistry
University of Chicago, 1985

Bachelor of Science
Chemistry
Ottawa University, 1983

COMMENTS

Extensive work-study experience in a variety of industry settings adds practical dimensions to my theoretical training. Upon request, references will be provided to substantiate my performance in those settings. **⑩**

Child-Care Worker

FOCUSED RESUME

General Strategy

Ms. Busch has a specific goal in mind that calls for presenting a rather specific set of strengths—she can do this most effectively by using the **Focused Resume** since it makes these qualities the central focus of her presentation. With it she is able to:

- show that she is formally trained for the position she seeks;
- qualify the level of position and the setting she most values;
- enumerate her five greatest strengths unencumbered by spreading them across a series of different positions;
- properly establish work experience; and
- verify important certification and affiliation.

Specific Points

❶ Legitimacy and professionalism are conveyed by her formal training at a known institution.

❷ Precisely what she seeks is noted up front—including private-sector setting that will make clear her commitment to business day-care.

❸ Institutional experience separates her from home child-care applicants.

❹ Directly addresses community concern with health and character.

❺ Demonstrates familiarity with child-care in a variety of settings.

❻ References alluded to—essential in such a sensitive position.

❼ Work history is brief, but establishes context for strengths noted above it.

❽ Verification of required licensure.

❾ Certification of personal health and character available.

❿ Member of national association that espouses professionalism and high standards.

Lois M. Busch

672 Pocatello Drive, Apartment 78
Lewiston, ID 83501
208-333-9075 (Residence)

EDUCATION

❶

Certificate
Child-Care
Boise Community College, 1993

POSITION DESIRED

❷ Child Care Director — Private Sector

STRENGTHS

- Six years of progressively more responsible experience as a child care paraprofessional in institutional settings. **❸**

- Established credentials verifying personal health, character, and professional status. **❹**

- Experienced in public education, private non-profit, and industry child care situations. **❺**

- Formal training in a certified public postsecondary institution.

- Proven effectiveness in working with children, parents, educators, and company management — references available. **❻**

EXPERIENCE

❼ 1997-Present: Assistant Director of Child Care Program, Amsel Industries, Wilmington, ID

1995-97: Child Care Aide, Main Street Methodist Church, Kinton, ID

1993-95: Teacher's Aide, Johnson Elementary School, Sioux, ID

COMMENTS

❽ Licensed Child Care Worker, Idaho County Board of Commissioners

❾ Health and Personal Background Certified

Member: National Association of Child Care Paraprofessionals

 ❿

Civil Engineer

WORK HISTORY RESUME

General Strategy

Mr. Choy is an engineer with a substantial list of substantive employment situations that fits the **Work History Resume** format well. With it he is able to convey that he has:

- a broad base of specific civil engineering experiences;
- a long, responsible history of upward movement on a well-defined career ladder;
- the appropriate formal education; and
- an array of career-related short courses that have kept him current.

Specific Points

❶ A **Summary** is appropriate in a long, reasonably detailed work history. It serves to draw out important specifics for preliminary attention.

❷ In a few bulleted statements he sketches the breadth of his experience.

❸ The work history relates an unbroken chain of responsible employment from college through present position.

❹ Quantified technical and supervisory experience lets his importance be adequately appraised.

❺ Mention of successfully dealing with specific environmental problems of his industry marks him as a progressive and sensitive technical manager.

❻ Reporting relationships tend to show relative status and are important in describing your place within an organization.

❼ Being both a competent engineer and a person who can relate to government and community concerns is a plus worth mentioning.

❽ Early experience within a major federal agency vouches for an ability to deal with such institutions successfully.

❾ Verification of holding the basic educational credential of his profession.

❿ Evidence of remaining current in his field by attending specialized training over the course of a long career, offsetting a lack of graduate study.

Winston K. Choy
387 Mililani Street
Honolulu, HI 96813
808-222-9988 (Office)
808-333-9075 (Residence)

Summary

(1) Civil Engineer with extensive infrastructure experience, including:

- Liaison with government and private environmental interests
- 26 years of increasingly responsible field experience
- Federal, state, and private workplace exposure
- Professional continuing education
- Significant design innovations
- Major supervisory roles

(2)

Experience

(3)

<u>June 1995 - Present</u>: **Senior Operating Engineer,** Hawaiian Cane Group, Inc., Honolulu, HI. Ranking civil engineer in charge of field irrigation, infrastructure, and fixtures for the number two sugar cane producer in the Islands. Supervise a staff of 129 professionals, technicians, and workers engaged in the design, installation, and maintenance of systems supporting the planting, growing, and harvesting of the crop on three islands. Directly responsible for conversion from immersion to drip irrigation resulting in savings of 32 million gallons of water per year. Developing mechanically induced, high temperature burn-off techniques to comply with EPA air pollution mandates and residential development complaints. **(4)**

<u>April 1988 - May 1995</u>: **Field Engineer,** Knaurhowser Timber Management Corporation, Pine Coast, NC. Led the engineering team responsible for grading, erosion, and fire control mechanics for a 300,000 acre plot of pulp and timber pines in Coastal North Carolina. Reported to Engineering Group Chief Engineer at Atlanta office. Personally responsible for maintenance and emergency response engineering for the full spectrum of plant maturities. Extensive coordination with local and federal fire resources, EPA regulators, and recreation managers. Successfully settled long standing controversy regarding All Terrain Vehicle (ATV) use on company properties. Supervised engineering and support staff team of 74, approximately two-thirds of them professionals. **(5)**

<u>January 1979 - March 1988</u>: **Staff Engineer,** California Department of Highways, Palo Alto, CA. One of 47 engineers staffing the expansion of the Interstate Highway environmental impact retrofit project. Team effort in developing innovative techniques for correcting undesirable impact of initial engineering on 300 cut and fill sites, 47 bridges, and 3,492 water distribution device faults along the 4,229 coastal highway segments of California Interstate highways. Working level liaison with government and private environmental interests. Led a team of 12 civil engineers and draftsmen. **(6)**

<u>June 1977 - December 1978</u>: **Civil Engineer III,** San Mateo County Maintenance Division. Working civil engineer supporting the parks and lands division of the county property maintenance group. Participated in design and approval of contractor implemented projects involving roads and infrastructure serving the county's 398 acre park system and adjoining properties. **(7)**

<u>June 1973 - May 1977</u>: **Lieutenant, Army Corps of Engineers,** Fort Belvoir, VA. Junior engineering officer participation on coastal wetlands survey group. Ultimately merged with teams responsible for design and placement of beach erosion devices on the Outer Banks. Supervised a civilian contract construction group. **(8)**

Education

Bachelor of Science
(9) Civil Engineering
University of East Texas, 1973

Comments

Participated in a series of applied career related short courses, including:

- 1975 - Army Corps of Engineers Advanced School for Coastal Problem Resolution, Charleston Regional Office, SC.
- 1978 - Environmental Coalition Associations Symposium, Mare Island, CA
- 1980 - Southwestern Highway Engineers Retrofit Annual, Tucson, AZ
- 1983 - Major Contractors' Annual Meeting, San Francisco, CA
- 1984 - The Environment and the Civil Engineer, Lake Louise, AL
- 1988 - Timber Management Engineers Regional Conference, Lumberton, NC
- 1995 - Agricultural Civil Engineering in the 1990s, Great Valley, CA

(10)

College Professor

FOCUSED RESUME

General Strategy

Ms. Dow is in the process of making the transition to a higher level of functioning in her present specialty—teaching history. The **Focused Resume** gives her the format to present her admirable work history and associated educational credentials, but, importantly, it also lets her focus on her strongest assets outside the context of the setting she wants to move from.

She *focuses* on her:

- objective of moving from the high school to the community college-level institution;

- ability to teach history to anyone, regardless of level or ability; and

- scholarly productivity.

Specific Points

❶ An **Objective** statement says in a sentence what she wants to do, at what level, and in what geographic area.

❷ Six years of teaching history are documented.

❸ Successful part-time experience teaching history at the community college level to which she aspires is demonstrated.

❹ Professionalism beyond that expected of a high school history teacher is shown— desirable traits for a college professor and apt to impress those reviewing her resume.

❺ Experience recounted in traditional work history fashion.

❻ Honors as an outstanding teacher validate her competence.

❼ Community outreach project is apt to be a well-regarded initiative at the college level where similar arrangements are valued.

❽ Adjunct position shows ability to function on college level with adults.

❾ Willingness to teach in a nontraditional setting is potentially important.

❿ Being a former community college student looks good for this position.

Cynthia M. Dow

9827 North Millwork Lane
College Park, MD 20740
240-922-9988 (Office)
240-373-9075 (Residence)

❶ Objective: To obtain a tenure track position teaching U. S. History at the community college level in the Central Atlantic region.

Overview

❷ • Six years of teaching history at a public high school to a cross-section of different ability level students.

❸ • Three years of teaching history at the community college level on a part-time adjunct faculty basis.

• Secretary-Treasurer of the Maryland History Teachers Association and active in public outreach historical promotions.

❹ • Published articles in *Mid-Atlantic History* in 1995 and 1997.

Experience

September 1993 - Present: **Teacher of history,** Prince George High School, Ableville, MD. Teach U.S. History to top 3 sections of eleventh grade students; World History to 2 mid-level sections of seniors; and 1 section of honors students on **❺** Contemporary Policy Issues. Voted teacher of the year twice, first runner-up for **❻** Maryland Teacher in 1998. Co-founder of Parents, Students and Business Leaders, a community foundation that raises non-public funds to augment the school budget for **❼** special equipment and events.

August 1996 - Present: Concurrent with full-time position noted above, assumed duties as **U.S. History teacher at Johnson County Community College.** **❽** Responsible for an evening class of working young adults at the campus and a study-release class of inmates at the college's outreach campus in Stanboard Correctional Institute.

❾

Education
Master of Arts
History
University of Maryland, 1993

Bachelor of Arts	Associate in Arts
History	Liberal Arts
Johns Hopkins University, 1992	Hagerstown Junior College, 1990

Computer Maintenance Specialist

FOCUSED RESUME

General Strategy

Mr. Garrett's IT resume addresses a specific job and specialized kind of work so it is best structured as a **Focused Resume,** which helps to:

- highlight specific kinds of technical skills;
- concentrate on building a logically ordered resume containing appropriate key words since information technology (IT) resumes are generally sent by e–mail in an unembellished text format and
- still create a strong core resume that is easy to adapt should aesthetics become important.

Specific Points

❶ The address element includes the most practical ways to contact him. An e–mail address is probably expected, especially in an IT environment.

❷ While it isn't essential, he includes a personal Web page because it tells a more complete story than his resume. See Point 10 for details.

❸ Immediately relates his technical expertise using keywords recognizable both to programs that evaluate them electronically and to hiring officials.

❹ Conveys both software and hardware familiarity.

❺ Work History substantiates his claims of experience and documents his progress through greater levels of responsibility.

❻ Work History accounts for continuous employment.

❼ Work History communicates the scope of his responsibilities with quantified information.

❽ Relevant part-time student employment.

❾ Professional certification is often on a par with college training in the IT field.

❿ Indicates why his personal Web page is worth examining.

GEORGE C. GARRETT

7341 Vandue Range
Charleston, SC 29401
803-721-9321 • FAX 803-721-1255
GCG294@aol.com
http://14507@collegeplacement.com

OBJECTIVE

Computer Maintenance Specialist working in the installation, maintenance, and support of PC networks.

TECHNICAL EXPERTISE

- Large PC network installation and support
- AS/400 and Novell Network qualified
- PC software integration including Windows 95, AS/400, Microsoft Office and Microsoft Exchange.
- Novell experience and certification
- Demonstrated troubleshooting skills

WORK HISTORY

1996-1999—<u>Computer Maintenance Specialist</u>. Fort Gordon, GA. Served as a civilian maintenance technician for the installation and support of a series of 30-station PC networks for the Army's BNCOC classrooms at a large technical training facility. Integrated Windows 95, AS/400, and a variety of other off-the-shelf and specialized software packages. Assisted instructors in modifying and operating the system to include extensive troubleshooting activities.

1994-96—<u>Computer Laboratory Assistant</u>. Student assistant working part time installing and maintaining college instructional and administrative LAN PC under the direction of instructors and certified maintenance personnel.

EDUCATION AND CERTIFICATION

College of the Low Country, Beaufort, SC
Associate of Science in Computer Studies, 1996
Novell Certified NetWare Engineer (CNE)

COMMENTS

Personal Web page includes links to work samples and links to previous employers.

Computer Operator

FOCUSED RESUME

General Strategy

Ms. Paris has the training and experience to do the job, but she has been out of the workplace for several years. She will use the **Focused Resume** to place the emphasis on specific, enduring skills lifted from the context of her somewhat dated work history.

With this approach she *focuses* on her:

- ability to use either of the two best-known families of computers;

- familiarity with the kinds of software most likely to be encountered in a new position; and

- overall quality of being a good worker in a team setting.

Specific Points

❶ Since her experience is not current, she begins by documenting her basic formal preparation to do computer work—her education.

❷ Establishes the fact that the most popular computer systems are familiar.

❸ Verifies that she knows the software and can use it in either environment.

❹ Traditionally presented work history showing dates of employment.

❺ Demonstrates that she has continued to be productive using her computer skills even while not employed in a regular position.

❻ Evidence of being able to coordinate her work with those who generate the input for her computerized efforts.

❼ Experience with a larger mainframe computer is mentioned to show versatility.

❽ Ability to work in the absence of immediate on-site supervision.

❾ Demonstrates ability to do more than just operate equipment.

❿ Brief explanation of her absence from the workplace.

Elizabeth R. Paris
856 Lincoln Way, Apartment 102
New Orleans, LA 70119
504-363-9075 (Residence)

Education

Diploma
❶ Data Processing
Dauphine School of Business, 1990

Strengths **❷**

- Trained in the operation of both IBM and Apple Macintosh families of personal computers and peripherals.
- Experienced in word processing, desktop publishing, database
❸ management, and spreadsheet software for Windows and Macintosh operating systems.
- Task oriented, independently productive worker with the proven ability to cooperate in team efforts.

Experience

June 1993 - 1995: **Data-entry operator** working from my residence as an independent contractor to major publishers. Enter author prepared text data into book formats using appropriate desktop publishing software on my **❺** Macintosh computer. Produced 4 books annually for the 3 year period. Excellent evaluations from authors and editors, with whom I coordinated closely. **❻**

❹ **June 1990 - May 1993**: **Computer Operator,** Middlesex County Library, Suffolk, NY. Responsible for the operation of the library's TI-5000 stand alone computer system used in catalog maintenance, ordering, lender **❼** record keeping, and payroll. Worked under the supervision of the Data Systems Manager who oversaw similar operations in 3 other county office complexes. Instrumental in bringing on line the library's first CD units for user **❽** research. Assisted in obtaining a Library of Congress grant for that project.

❾ **Comments:** I left the workplace in order to be in the home during my child's early years and I now want to return to a traditional career path.

❿

Computer Programmer

WORK HISTORY RESUME

General Strategy

Ms. Leone is an entrepreneurial professional with several years of valuable experience that she wants to present to like-minded people. Since her experience is traditional, in good order, and descriptive of her talents, she appropriately elected to use the **Work History Resume,** although she inserted a Technical Expertise section to highlight her technical skills.

With this presentation she can:

- show what she has to offer and what she aspires to achieve;

- show her technical expertise and detailed work history; and

- comment on her inclination toward participating in a business on a speculative basis.

Specific Points

❶ Key to her presentation is the fact that she is prepared technically—has the right degree.

❷ Next she summarizes her dual experience in the manufacturing and user communities.

❸ In the **Overview,** she addresses her orientation toward taking a participating position in a high-tech start-up—trading talent for future profits.

❹ Highlights her technical expertise in a separate section.

❺ Describes a large applications project that she oversaw that was commercially successful.

❻ Uses quantifiable measures of her success in helping the firm make money by using applied computer capabilities.

❼ Her knowledge made a computer fit the marketplace profitably.

❽ Experience working in the national systems programming community.

❾ Bonus as verification of the value of her contributions.

❿ A brief recap of willingness to take a business risk and what she might contribute to the success of a start-up.

Raye F. Leone
8734 Woodland Avenue
Louisville, KY 40294
502-222-9988 (Office)
502-333-9075 (Residence)
rfleone@worldnet.att.net

Education

① Bachelor of Science
Computer Science
Kentucky State College, 1988

Overview

② Six years of combined systems and applications programming experience in both the computer manufacturing industry and a major commercial user's organization. Seek stable, entrepreneurial start-up willing to trade ownership participation for exceptional technical contributions. ③

Technical Expertise ④

- Installed and tested software and provided corrective maintenance
- New software problem diagnosis and resolution
- DBA for Oracle 7.0 on IBM mainframe running MVS/ESA
- Product customization, user support, and tuning
- Experienced in use of IBM SMP/E installation utility

Experience

June 1992 - Present: **Director of Computer Applications,** Seemans Regional Office Supplies, Louisville, KY. Assumed newly created position with major ($437 million annual sales) regional office supply firm. Tasked with computer order placement and remote technical support for a field sales force of 143 professionals covering the Southeastern U.S. Successfully acted as systems analyst, applications programmer, and ⑤ interacted with supplier systems programmers to achieve an industry recognized ⑥ breakthrough system of laptop/modem support sales. Development costs recovered in 16 months. Sales staff turnover reduced 38 percent in last year. Lost sales attributable to support lag reduced to less than 4 percent after 14 months.

June 1988- May 1992: **Systems Programmer,** Comtrack Computer Corporation, Waco, TX. Adapted existing operating systems to fit the unique needs of Comtrack's market ⑦ niche—the traveling technical sales representative. Worked in cooperation with applications programmers in the Seattle and Atlanta software markets supporting conversions of popular products to Comtrack operating systems. Created the conversion and installation systems provided with new Comtrack desktops that strengthened marketing and accounted for a substantial share of the firms $38 million ⑧ of crossover sales last year. Consistently earned performance bonuses for outstanding contributions. ⑨

Comments

Offer a solid base of user and manufacturer experience, excellent technical credentials, and a willingness to take reasoned business risks.

Computer Sales Representative

FOCUSED RESUME

General Strategy

Mr. Winters is just out of college, has all the right training, and some good part-time experience, but lacks a history of full-time employment. In order to show what his strengths are, he has decided to use a **Focused Resume.**

In this case the *focus* will be on:

- a college education that directly and practically prepared him for technical sales;
- seasonal jobs that have already given him a start in the business; and
- a technical background sufficient to let him sell authoritatively.

Specific Points

1 Specific college training in the technical sales specialty.

2 Identification of the technical sales market segment that he aspires to serve—small-business and personal computers.

3 Demonstrated experience in the business beyond the sales floor.

4 Seasonal sales of relevant software for a nationally franchised outlet.

5 Specific experience dealing with small-computer users as customers.

6 Hands-on technical experience in a laboratory setting—transferable skills include demonstrating computer equipment.

7 Success as a salesperson in the technical market.

8 A practical way to demonstrate link between college activities and potential success as a professional in technical sales.

9 Recognition of the career ladder and a motivation to climb it.

10 An understanding of the compensation system and subtle confidence that he will prosper under it.

Roscoe V. Winters
8037 Mahaney Avenue
Norwich, CT 06360
860-345-9075 (Residence)

Education

1 Associate in Science
Technical Merchandising
Mitchell Community College, 1999

2 **Objective:** To obtain a technical marketing position with a major retail vendor of personal and small business computers.

Strengths

- Three summers of full-time employment in The Computer Shed, a retail computer outlet of the Systems Computing Corporation of Sunnyvale, CA. Performed **3** backroom assembly, stock maintenance, and inventory for their line of desktop and laptop computers.

4 - Christmas seasonal employment as a floor sales representative at The Software Place, a nationally franchised purveyor of off-the-shelf applications software to **5** small commercial users and individuals.

6 - College work-study experience as a computer laboratory assistant to the professor of data processing technology at Mitchell Community College. Spent 15 hours weekly assisting in the set-up and operation of the lab sessions in which students from non-computer disciplines learned the basics of practical computer use.

- Junior Salesperson of the Year Award 1998, Technical Magazine and Book Direct Sales Organization. Award included a $500 tuition grant and was earned by **7** leading the Northeast region in subscription sales on behalf of the Campus **8** Computer Users Club.

Comments

9 Highly motivated for a career in technical merchandising with aspirations for management after acquiring experience. Planning to pursue continuing education in the related technologies. Receptive to incentive-based compensation.

Computer Systems Analyst

FOCUSED RESUME

General Strategy

Ms. Alamitos has a lot of strengths and she can demonstrate achievement, but it comes across more boldly if extracted from the four relatively brief periods of employment that constitute her work history. Her best bet is to use the **Focused Resume** in order to concentrate the reviewers' attention on her strong points and not make them dig it out of the several places where she acquired it.

Her correct choice of resume will present her as someone with:

- a strong educational background for being an analyst;

- experience that spans several important user-group industries;

- valuable familiarity with systems of great commercial potential; and

- a set of significant achievements as a systems analyst.

Specific Points

❶ Her combination of degrees is particularly strong and worth highlighting.

❷ **Overview** emphasizes that ideal preparation and adds her broad, if brief, experience in large-market industries—also names the position she wants in terms readily understood in her specialty.

❸ Specific industry groups and perspectives detailed.

❹ Details her technical expertise in the midst of her overall strengths.

❺ Gives practical application to her dual-track education.

❻ Award indicates success and offsets short tenure in the position.

❼ A specific project with tangible results achieved.

❽ A systems analysis case history in capsule form.

❾ Employment gives a chronology of significant positions.

❿ Summary format provides dates, but after strengths and achievements have already been made clear—instead of along with them as would have been the case in a work history resume, for example.

Louise S. Alamitos

8231 Fairway Drive
Costa Mesa, CA 92628
714-222-9988 (Office) • 714-333-9075 (Residence)
lalamit@westnet.com

Education

①

Bachelor of Science
Business Administration
California State University, 1987

Associate in Science
Computer Sciences
Palomar Junior College, 1985

② **Overview:** Rigorous business training backed by technical credentials in computer sciences. Experienced in major industry segments of business systems analysis including banking, government, and manufacturing. Seek Lead Analyst position with services company catering to a cross-section of such clients.

Strengths

- Broad systems experience across the government, defense contractor, commercial and consumer banking industries.

- Perspectives of government contract review authorities, major industry bidders, and funding sources.

④
- Installation and administration of OS/2 and UNIX/LANs with IBM architecture using TCP/IP and IPX protocols and RS6000 administration.

- Outstanding ability to extract and relate requirements to non-systems managers and decision makers.

⑤
- Knowledge of computer and business fields enhances ability to convey business system requirements to computer programmers.

Achievements

⑥
- Commerce Department Junior Analyst of the Year Award, 1988, for contributions to advanced industry sampling model.

⑦
- RWC bonus system restructured on the basis of cost-benefit analysis conducted by my project group resulting in reallocation of 73 percent of middle-management bonus dollars.

⑧
- Billing errors reduced by 39 percent and customer complaints reduced 78 percent at SuperCard after sampling-based analysis of historical problems data revealed correctable procedural errors.

Employment

⑨ Senior Analyst, Card Services Division, SuperCard, Inc., San Francisco, CA, December 1992 - Present. **⑩**

Systems Analyst, Bank of the West, San Diego, CA, June 1990 - November 1992.

Specifications Analyst, Rocket Weapons Corporation, Reston, VA, July 1989 - May 1990.

Junior Systems Analyst, U.S. Department of Commerce, Washington, DC, June 1987 - June 1989.

Corrections Officer

WORK HISTORY RESUME

General Strategy

Mr. Gregg has a logical progression of jobs in the law enforcement and security areas that are easily described in the traditional **Work History Resume** format. What he has done relates directly to the job on which it was done and this approach to describing his abilities will:

- show that he is trained for security work;
- verify in specific settings that he has gained valuable experience that relates directly to his occupational objective; and
- convey the unique nature of his circumstances and just what he is trying to achieve.

Specific Points

1 He has formal postsecondary training at the college level in the corrections field that matches his goal directly—a strong point worthy of prominence.

2 Since he is seeking another federal job, it is relevant to establish that he is already on the register—a part of the federal employment system.

3 His experience as a security officer—shift supervision in a secure environment—is compatible with the corrections job he seeks.

4 A responsible position, related to his field and indicative of good character.

5 Jail house supervision is relevant and worth mentioning.

6 Experience in prison disturbance control is also a strength to note.

7 Honorable military service is a plus in his line of work.

8 Guard duty, even in a diplomatic setting, has relevance for the job sought.

9 **Comments** is a good place to explain his situation briefly—in case the cover letter gets separated from the resume.

10 No concern about privacy since a change is mandated, so he correctly asks that his resume be passed along to anyone who might be able to help him.

Thomas G. Gregg
8309 Agassette Circle
Dobbs Ferry, NY 10522
914-222-9988 (Office)
914-333-9075 (Residence)

Education

1 Associate in Science
Corrections
Myrth Valley Community College, 1989

Employment

2

3 <u>June 1997 - Present</u>: Security Officer, Meredith Air Force Base, NY. GS-9 position as an Air Force civilian law enforcement officer charged with maintaining gate security. Supervise a shift consisting of 6 USAF enlisted security police and 2 civilians.

4 <u>June 1993 - May 1997</u>: Deputy Sheriff, Grapevine County Sheriffs Department, NY. Performed general duties in a mid-sized, rural law enforcement organization. Obligations included serving court papers, crowd and traffic control, and supervision of the county jail, as one of three officers on rotation. Augmented prison authorities in controlling major disturbance at Northern State Prison in 1985. ← **6** **5**

7 <u>July 1989 - May 1993</u>: United States Marine Corps, Quantico, VA. Served as an enlisted combat Marine. Left active-duty as a Corporal selected for Sergeant, a rank assumed in the Reserve. Experience included two years as an embassy security guard in Europe.

8

9 **Comments:** Due to the general reduction of forces occurring internationally, Meredith AFB is scheduled for deactivation in the spring. I am interested in transitioning to a law enforcement position within a federal corrections institution. A completed Form 171 and references are available upon request. Please feel free to share this resume with other agencies.

10

93

Credit Manager

WORK HISTORY RESUME

General Strategy

Mr. Masden has an array of work experiences that serve to verify his preparation for the next step on his career ladder. The **Work History Resume** is ideal for showcasing his steady rise in this conservative line of employment.

His resume will show that he:

- has made the necessary career steps to assume a more responsible position in the same line of work.

- has a college degree and has compensated for its nonbusiness nature by taking a number of specialized courses in his occupational field.

Specific Points

❶ A terse **Summary** is all that is needed to set the stage for his presentation, which simply says: "I'm ready for the next step."

❷ The stature of his current employer is established in order to convey his own responsibilities impressively.

❸ It is important to indicate the kinds of client companies that he has experience analyzing.

❹ Implementing systematic procedures was a specific and successful practice that he was responsible for and it is properly mentioned—with results.

❺ Even more dramatic bottom-line savings are shown by this example of his work.

❻ A brief but understandable picture of his credit analysis experience at the bank.

❼ Knowledge gained in this position has obvious value in future credit analysis roles, so that is implied in this entry.

❽ A responsible entry-level position in credit analysis.

❾ A less-than-ideal college degree is noted, but not emphasized.

❿ His strong suit is specialized training courses within the credit industry.

Edmund S. Masden

784 East Main Street
Cheyenne, WY 82009
307-222-9088 (Office)
307-333-9075 (Residence)

(1) Summary: Experienced credit manager seeking growth opportunity.

Experience

June 1997 - Present: Credit Manager, Watkins Wholesale Restaurant Supply,
(2) Greensboro, WY. Responsible for data collection, interviews, analysis, and credit
approval recommendations for a $4.5 million annual sales wholesaler. Clients include **(3)**
national franchise, small start-up, and established traditional restaurants and
institutions. Default rate reduced 39 percent during the second year of implementing
National Credit Rating Standards procedures under my direction. Implemented
Quick-Screen, a procedure for preempting poor risks without the inefficiency of **(4)**
extensive application and credit analysis—resulting in savings averaging $14,000 per
quarter for the past 18 months. **(5)**

June 1993 - May 1997: Credit Analyst, Bank of Northwest Wyoming, Suffolk, WY.
(6) Worked as the main officer analyst of small business and consumer credit
applications. Maintained a case load of 45 active files per week, resolving 80 percent
within that time frame. Knowledge of credit network protocols and ability to digest
elaborate business plans quickly. Supported the lending efforts of 6 commercial and 9
(7) consumer lenders.

July 1989 - May 1993: Credit Clerk, Wilcoxson Consumer Finance, North Woods,
(8) WY. Assisted the local office manager and secretary in the operation of a store-front
consumer lending business. Took credit applications from walk-in clients and
conducted rapid credit checks to approve high-risk/low-amount unsecured consumer
loans.

Formal Education

(9) BA, Art History
Smith University, 1993

Specialized Credit Training

- 1993—Two week training session at the American Consumer Training Academy,
Washington, DC, in basic credit analysis.

- 1994–95—Completed the correspondence version of the National Credit
(10) Association's Basic and Intermediate Credit Management Courses and earned their
Certified Credit Manager (CCM) designation.

- 1997—Advanced Credit Analysis and Management Course, Wholesale Merchants
of America, 2 weeks of resident and 6 months of correspondence learning,
Chicago, IL.

Customer-Service Representative

FOCUSED RESUME

General Strategy

Ms. Falls has been out of the regular workplace for many years and wants to present her assets outside the context of chronologically listed jobs. The best format for her situation is the **Focused Resume** because it will allow her to:

- make a pointed case for an accumulation of valuable experiences gained outside the traditional workplace;

- show that she can demonstrate achievements there that are relevant to potential success in the full-time job she now seeks; and

- present herself as a worthwhile applicant with the motivation, training, and ability to succeed in a regular position after a long absence.

Specific Points

❶ A strong **Summary** says it all briefly, but convincingly enough to get the reviewer to read on to the specifics of what she has to offer.

❷ Her planned transition is designed to take full advantage of current skills in telephone-based sales and services.

❸ A core of retail merchandising experience is timeless and a valuable base.

❹ Volunteer work on a local telephone hotline is relevant experience.

❺ More valuable is her home-based telemarketing of commercial services.

❻ Productivity vouched for by incentive awards.

❼ Further evidence of initiative and effectiveness as a persuasive telephone personality.

❽ Weak employment history seems less important after the relevant strengths have already been extracted and sold in the preceding parts of the resume.

❾ Initiative to get a current education in merchandising is a good endorsement of attitude and potential, plus assurance that she knows the latest trends and terms.

❿ A closing word of explanation that clarifies situation and goal.

Kathleen T. Falls
3179 MacCline Street
Milwaukee, WI 53203
414-333-9075 (Residence)

Summary

(1) Woman with formal training in merchandising returning to workplace after 18 years as full-time housewife. Seeking a telephone customer service/sales representative position with a national retailer to build on base of successful, current, part-time (2) telemarketing experience.

Relevant Experience

(3) • Five years as a retail clerk and department head for F. A. Olson Department Stores, Milwaukee, WI.
• Suicide Hotline of Montgomery County telephone volunteer for 6 years. (4)
• Home-based telephone marketing person for *SignCard* of Wisconsin for 34 months
(5) selling credit card registry, buyers club, and private club privileges to gold card holders.

Accomplishments

(6) • Won three incentive trips during as many years in peripheral bank card services telemarketing.
• Voted Volunteer of the Quarter for the community hotline dealing with teen suicide
(7) potentials.

Work History

(8) <u>1996 - Present</u>: Part-time telemarketing person with *SignCard* of Wisconsin, Wisconsin State Bank, Milwaukee, WI.
<u>1981 - Present</u>: Full-time housewife and mother with heavy involvement in community affairs.
<u>1976 - 1981</u>: Retail sales and department manager, F. A. Olson Department Stores, Milwaukee, WI.

(9) Education

Certificate
Merchandising
Milwaukee Community College, 1999

Comments: Never far removed from the mainstream of commercial and community activity during the raising of my family, I returned to college during the past year to ensure currency in my skills. Highly motivated to build a successful full-time telemerchandising career now that time is available. (10)

Database Administrator

FOCUSED RESUME

General Strategy

Ms. Hayle's IT resume addresses a specific job and specialized kind of work so it is best structured as a **Focused Resume** which helps to:

- highlight specific kinds of technical skills;

- concentrate on building a logically ordered resume containing appropriate key words since information technology (IT) resumes are generally sent by e–mail in an unembellished text format; and

- still create a strong core resume that is easy to adapt should aesthetics become important.

Specific Points

❶ Especially in an IT environment, an e-mail address is expected as a practical means of initial contact. It is disclosed automatically when a resume is transmitted by e–mail, but she includes it here for clarity.

❷ While not essential, her personal Web page tells a more complete story than her resume and cover letter, so it can be useful to the reviewer.

❸ Shows her technical experience using keywords recognizable both to programs that evaluate resumes electronically and people who read them.

❹ Experience presentation is focused on the job announcement and how she meets the employer's requirements.

❺ Work History substantiates her claims of experience and documents her progress through greater levels of responsibility.

❻ Work History accounts for her continuous employment since college.

❼ Work History also communicates the scope of her responsibilities and includes additional keywords that respond to employer requirements.

❽ Actual work in her area of professional certification is valuable.

❾ Professional certification is often on a par with college training in the IT field.

❿ Says why her personal Web page is worth reading.

SHELLY J. HAYLE
4419 North Main Street
Milwaukee, WI
414-484-9876 • FAX 414-484-2541
SJH@worldnet.att.net
http://www.attpwp.13987.net

1   **2**

OBJECTIVE

Database Administrator responsibilities that include supervising data modeling and logical and physical database administration.

TECHNICAL EXPERIENCE   **3**

4
- Data Warehouse design, development, and support
- Database tuning and troubleshooting
- Leadership of system development projects and LDD translations
- Informix qualified
- Novel and Oracle certification

WORK HISTORY   **5**

6   **7**
1996–1999—<u>Database Administrator</u>. CoMax Computer Support Services, Ltd., Menomonee Falls, WI. Provided SYBASE DVA administrative support for day-to-day operations at the firm's operations center. Responsibilities specifically included passwords, database modifications, storing procedures, writing triggers, keeping error logs, creating a database, and restoring from backup.

1994–96—<u>LAN Administrator</u>. Spectrum Services, Inc., Mequon, WI. Worked with NT Server Technology, Windows 95, and MS Office 95 applications software. Provided user support and implemented Novell NetWare and Windows NT network standards in multi-protocol and multi-server environments.

8

EDUCATION AND CERTIFICATION

9
Marquette University, Milwaukee, WI
Bachelor of Science in Computer Studies, 1994
Novell Certified NetWare Engineer (CNE)
Oracle Certified Database Administrator (DBA)

COMMENTS

See my Web page for links to CoMax and Spectrum, sites that continue to reflect my work.   **10**

Dental Assistant and Hygienist

WORK HISTORY RESUME

General Strategy

Ms. Wilkinson is applying for a paraprofessional position within a narrow, well-defined specialty. Her training and experience are nicely conveyed in the traditional **Work History Resume** even though her employment record is relatively brief.

Her resume will be used to:

- highlight the special educational preparation;

- note her professional certification; and

- show a record of successfully applying her talents and defining a specialty.

Specific Points

❶ **Seeking** quickly frames the limits of what she wants to do and where.

❷ The applied degree in dental assisting from an accredited program is a strong asset worth placing at the top of her list of qualifications.

❸ Professional certification is almost more valuable than a degree in many specialties—it constitutes approval to practice and a valued measure of job competency.

❹ Experience is very specific in this case and lends itself to point-by-point statements.

❺ Portrayal of the size and specialized nature of the practice she supports.

❻ Statement of the kinds of procedures performed is especially necessary, considering her goal.

❼ Describes how she has prepared for the specialty—vendor schools valued.

❽ The extent of her interest in advanced technology use is conveyed by mentioning the latest computer simulation and design procedures.

❾ Specific professional references are essential here and they are listed.

❿ A brief, easily understood reason for leaving is given in closing.

Cher W. Wilkinson
1123 Marshall Avenue
Shepherdstown, WV 25443
304-222-9988 (Office)
304-333-9075 (Residence)

Seeking: Full-time position with an institutional dental plan or health management
❶ organization in the greater Washington area having an advanced cosmetic dentistry
practice.

Education

Associate in Applied Science
❷ Dental Technology
Huntington Junior College, 1993

ADA Board Certified
❸ Cosmetic Dental Assistant (CDA)
1997

Experience

April 1985 - Present:
❹
- Dental Assistant in a one doctor family practice. ❺
- In the past 18 months it grew from 10 percent to 68 percent cosmetic dentistry clients.
- Primarily bleach and bonding, with increasing attention to porcelain caps and ❻ reconstructive alterations.
- Extensive reading and attendance at vendor-sponsored workshops on the latest
❼ cosmetic dentistry assisting techniques.
- Routinely assist in acid-prep cleaning and heat finishing of final applications.
- Trained and experienced in aesthetic approximations technology and related computer modeling where CAD/CAM applications are being used in the preparation of dental prostheses. ❽

Reference: Ruth A. Flausmun, D.D.S., College Park Professional Center, Suite 305,
Sheppardstown, WV 25442, 304-222-9988.

June 1993 - March 1995:
- Traditional dental assisting position in a two doctor practice. ❾
- Prepare materials for various treatments.
- Take and develop X-rays.
- Chair-side assistance in standard practices.
- Cleaning and scaling.

Reference: William J. Schwartz, D.D.S., Johnson & Schwartz, P.C., 309 Middletown
Pike, Hagerstown, MD 22501, 301-743-9099.

Comments: Present employer relocating her practice to California.

Editor

WORK HISTORY RESUME

General Strategy

Ms. Jason has a solid record of traditional workplace experience in her profession and it can be well presented in the **Work History Resume.**

She uses the resume to accomplish:

- an effective **Overview** of her experience;
- a detailed enumeration of duties in various positions;
- a suitable college degree; and
- **comments** that relate her special orientation and goal.

Specific Points

1 The New York address has significance in certain fields—publishing is one.

2 Her work is described sufficiently in the **Overview** to allow efficient screening by other professionals in her business.

3 **Experience** in her case is an objective detailing of times, tasks, and firms.

4 Quantification is important even in the arts—it defines level of responsibility and places achievements in a meaningful context.

5 A signal accomplishment is a strong way to end a particular job description.

6 Similarly quantified achievement portrays work in another setting.

7 Showing specific instances of measurable success strengthens credibility.

8 Verification that she performed well at the working level before entering the higher echelons of editorial work.

9 A worthy college background for an editorial career.

10 **Comments** frame her real objective and distinguish her for those entrepreneurial publishers she has decided to target with her resume.

Christine A. Jason
873 West 49th Street
New York, NY 10019
212-222-9988 (Office)
212-333-9075 (Residence)

Overview

More than a decade of successful editorial experience in trade book divisions of national and regional presses. Outstanding record of productivity in acquisitions, development, and market penetration.

Experience

June 1997 - Present: *Executive Editor, Business Books Division, Delconte & Sons, Inc., New York, NY.* Supervise 12 acquisitions and developmental editors and a supporting staff of 18 individuals, 9 professional and 9 clerical. Responsible for bringing Delconte into the modern era of published how-to-do-it books for the small business market. Increased market share by 47 percent in last 14 months. Products of this division opened airport and mass discount retailers to Delconte books where sales now account for 15 percent of the firm's gross sales.

June 1993 - May 1997: *Senior Editor, Bicycle Books, Inc., Irvine, CA.* Managed the acquisitions editing division of this New Age regional press generating an average of 23 new trade titles annually in the career choice and health foods niches that constitute its areas of specialization. Highly successful in efforts to identify fresh ideas among first-time authors and generate successful books using developmental editing techniques. Ratio of break-even titles increased from 2-in-3 to 7-in-8 during my tenure.

July 1989 - May 1993: *Project Managing Editor, Multi-Title Press, Inc., New York, NY.* Worked as a developmental editor in the new author acquisitions department of the paperback trade division of the number 3 seller of such books nationally. Participated in the successful development of such solid national sellers as J. K. Wilson and Carol Minor Jones.

June 1988 - June 1989: World travel following college graduation.

Education

Bachelor of Arts
Liberal Arts
Metropolitan University, NY 1988

Comments: Primarily interested in acquiring participating status in a contemporary trade start-up or small house with potential for specialized growth in association with aggressive national distributor. Entrepreneurial orientation and financially positioned to consider delayed compensation for the right opportunity.

Electronic Engineer

COMPETENCY CLUSTER RESUME

General Strategy

Mr. VanGogh has a powerful combination of operational and research-and-development experiences that are best presented in a **Competency Cluster Resume.** His particular goal is to make the transition from the military to the civil aviation side of the industry and his most convincing case is made by addressing aggregates of talent valued in both sectors.

His resume is structured to show:

- solid college credentials in his specialized technical field;

- specific, successful experience in three major competency areas;

- achievements that would be meaningful anywhere in the industry;

- a record of continuous employment in the field; and

- a brief statement reaffirming his objective and why it makes sense.

Specific Points

❶ Address has relevance in this case since the civil aviation industry is largely found in the Seattle area—he is available without relocation expenses.

❷ College degrees clearly relate to the professional goal and establish him as a qualified applicant.

❸ Tells how he has implemented successful applications.

❹ Credible as a manager with quantified measures of his experience.

❺ Implications of familiarity with federal regulators and space technology.

❻ Important operational experience adds to technical preparation.

❼ An example of applying military knowledge to a civil aviation application.

❽ Tangible evidence of excellence in his work.

❾ A respectable work history that accounts for all time periods since college.

❿ **Comments** concludes his personal presentation with the goal statement.

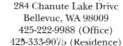

Robert P. VanGogh
284 Chanute Lake Drive
Bellevue, WA 98009
425-222-9988 (Office)
425-333-9075 (Residence)

Education

Bachelor of Science
Electrical Engineering
University of Seattle, 1990

Master of Science
Electronic Systems Engineering
University of Seattle, 1996

Applications Experience

- Used night flying and terrain avoidance radar systems as an operational crew member flying F-15s in all weather simulated combat environments.
- Revised Huguenot calibration procedures for standardization of LanSat-based night navigation equipment on transport aircraft.
- Implemented total auto-pilot integration sub-sets for all J-79 systems in use, military and civilian, during the mid-1990s.

Managerial Experience

- Led a team of 4 engineers and 5 technicians supervising the installation of retrofit SatSys decoders on the commercial passenger fleet of Divided Airlines, Inc. over a period of 17 months.
- Quality assurance engineer in charge of 35 technical inspectors in the Final Phase Division of Wilson & Bell Avionics responsible for satisfying FAA mandates on all KeyStat installations.

Research and Development Experience

- Flew debugging missions as an EWO in F-15 aircraft for the operational testing and calibration of BV-3 Birdseye radar systems during their first all weather night tests.
- Master's thesis focus was an unclassified cross-talk translation of military to civilian night wind shear avoidance systems.
- Developed first solid state blind-flight ergometer with sufficient deviation tolerance to satisfy FAA and military STANBOARDS.

Achievements

- Twice received the USAF Commendation medal for contributions to night flying safety, first as an active-duty aviator, then as a contract engineer.
- Reduced material costs 86 percent on EWSD's crossover shear detection night goggles by implementing first industry use of SeepTAC-4 in such applications.
- Secured 14 contracts with a total value of $83 million during 6 years as a contractor's engineer.

Employment

November 1998 - Present: Senior Engineer, Wilson & Bell Avionics Corporation, Bellevue, WA.
June 1996 - October 1998: Project Engineer, Electronic Warfare Systems Division, Elliot Systems, Inc., Los Angeles, CA.
September 1995 - May 1996: Full-time graduate study.
June 1990 - August 1995: Lieutenant, United States Air Force. Electronics Warfare Officer, F-4 Phantom, Tactical Air Command.

Comments: Objective is to make the transition from aerial weapons systems applications to civil aviation. Experience and training in non-visual systems is universal to both sectors.

Emergency Medical Technician

WORK HISTORY RESUME

General Strategy

Ms. Ward is creating her resume to obtain a teaching job in the field in which she is now a practitioner. Since her employment has been in a logical career pattern and it describes her strengths well within the context of the jobs held, she is advised to use the **Work History Resume** format.

Her resume will feature her:

- education and certification for a specialized service;
- six years of experience actually practicing her paramedical skills; and
- efforts to make the crossover to teaching.

Specific Points

❶ The EMT associate degree is the key to her training and is featured prominently.

❷ **Overview** is used for the dual purpose of noting professional certification and previewing her work history.

❸ **Experience** accounts for all periods of time and distinguishes full and part-time positions clearly for the reviewer.

❹ Position and job title describe her duties fully to those who know the field.

❺ Level of responsibilities within that position need further amplification that is given by noting team rank and describing duties beyond the expected.

❻ Position is self-descriptive to those familiar with the region's services.

❼ Amplification includes team size and precise mission, including breaking down categories of response.

❽ Part-time experience especially relevant since it represents the desired crossover.

❾ The award for valor adds stature in this business.

❿ Goal clarification and statement of moral commitment to the helping profession.

Dorothy L. Ward

783 Shoreline Drive
Newport News, VA 23606
757-222-9988 (Office)
757-333-9075 (Residence)

Education

Associate in Applied Science
① Emergency Medical Technology
Hampton Area Community College, 1993

② Overview

Board certified Emergency Medical Technician with 6 years of urban mobile trauma unit response experience.

Experience

Full-time: **④**

June 1997 - Present: *Emergency Medical Technician, Eastern Beach Community Rescue Team*, Eastern Beach, VA. Response vehicle team captain assigned to street duties similar to those described below, but with **⑤** approximately one-third of time devoted to dispatcher training and assistance in telephone administered trauma management.

③ June 1993 - May 1997: *Emergency Medical Technician, Woodside Fire and Rescue Service*, Tidewater, VA. Member of a two-person response team **⑥** answering calls in a 300 square block segment of Southeast Tidewater. Emergencies attended included 34 percent vehicle accidents, 48 percent **⑦** violent crime, 9 percent drug overdoses, and 9 percent routine medical emergencies such as heart attacks and illnesses.

Part-time: **⑧**

October 1995 - Present: *Instructor* of American Red Cross advanced First Aid, Cardio-Pulmonary Resuscitation (CPR), and EMT certification training at Bayside Community College during the fall and spring terms.

Comments

⑨ Recipient of the Governor's Award for Lifesaving as a result of 1994 recovery and resuscitation of automobile accident drowning victim.

Reason for Leaving

Seeking a full-time teaching position where my skills and experience can be conveyed to others.

⑩

Employment Counselor

COMPETENCY CLUSTER RESUME

General Strategy

Mr. Richards has mixed two types of employment—business and public. He is crafting a resume that will help him take the best of both and gain a position in the private sector that will satisfy both his love of counseling and desire to profit. In his situation, the **Competency Cluster Resume** will make the strongest case by presenting his most attractive attributes apart from their somewhat restrictive settings.

His resume will describe:

- his education;
- the clusters of business and counseling skills he has acquired; and
- how he now wants to pull them together as an executive recruiter.

Specific Points

❶ The degrees show the counselor side of his assets.

❷ **Objective** says he is more complex than his education indicates—he has both business and counseling interests and sees how to combine them profitably.

❸ The first competency cluster to establish is business and sales—this will balance any skepticism about him being an academic not hardened to the business world.

❹ Counseling experience is put in the context of the employment marketplace.

❺ Again, a link is established between counseling and job seekers.

❻ Implication that he can bring desirable professionalism to recruiting.

❼ State licensure verified.

❽ Specialized licensure relevant to recruiting is noted.

❾ Both counseling and business experience are established by employment record.

❿ Goal expresses motivation for the change.

Perry L. Richards

891 Triad Square
Montpelier, VA 23192
804-222-9988 (Office)
804-333-9075 (Residence)

Education

Bachelor of Arts		Master of Education
Psychology		Counseling
Southern University, 1993		Maryland University, 1997

Objective

2 To apply professional training, licensure, and combined counseling/business experience to a fee-based position in a professional executive recruitment organization.

3 • **Business Experience** — Four years as a professional marketing representative for a major pharmaceutical firm. Interacted heavily with professional clients and business associates.

4 • **Counseling Experience** — Two years as a full-time counselor with the Virginia Employment Service. Counseled adults on job opportunities and assisted **5** arranging training, interviews, the preparation of resumes, and good work practices. One of 9 counselors in a rapidly expanding urban job market. Most clients were high school graduates with little technical or business training or experience.

• **Training** — Psychology degree augmented by a master's degree in educational counseling with a concentration on employment counseling.

• **Supervision** — **6** Practicum experience in master's program consisted of 600 hours of supervision by fully certified professional counselor in an Employment Service Office. Administered in accordance with the requirements for Virginia licensure.

• **Licensure** — **7** Licensed Professional Counselor, Virginia Board of Professional Counselors, General certification with specialization in Employment Counseling. Initially licensed in May 1998.

8 Certified Personnel Counselor (CPC), National Association of Personnel Consultants, Alexandria, VA.

Employment

June 1997 - Present: Employment Counselor, Virginia Employment Commission, Mount Scenario, VA.

9 June 1993 - May 1997: Medical Sales Representative, Lampton & Boxworth Pharmaceuticals, Inc., Baltimore, MD.

June 1993 - May 1997: Full-time graduate study.

10 **Comments:** Entrepreneurial inclination and strong interest in the private sector motivate me to adapt my counseling and occupational choice training to a career in executive recruitment. Seek commission-based incentive pay not available in institutional counseling settings.

Environmental Technician

WORK HISTORY RESUME

General Strategy

Mr. Lee has a set of experiences that conform to the positions and time periods in which they were acquired. In the absence of strong assets that would stand out as aggregate qualities, he is advised to present himself in the context of the standard **Work History Resume.**

His employment history will reveal:

- a candidate looking for an environmental position in the private sector;

- a work history that stems from a logical beginning and progresses through contemporary environmental issues; and

- the basic technical education to support his professional efforts.

Specific Points

❶ **Introduction** serves as a headline stating who he is and what he wants.

❷ Experience relates an unbroken chain of employment dating from college graduation.

❸ Current position is public, but presented in such a manner as to appeal to developers—his target job market.

❹ Specific reference is made to future residential development projects.

❺ More evidence of competency in the region's environmental concerns.

❻ Notes that his efforts have produced profit centers for his employers in the past—the test he developed continues to earn money for the consulting firm.

❼ Shows that he can think like a regulator—he has been one.

❽ Chemistry teaching is a logical springboard for environmental employment.

❾ The right degree is presented—no elaboration needed.

❿ A career value judgment is communicated in his reason-for-leaving statement—he is more comfortable in the private sector and wants to establish himself there.

Winston K. Lee
45 Harriston Boulevard
Ogden, UT 84404
801-222-9988 (Office)
801-333-9075 (Residence)

(1)

Introduction

Experienced environmental scientist seeking private sector position.

Experience

(3)

1997 - Present — Environmentalist III, U. S. Environmental Protection Agency, Ogden Field Office, Ogden, UT. GS-13 scientist participating in an industry/river management project in North Snake Development Region. Major project management responsibilities. Benchmarks being established for luxury recreational development communities. Template analysis initiated at outset under my direction. **(4)**

(2)

1993 - 1997 — Environmental Consultant, Eco-Systems Consulting Corporation, Denver, CO. Consulting chemist working in **(5)** conjunction with engineers on the correction of mining-related pollution problems in southern Colorado. Devised tests and neutralization procedures that are now proprietary and constitute standards in the industry. **(6)**

1990 - 1993 — Staff Environmentalist, Oregon Department of Fish and Wildlife, Portland, OR. One of three scientists monitoring industries for compliance with state regulations regarding the discharge of materials potentially harmful to wildlife. **(7)** Visual inspection and chemical testing of suspicious effluents.

1986 - 1990 — **(8)** Chemistry Teacher, Portland High School, Portland, OR. Instructor of general chemistry.

Education

(9)

Bachelor of Science
Chemistry
Utah State University, 1986

Reason for Leaving: Desire to return to private sector employment either in a consulting capacity or as an employee of an environmentally sensitive real estate development firm.

(10)

Financial Analyst

WORK HISTORY RESUME

General Strategy

Ms. Robinette has selected the **Work History Resume** to present her string of responsible positions in the investment management profession. With it she will attempt to convey that she:

- has the right degrees and professional certification;
- currently holds one of a series of impressive positions in her field; and
- knows when it is time to move on.

Specific Points

1 College majors are relevant in a specialized field such as finance.

2 Professional certification is a benchmark in institutional investment firms.

3 **Experience** is presented straightforwardly with connecting dates and a full description of duties related to each position.

4 Since her job market is national, she describes the dollar size of her present department so those unfamiliar can better judge her status.

5 Details can be tersely presented and still say a lot within an industry group—types of clients, investment orientation, etc. quickly categorize a financial analyst.

6 Most organizations value business development (selling) skills, so mention them.

7 Computer literacy is essential and it is wise to verify it.

8 Short tenure in this position is explained—references would verify.

9 Other rather standard duties duly noted on her way up the career ladder.

10 Comments used to communicate two important points: (1) She is realistic about heading for a more favorable economic climate, and (2) her performance as a money manager will be of interest so it is volunteered.

Darlene W. Robinette
96 Galveston Lane
Houston, TX 77071
281-222-9988 (Office)
281-333-9075 (Residence)

Education

①

Bachelor of Science
Business Administration
Smith University, 1975

Master of Business Administration
Finance
University of Texas, 1986

Chartered Financial Analyst (CFA) 1991

②

Experience

④

<u>April 1993 - Present</u>: **Vice President & Trust Investment Officer, National Bank & Trust of Eastern Texas, Houston, TX ($1.5 billion trust department).** Senior portfolio manager in a group of 6; managing both fixed and equity in collective and other funds (personal, pension, and endowment). Responsible for all fixed income funds (aprx $300 million personal/$100 million employee benefits); responsible for most equity funds (aprx $400 million personal/$20 million employee benefits); foundations and charities account for an additional $75 million. Involved in business development activities, including presentations to support new business and existing accounts—also cooperative development projects with other elements of the trust department. Handled installation of IBM-AT dedicated to investment function; computer literate and proficient with DOS, LOTUS, asset allocation programs, Microscan, LOTUS Financial, Norton Utilities, communications, and disk maintenance.

⑤ ⑥ ⑦

<u>June 1992 - March 1993</u>: **Vice President & Trust Investment Officer, United Bankshares Trust, Fort Worth, TX ($580 million trust department).** Chaired the investment committee. Lowered transaction costs 32 percent. Implemented standard investment procedures. Established a research capability and client newsletter. Brief tenure accrues to inability to adapt to the culture and lifestyle of the area.

⑧

<u>July 1989 - May 1992</u>: **Assistant Vice President and Trust Investment Officer, Chicago Retail Trust Bank, Chicago, IL ($250 million trust department).** Senior investment officer responsible for setting overall investment posture; conceived and implemented a new common trust fund, revised others. Organized and conducted investment conference for 200 members of the local professional community. Implemented formal procedures to control commission use and allocation. Established investment management goals, including performance measurement techniques. Wrote monthly economic/investment commentary for distribution to 300 regional bankers, government officials, corporate officers and selected clients.

⑨

<u>Eight previous years</u>: **Retail stockbroker,** Scott & Delmonico, Inc., Milwuakee, WI.

Comments: <u>Reason for leaving</u> relates to the declining economy of the region where oil, gas, and space programs show little promise in the near future. <u>Investment performance</u> for the past five years: 14th percentile equities; 23rd percentile fixed income; 19th percentile combined.

⑩

③

Food Technologist

FOCUSED RESUME

General Strategy

Mr. Boyd has held a series of positions in the food processing industry, but wants to stress his particular strengths rather than just describe each job. The recommended format for this is the **Focused Resume.**

Using this resume vehicle he will be able to *focus* on:

- special capabilities that he has developed that would be of value across the industry;
- several substantial achievements; and
- an overall work history into which these highlights logically fit.

Specific Points

❶ The ideal degree for his specialty is noted.

❷ Professional certification is valuable—often can offset graduate study.

❸ **Overview** states what he has to offer—stresses production *and* R & D.

❹ **Capabilities** are the statement of aggregate skills that might get lost when spread across the several jobs in which they were acquired.

❺ Familiarity and success in dealing with government in this regulated industry.

❻ Language capability important in this business.

❼ Sensitivity to marketing concerns is an asset as he aspires to higher, more general management positions.

❽ Specific evidence of excellence and quantified, verifiable savings are strong points.

❾ Had a team-member role in establishing an industry standard—mention it.

❿ The work history stands alone, now that the strengths have been extracted and presented with emphasis in their own right.

Donald C. Boyd
78 Overton Way
Memphis, TN 38112
901-222-9988 (Office)
901-333-9075 (Residence)

Education

1 Bachelor of Science
Food Technology
East Memphis University, 1990

2 Certified Food Technologist (CFT)
1993

3 **Overview:** Nine years of progressively more responsible food processing industry positions involving both production and research and development.

4 Capabilities

5 • Experienced in FDA-based texture and temperature testing technology as it applies to juice, convenience meals, and bulk vegetable preparation.

6 • Supervision of processing personnel and team leaders—native language capabilities in Spanish.

7 • Participation in sales, advertising, and marketing research—included regular consultation with ad agency personnel regarding verifiable claims of nutritional content and taste validity.

Achievements

8 • Recipient of the 1997 Golden Platter Award from the convenience food marketing association for excellence in technical support consultation.

• Top bonus award 1994 earned for equipment selection recommendations that resulted in savings of $138,000 over previous year's operations due to 24 percent reduction in contract staff maintenance costs.

9 • Member of a three person team credited with the 1998 discovery of the frozen gravy stabilization technique (FGST) now the standard of the convenience food industry.

Employment

November 1997 - Present: Food Chemist, Dinner Time Frozen Foods, Memphis, TN.

10 January 1993 - October 1997: Production Supervisor, Minuterite Natural Juices, Inc., Ocala, FL.

July 1990 - December 1992: Junior Food Chemist, King of Vegetables Processors, Salinas, CA.

Fund Raiser

FOCUSED RESUME

General Strategy

Mr. Oden is a private fund raiser for private colleges. He uses a resume to make his services known and to present his firm for consideration as the institutions select those who will assist them in the coming year. His employment record is relevant, but this specialized need is best met by the **Focused Resume.**

The resume will focus attention on:

- his own prestigious college background;
- the style of his work, as much as its substance; and
- respectability by association.

Specific Points

1 The Yale degree constitutes instant endorsement for his work and is featured prominently as is his most appropriate major in marketing.

2 **Summary** says what he does, with whom, and for how long.

3 Dollars and cents results couched in tasteful terms.

4 The promise of a commercial quality campaign that won't look that way.

5 Clients identify and classify the practitioner in this business.

6 Employment history is given a classier name with the implication that he has been more than a mere employee.

7 His own firm is identified—little description needed here since the whole resume is focused on defining that image.

8 A campus development (fund raising) position adds to credibility.

Five years in big-time advertising circles brings commercial respectability.

10 The solicitation itself is tastefully and briefly held for last. Cover letter also amplifies the purpose of this communication—to seek additional clients.

Ronald P. Oden
43 Aiken Avenue
Charleston, SC 29403
803-222-9988 (Office)
803-333-9075 (Residence)

Education

❶ Bachelor of Science
Marketing
Yale University, 1984

❷ Summary: Experienced marketing professional with 6 years of outstanding performance as an institutional fund raiser in the private college sector.

Performance Characteristics

- Ambitiously realistic goal setting with institutional leaders and mentors.

- Alumni participation rates consistently exceed industry standards by 25 percent or more.

❸
- Noted for tastefully conducted, professional campaign with the impact of a commercial promotion, the feel of a traditional appeal. **❹**

- Goals consistently exceeded by an average of 15 percent.

Current Client List

❺ Alverno College, Texas
Asbury College, Maine
Bard University, New Mexico
Defiant College, Kentucky
Hope University, South Carolina
Rockhurst Academy, Michigan
Sacred Dominican University, Indiana
Whitman College, California

Present and Prior Affiliations

1993 - Present: President and Chief Executive Officer, Ronald P. Oden and **❼**
Associates, Ltd., Charleston, SC.
Consultants to the annual giving and special project financing of private institutions of higher education nationally.

❻
1990 - 1993: Director of Development, Witherspoon College, NH. **❽**

1985 - 1990: Associate, The John Melon Krumpright Agency, New York, NY. **❾**

Comments: Currently accepting invitations for proposals for the 1999–2000 college giving year. I would welcome the opportunity to consider your needs.

Graphic Designer

COMPETENCY CLUSTER RESUME

General Strategy

Ms. Lyle is a graphic artist with a continuous work history, but she is more interested in establishing an array of special competencies. The way to do that is to use the **Competency Cluster Resume** in which the skills gained in several settings are pulled together and presented as one.

This resume will be directed toward:

- identifying her as a technologically up-to-the-minute artist;
- establishing her solid foundation in traditional settings; and
- pulling it all together around the right awards, credentials, and past affiliations.

Specific Points

❶ Since she has the equipment and graphic art is her field, a modest amount of style is added to the resume with lines and unusual type faces.

❷ **Competencies** establishes her three main skill areas.

❸ Computer graphics is highlighted, since it is a highly marketable specialty. Demonstrating familiarity with Internet applications is particularly desirable.

❹ Enough technical jargon is used to communicate understanding.

❺ No computer-capable graphic artist would be complete without desktop publishing credentials, so they are established.

❻ Confirmation that all the technology is underwritten by the skills of a basic artist.

❼ Awards selected to show across-the-board excellence.

❽ Employment history is continuous and correct.

❾ Her degree is the right one and from a respected institution.

❿ **Comments** clarifies what she is out to accomplish with her career move.

Patricia D. Lyle
51-C Mount Pleasant Drive
Providence, RI 02908
401-222-9988 (Office)
401-333-9075 (Residence)

° Competencies °

Computer Graphics

Color and B&W graphics capabilities using Aldus Freehand on the Power Macintosh G3 computer system. Experienced in using both text and graphic scanners. Preparation of products using PhotoGrade and FinePrint technologies for photorealistic images and text. Expert at trace modification art and logo design. Expert user of Adobe Systems' Page Mill 2.0 HTML editor and associated Web–authoring software.

Desktop Publishing

Oversized Radius screen used for layout of single illustration and multipage publications with desktop publishing software, principally PageMaker. Experienced in brochure, tabloid, magazine, and newspaper layout—expert integration of graphics, including photography.

Drawing Board Artist

Nine years of combined college and commercial experience. Began as illustrator and paste-up person for university publications. Followed by three years of newspaper and two years of national magazine advertising and story art.

° Awards °

- Computer Monthly Magazine, 1998 First Place Award for Commercial Graphics
- The New England Gazette Syndicate, 1995 Award for Excellence in Advertising Graphics
- Numerous collegiate graphic arts and journalism awards.

° Employment °

1997 - Date: Senior Graphic Artist, Rhode Island Weekends Magazine, Providence, RI.
1995 - 1997: Paste-up and Insertion Technician, The Providence Daily, Providence, RI.
1993 - 1995: Free-Lance Artist/Photographer

° Education °

Bachelor of Arts
Commercial Design
Rhode Island College of Design, 1993

° Comments °

Interested in taking combined artistic, journalistic, and commercial experience and applying it in a computer-equipped graphic arts studio.

Heating, Air Conditioning, and Refrigeration Mechanic

FOCUSED RESUME

General Strategy

Mr. Blackwell is a recent technical graduate who needs to emphasize his strengths independent of a traditional employment listing. His best choice is the **Focused Resume,** which will allow him to:

- highlight his excellent technical education;
- show that he has had significant work experience, if not regular jobs; and
- indicate that he has excelled in several categories that have relevance for occupational success.

Specific Points

1 The right degree for his specialty from a respected local junior college.

2 **Introduction** establishes him as a properly prepared recent graduate with references ready to vouch for his potential.

3 In the absence of a full-time work history, the resume properly focuses on academic preparation, experience related to training, and evidence of excellence—awards.

4 In his urban market, the specialized skills can be attractive to a large firm.

5 Summer work with a respected firm adds credibility and potential references.

6 Evidence of ability to deal with older equipment as well as the most modern.

7 Work-study experience provided experience and showed initiative.

8 Quantification of the situation helps others judge its relevance to them.

9 Awards provide unbiased endorsement of excellence and promise.

10 Note shows awareness of the next steps to take professionally and the fact that they are being actively pursued.

Harold S. Blackwell
45 Cheney Creek Road
Philadelphia, PA 19153
215-333-9075

Education

❶ Associate in Applied Science
Heating, Air-Conditioning, and Refrigeration Technology
Philadelphia Junior College, 1999

❷ **Introduction:** Recent graduate with up-to-the-minute technical training and work-study experiences with latest commercial and institutional cooling and heating units. Excellent trade and academic references available. Seek growth opportunity in my field.

Academic Preparation

- Completed a two-year, 90 quarter hour, Heating & Cooling Institute accredited course of study concentrating on commercial and institutional installations.
- **❹** Specializations included plant failure diagnostics, passive heat loss control, and third generation heat pump installation and maintenance.

Work Experience

- **❺** Two summers of full-time employment with Jones & Whitman Engineering, Inc., installing new heating and air-conditioning plants in commercial buildings. Last three weeks of each summer spent servicing, in preparation for the heating season, existing heating systems ranging in age from new to 20 years. ◄── **❻**
- **❼** 17 hours weekly college work-study experience with the maintenance department of Philadelphia Junior College District. Assisted in the maintenance of 4 separate heating, air-conditioning and refrigeration systems
- **❽** serving the 327,000 square foot facility.

Awards

- **❾** Quail Industries Student Trouble-Shooter of the Year Award for 1999, presented at their annual meeting in Washington, DC.
- Honors Graduate, Philadelphia Junior College, Technical Division, 1999

❸

Note: Currently pursuing National Association of Heating, Air-Conditioning, and Refrigeration Technicians' professional certification. Anticipate having the Certified NAHACRT designation in minimum time following three years of qualifying full-time work experience and supervision. **❿**

Hospital Administrator

WORK HISTORY RESUME

General Strategy

Ms. Munford has held only two full-time positions, but they are sufficiently well defined to describe her capabilities and accomplishments. She has selected the **Work History Resume** in order to show:

- the right degrees for a career in hospital administration;
- solid, successful experience in the number-two slot at a major hospital; and
- prior experience that adds to her credibility in managing resources.

Specific Points

❶ The undergraduate degree in Business Administration would be adequate.

❷ Add a master's degree in Hospital Administration and you have a combination worthy of leading the resume.

❸ **Overview** tells the reviewer what is to come and the presenter's objective.

❹ **Employment History** is brief, but totally relevant—also accounts for all dates.

❺ Position is clarified beyond title to show full responsibilities.

❻ The institution is described to convey the scope of what she manages.

❼ Strength in hospital personnel management is verified.

❽ Familiarity with hospital accreditation is noted.

❾ Since it is highly relevant, military experience is detailed.

❿ Commendation for excellent performance is worth noting.

Dea S. Munford
84 Newburg Avenue
Eugene, OR 97405
541-222-9988 (Office)
541-333-9075 (Residence)

Education

❶

Bachelor of Science
Business Administration
Smithson University, Oregon 1989

❷

Master of Science
Hospital Administration
Oregon State University 1994

❸ **Overview:** Experienced administrative officer with nearly ten years of institutional finance and personnel management experience, 5 of them in a hospital setting. Desires to assume chief hospital administrator position in a mid-size urban institution.

❹ Employment History

❺ 1994 - Date: *Assistant General Administrator,* Eugene Memorial Hospital, Eugene, OR. • Second ranking administrative officer in a 375 bed, 84 doctor general care facility serving a suburban population of 123,000 residents. **❻** • Manage a budget of $22 million dollars annually. • Responsible for staff liaison and labor contracting. • Major role in rate negotiations with insurance **❼** carriers. • Designated coordinator of combined annual giving and community volunteer program. • Achieved outstanding results in all areas including: 38 percent reduction in nursing staff turnover, contracts maintained within CPI guidelines, and hospital restored to full accreditation after 2 years of probation.

❽

1993 - 1994: Full-time graduate study.

❾ 1989 - 1993: *Personnel and Finance Officer,* United States Navy, Norfolk and San Diego. • Officer in charge of personnel and financial records management for carrier squadrons 9 and 37 out of the ports of Norfolk and San Diego. • Accountable to senior managers and commanders for a bi-weekly payroll of $678,000 dollars. • All personnel records maintained according to Navy regulations. • Navy Commendation Medal awarded upon **❿** change of command and return to inactive reserve status.

Hotel Manager

WORK HISTORY RESUME

General Strategy

Mr. Brown has pursued the expected career ladder and each position provides a forum for his accomplishments at that level. His choice of the **Work History Resume** is a correct one.

The resume will be structured to show:

- a degree directly related to the job pursued;

- a career path that moves logically from entry level to management; and

- an explanation of why he wants to make a career move now.

Specific Points

❶ Hotel Management degree from Cornell is worth featuring.

❷ **Introduction** notes length and level of service in the industry.

❸ **Experience** is a textbook example of upward mobility in the hospitality industry.

❹ Clarification of reporting authority within the organization and the nature of the property managed are both important in establishing his level.

❺ Verifiable measure of excellence noted.

❻ Quantified depiction of the property and his role in its management are needed.

❼ Success in managing a specialized profit center is worthy of note.

❽ Valuable to demonstrate success in a turn-around situation—even at this less-than-comprehensive management level.

❾ States what it would take to entice him to move on.

❿ Shows that he is continuing to build his industry credentials.

Darrell T. Brown
763 Boone Street, NW
Norman, OK 73070
405-222-9988 (Office)
405-333-9075 (Residence)

Education

Bachelor of Science
Hotel Management
❶ Cornell University, 1991

❷ **Introduction:** Nine years of successful experience in positions of growing management responsibility in commercial chain hotels catering to up-scale business travelers in the continental United States.

❸ **Experience**

1997 - Present   Manager, Hildome Resident Business Suites, Norman, OK.
❹ Site Manager responsible to a Regional Manager for the complete operation of a 214 unit suites-only business travel facility near the university research park. Supervise a food and beverage manager and housekeeping manager in addition to contract grounds maintenance services and security. Led the region past 3 quarters in ratio analysis profitability. ❺

1994 - 1997   Assistant Manager, Airport Inns of America, O'Hare International Airport, Chicago, IL. Reported to the General Manager while
❻ serving as the second in charge of the total management of this 387 room middle market business traveler's airport hotel. Special duties included group and convention sales staff supervision. An ❼ area in which O'Hare achieved a 500 percent increase in bookings during my tenure.

1991 - 1994   Food and Beverage Manager, Lakeside Inn and Conference Center, Avalon Lake, NY. Assumed management of a failing restaurant, conference, and room service operation in this 277
❽ room business resort facility and turned it into a profit center in 17 months. Converted kitchen from traditional preparation to local chef's entree supplemented by top quality prepared supporting products. Reduced staff by 65 percent, reinvested proceeds in upgrading chef and investing in state-of-the art high intensity cooking facilities.

❾ **Comments:** Reason for leaving—To pursue multiple unit, regional management responsibilities with a major national business property. Continuing Education— Enrolled in the final section of the Hotel Managers Institute remote learning series leading to designation as a Certified Hotel General Manager (CHGM). Completion expected next summer.
❿

Insurance Agent

WORK HISTORY RESUME

General Strategy

Mr. McClay has moved successfully and profitably up the insurance sales career ladder. The jobs he has held are perfect devices for displaying his talents and the nature of his accomplishments. He is well advised to present himself on the strength of his professional positions arrayed in a standard **Work History Resume.**

His resume will be used to:

- show a logical insurance career path;
- classify himself as a successful group sales agent; and
- state his objective of achieving participating status in an agency.

Specific Points

❶ **Overview** is used to identify his segment of the industry.

❷ His objective of becoming a business partner in an agency is also noted up front.

❸ Experience is arrayed to show movement in timely fashion from individual sales to major group sales.

❹ His present position is described in the terms of the industry.

❺ Ability to train and manage other agents is an attractive partner quality.

❻ Results that can be shown in profit-generating numbers are impressive.

❼ Another successful group sales situation is described quantitatively.

❽ Clients and products are described and measures of success noted.

❾ Power as a one-on-one salesman is always worth establishing, as are the basic certifications of the industry and the fact that they have been achieved.

❿ The college degree is a basic credential worth noting—nothing to stress.

Robert J. McClay

12-F Devils Lake Avenue
Columbus, OH 43209
614-222-9988 (Office)
614-333-9075 (Residence)

①

Overview: Twelve years of successful group sales with life and health products of a single underwriter in the institutional non-profit segment of the market. Seeking partnership interest in an agency engaged in these aspects of insurance marketing. **②**

Experience

③

June 1997 - Present: *Senior Group Sales Agent,* The Haas Agency, Suite **④** 300, Embassy Square, Columbus, OH. Manager in charge of 4 salespersons concentrating on the colleges in North Central Ohio and Western Pennsylvania. Duties include training and motivation for those under my **⑤** supervision and sales presentations to principal client institutions. 1998 revenues for my segment exceeded 1997 by 300 percent. New accounts ◄**⑥** added in 37 colleges and universities previously serviced by national firms.

June 1993 - May 1997: *Group Sales Representative,* Wilcox & Wilson Insurance Agency, Inc., One South River Front Road, Columbus, OH. Lead group sales representative for the number one volume firm for non-profits in Columbus. Served hospitals, professional organizations, and governmental **⑦** entities within a 50 mile radius of Columbus with life and health packages. Multi-Million Dollar Roundtable member 1994 through 1997, logging higher combined sales than all but 17 other similarly situated agents in the Eastern **⑧** United States.

July 1987 - May 1993: *Agent,* Ohio Life and Casualty, Cleveland, OH. Sale of individual life and casualty products to professional clients in the greater **⑨** Cleveland market. Exceeded company production records for a new hire agent in 13 months and opted to enter their group sales division where I remained until 1993, learned the business and earned all relevant professional licenses, certifications, and designations.

Education

⑩ Bachelor of Arts
Liberal Arts
Clarkson University, Pennsylvania, 1987

Interior Designer

FOCUSED RESUME

General Strategy

Mr. Gilbert has done some things that make him attractive as a decorator and they are best viewed when pulled together from their separate occupational experience sources. To do this he has correctly selected the **Focused Resume** format.

His resume will have the objective of *focusing* the reviewer's attention on those several qualities and experiences that constitute his main assets:

- academic credentials appropriate to his field;

- urban experience; and

- commercially successful accomplishments in various settings.

Specific Points

❶ A traditional college program in the arts is offered as a basic credential.

❷ Specialized training in a recognized design institution adds an important dimension.

❸ **Strengths** all cater to the large urban market to which he again aspires.

❹ Points out the power combination of training he possesses.

❺ Experience is confirmed in accepted settings and situations.

❻ **Accomplishments** show that he is commercially successful.

❼ Versatility is evidenced in a range of projects that reach from an institutional setting to a piece of commercial equipment to a prestigious home.

❽ Magazine article recognition is important endorsement.

❾ Work chronology is necessary, but requires no elaboration beyond that given above.

❿ **Comments** describe desire to return to urban market.

Thomas K. Gilbert

32 Bismark Drive, NW
Minot, ND 58701
701-222-9988 (Office)
701-333-9075 (Residence)

Goal: To obtain a decorator's position with an established urban interior design studio.

Education

① Bachelor of Arts
Art History
Smith University, 1983

② Certificate
Interior Design
New York School of Design, 1987

③ Strengths

④ • Educated in the classic art tradition, yet specifically trained in the practical aspects of the contemporary design industry.

• Two years of full-time experience with the commercial design firm of Winston Interiors, Ltd., New York.

⑤ • One year of teaching and working as a free-lance interior designer with residential clients in an urban setting.

• Three years of part-time commercial design work on referral basis while a full-time student at the New York School of Design.

⑥ Accomplishments

• Redesigned the Minot Air Force Base Officers Club which subsequently won the 1989 Strategic Air Command Award for Non-Appropriated Funds Facilities Improvement.

⑦ • Credited with the selection of colors and textures used in the bulkhead tapestries for the new Trunpet Shuttle 727D airliners while a Winston Associate in 1988.

• Residential design of the William S. Peed apartment in New York, done on a free-lance basis while a student, featured in NY Apartment Living Magazine, June 1984.

Chronology **⑧**

1988 - Present: Self-employed interior designer, Minot, ND.
1987 - 1988: Commercial Design Associate, Winston Interiors, Ltd., New York.
⑨ 1984 - 1987: Full-time student in interior design, New York.
1983 - 1984: Teacher of Art History, Darien Saints Preparatory School, Darlen, CT.

Comments: After returning to small town environment and opening my own studio, am convinced that the best opportunity to reach my potential is in the city.

Internet Security Engineer

FOCUSED RESUME

General Strategy

Mr. Wagoner's IT resume addresses a specific job and specialized kind of work so it is best structured as a **Focused Resume** which helps to:

- highlight specific kinds of technical skills;

- concentrate on building a logically ordered resume containing appropriate key words since information technology (IT) resumes are generally sent by e–mail in an unembellished text format; and

- still create a strong core resume that is easy to adapt should aesthetics become important.

Specific Points

❶ An e–mail address is expected; a personal Web page is optional. He includes it because it adds to information already available in his resume and cover letter.

❷ Because the position involves managing or interacting with others, he acknowledges non-technical skills and expectations in his overview.

❸ Shows his technical experience first using keywords recognizable both to programs that will evaluate his resume electronically and people who will read it.

❹ The experience section focuses on the job announcement and matches his preparation to the employer's requirements.

❺ Work History substantiates claims of his experience and documents his progress through greater levels of responsibility.

❻ Work History accounts for continuous employment from graduation through his current position.

❼ Work History also communicates the scope of his responsibilities and includes additional keywords that respond to employer requirements.

❽ Work experience in your area of professional certification is flagged.

❾ Paints word pictures of his work environments that show the scope of his responsibilities.

❿ Professional certification is on a par with college training in the IT field.

①

LAWRENCE A. WAGONER
117 Sheridan Drive
Menomonee Falls, WI 53051
414-552-0336 · FAX 414-522-2851
lawagoner@nucleus.com
http://www.conceptlaw@nucleus.net

OBJECTIVE

② Internet Security Engineer position with responsibilities for design, consultation, and integration efforts supporting new security capabilities for commercial Internet services.

TECHNICAL EXPERTISE **③**

④
- 8 years of programming and design experience
- Understanding of security architecture design for the Internet
- Knowledgeable of public key cryptography and infrastructure, digital certificates, single sign on, S/MIME, SSL using mutual authentication and Virtual Private Networks
- Implementation of cryptographic solutions
- Experience with LDAPv3, direct services, SSL hardware, SET, CORBA/IIOP, UNIX, NT, and PKSC.

WORK HISTORY **⑤**

1995-1999—<u>Internet Security Engineer</u>. GenCo Information Services, Milwaukee, WI. Hands-on management experience with Internet security and IP networks. Managed firewalls, conducted IP network threat analysis and implemented protection strategies. Used DES MD5, IPSEC, TCP/IP Perl and Unix. Extensive familiarity with distributed systems and IP sockets.

⑥ 1992-95—<u>WebMaster/Web Engineer</u>. Micro Modeling Technologies, Inc., Waukesha, WI. Oversaw technical and maintenance requirements for the company's Web sites. Responsible for the day-to-day operation of the server (MS and Netscape), monitoring performance, usage statistics and log files, adjusting configuration settings, and as-needed backing up the system. Handled Web site security to include permissions. Worked extensively with authoring tools, image editing utilities, templates, style sheets, CGI scripts, and publishing back-end DB information on the web. **⑦**

1989-92—<u>Programmer/Analyst</u>. E. F. Thomas, Companies, Ltd., Elkhorn, WI. Hands-on development experience using C, C++, SL, Oracle, UNIX. Internet development experience in a client/server environment. Implemented software development methodologies and relational database concept. **⑧**

⑨
EDUCATION AND CERTIFICATION

- Marquette University, WI: Master of Science, Information Systems, 1989
  Bachelor of Science in Computer Studies, 1987
  - Oracle Certified Database Administrator (DBA)
    - Novell Certified NetWare Engineer (CNE)

⑩

Landscape Architect

WORK HISTORY RESUME

General Strategy

Ms. McGee has a very straightforward presentation to make that involves two periods of employment that directly represent her skills and interests. For that objective, nothing is better suited than the **Work History Resume.**

She will rely on her resume to:

- communicate her basic education and experience; and
- recount specific projects that speak to her ability to handle both the technical and public relations work associated with the position she seeks.

Specific Points

❶ Landscape architecture is the ideal degree and worthy of prominence in this brief resume.

❷ The **Objective** is used to identify a specific position for which she is applying.

❸ **Experience** is brief and pointed since it is directed toward a specific objective.

❹ Present position title endorses her as a player in the local restoration community.

❺ Her public position will not be that different from the proposed foundation position she seeks, so the comparison is appropriate.

❻ Among her present duties are two that will attract attention in the resume screening process: A successful role in articulating a restoration's outcome on the Internet, and the ability to relate to the commercial sector of her non–profit industry.

❼ Experience obtaining grant money is going to be an attractive quality.

❽ Commercial developers will be involved in the Lowlands project and this shows she is familiar with how they work.

❾ Specific roles in community development will be valuable.

❿ Ability to work with community and government groups will be essential, so it is worth providing evidence that she can do this.

Wanda H. McGee

87 New Bern Road
Greenville, NC 27858
252-222-9988 (Office)
252-333-9075 (Residence)

Education

❶

Bachelor of Science
Landscape Architecture
South Carolina University, 1993

❷ **Objective**: Applying for the position of Landscape Architect II with the Historic
Lowlands Foundation, Charleston, SC.

❸ Experience

❺ May 1996 - Present: *Resident Landscape Architect*
Old Town Historical Society, Greenville, SC. **❹**

❻
- Report to the City Manager and responsible for the design and management of public green spaces within Greenville.
- Close working relationship with Park Authority, Department of Highways, and other agencies impacting the green spaces.
- Coordinated park restoration project which involved excavation and reestablishment of an historic garden in downtown district.
- Provided technical and cost estimate support for local resident drive to save the vintage peach trees lining Woodrow Marsh Avenue in suburban Greenville. **❼**
- Secured federal grant for the study of requirements and funding needed for the restoration of Meeting Square Gardens, private residential plots adjoining the town square.
- Coordinated with the city's Web page designer in adding an award–winning historic landscape feature which was hyperlinked by travel agencies and prominent landscape firms serving the restoration industry.

June 1993 - April 1996: *Architectural Design Assistant-Exterior*
Bantum Development Company, Atlanta, GA. **❽**

❾
- Layout and specifications designer for major developer in the greater Atlanta area.
- Reported to the Chief Landscape Architect and responded to requests for assistance with land treatments beyond the walls of project structures.
- Liaison with community and government environmental and preservation groups.

❿

Legal Assistant

COMPETENCY CLUSTER RESUME

General Strategy

Ms. DeMagio has an acceptable, but undistinguished work history. It will make a stronger presentation if her competencies are extracted and showcased instead of her jobs. To do that she will use the **Competency Cluster Resume.**

In making the most of her skills, she will use her resume to:

- show that she can prepare all sorts of materials for legal cases; and

- demonstrate that she can prepare individual and corporate legal documents.

Specific Points

1 The starting point for her paralegal resume is an associate degree in the field.

2 **Competencies** constitutes a three-item summary with supporting detail.

3 All of the basic skills of paralegal case preparation are acknowledged here.

4 Affidavit taking can constitute a specialty in its own right.

5 Document preparation is a mainstay of the paralegal, so it is supported here.

6 Depending on the concentration of the hiring firm, it may be more important to have corporate skills, so they are developed separately.

7 The employment history shows steady, relevant employment.

8 Both corporate and institutional experience are available, so they are cited.

9 Private-practice experience still represents a large segment of the potential employers, so it is covered separately.

10 Professionalism is shown by the appropriate affiliations.

Joanne G. DeMagio

7-B Flushing Drive
Plattsburg, NY 12903
518-222-9988 (Office)
518-333-9075 (Residence)

Education

❶

Associate in Science
Paralegal Technology
Junior College of Staten Island, 1993

Competencies

Case Preparation

❸

- Background work for cases pending before the courts.
- Researched appropriate laws, judicial decisions and drafted written opinions.
- Prepared preliminary arguments and pleadings.
- Obtained affidavits. ← ❹

Document Preparation

❺

- Prepared draft contracts, mortgages, separation agreements, tax returns, estate and trust instruments.

Corporate Support

❻

- Assisted in preparing employment applications, contracts, shareholder agreements, employee benefit plans, loan documents, and annual financial reports.

❷

Employment History

June 1997 - Present: Legal Assistant, The Kilgore Corporation, Plattsburg, NY.

❼ ❽

June 1993 - May 1997: Legal Aide, Trust Company of Northwest New York, Irvington, NY.

May 1993 - December 1994: Legal Technician, Joseph, Joseph, and Wilkins, Attorneys at Law, Ithaca, NY.

❾

Professional Memberships

National Association of Legal Assistants
State Bar Association, Legal Assistants Division

❿

Library Technician

COMPETENCY CLUSTER RESUME

General Strategy

Mr. Warden is a recent liberal arts graduate at the associate degree level. His challenge is to portray himself as what he legitimately is—a rather well-trained library technician. With neither the degree title or full-time work experience to support his claim, he is well advised to present himself in the context of a **Competency Cluster Resume** that can:

- highlight his various less-than-formal, but valuable library experiences; and

- explain that his degree is more than it appears to be.

Specific Points

1 With no full-time position, it would be inappropriate to list an office phone.

2 Experience is arranged in such a manner as to show two strong clusters of highly relevant library experience.

3 One dimension is the technical services area addressed here.

4 Specific experience includes the latest technology—CD/ROM disk.

5 Experienced in the clerical aspects of library work.

6 Further evidence of involvement with library technology.

7 The second major cluster is user services, developed here.

8 Examples include both front desk and telephone work assisting the public.

9 Degree is noted and clarified effectively with verification offered.

10 Professional affiliation is useful even at the entry level.

Barry W. Warden
98 Levermour Street
Las Cruces, NM 88004
505-333-9075 (Residence)

❷ Experience

TECHNICAL SERVICES ❸

- Assisted faculty and students in the use of the library's newly installed CD/ROM databases for card catalog, periodicals and newspapers.

- Prepared documents for shipment to microfilm copying service.

- Validated information requests for technical research.

- Participated in the conversion of library catalog holdings to electronic media.

USER SERVICES ❼

- Manned New Mexico Library Consortium Hotline as a volunteer responding to statewide inquiries about library use and resources.

- Work-study desk clerk 20 hours per week at the college library for two years of full-time study.

Education

❾ Associate in Arts
Portales Community College, 1999

Comments

Degree in library technology not approved at Portales Community College, but took a concentration of 15 semester hours in related courses. See college transcript for verification and specifics.

❿ Professional Affiliation

Associate Member: American Library Association

Manufacturers' Sales Representative

COMPETENCY CLUSTER RESUME

General Strategy

Ms. Black is an engineer and a salesperson. Her objective is to convey both technical competency and the ability to sell this class of products and services. Since only one of her three positions deals with sales, she has correctly elected to present herself in the framework of the **Competency Cluster Resume.**

Her use of the resume is to:

- demonstrate field sales competency with technical clients;
- show familiarity with the field and manufacturing aspects of her product line; and
- establish credibility as a serious sales professional.

Specific Points

❶ Since she is seeking a sales rep position, her address may have some relevance—in this case it is a good jumping-off point for working her desired territory.

❷ Overview tells the story of her dual experiences and her objective of joining an appropriate manufacturers' rep agency.

❸ **Competencies** is used as a heading to highlight her three areas of greatest strength.

❹ Technical selling is the lead item since it points directly to what she seeks.

❺ Knowledge of codes, estimating, and field sales support technology are rightly stressed.

❻ This item establishes that she can relate to customers—she's been there.

❼ She knows the product line from the manufacturing perspective—strong selling point in the field.

❽ Employment history covers all that is necessary to say—emphasis has already been placed earlier in the resume.

❾ Appropriate technical degree noted.

❿ Affiliations reflect commitment to professional sales career.

Frances C. Black

2-A Cinnaminson Road
Hackettstown, NJ 07840
908-222-9988 (Office)
908-333-9075 (Residence)

Overview: More than 6 years of combined civil engineering experience in the manufacturer, contractor, and sales representative sectors. Seeking an expanded manufacturers' representative opportunity in association with an established agency.

Competencies

TECHNICAL SALES

- Market a full line of heavy drainage and conduit products to contractors in the New York, New Jersey, and Eastern Pennsylvania region.
- Experienced estimator familiar with various codes and ordinances as well as the product line.
- Accomplished user of the laptop computer for on-site demonstrations and estimates and remote order placement and field support communications via modem.

FIELD ENGINEER

- Supervision of survey and design crews in the construction of interstate highway systems.
- Specifications engineer for the district office of a state highway department with field verification responsibilities.

MANUFACTURING

- Design and testing of pre-cast concrete components for highway drainage systems.
- Familiarity with the materials and manufacturing processes involved in producing pre-cast civil engineering components.

Employment History

November 1997 - Present: Manufacturers Representative, Norton & Associates, Inc., Denville, NJ. One of three independent contractor sales representatives coordinated by the Norton agency.

April 1995 - October 1997. Field Engineer, New Jersey Department of Highways, Dover District Office, Dover, NJ.

August 1993 - March 1995: Staff Civil Engineer, Concrete Castings, Ltd., Edison, NJ. Design and testing for largest manufacturer of pre-cast drainage system components in New Jersey.

Education

Bachelor of Science
Civil Engineering
Fairleigh Dickinson University, 1993

Trade Affiliations

Women in Sales
Manufacturers Agents National Association

Medical-Records Technician

FOCUSED RESUME

General Strategy

Mr. Webb has had three jobs, all in his field of Medical-Records Technology, but they amount to an unfocused summary of his true capabilities and achievements. When he put it all together in a **Focused Resume,** here is what he was able to accentuate:

- the right degree and professional certification;

- an aggregate of valuable experience and a goal to match; and

- a clearly presented set of capabilities and achievements.

Specific Points

1 The associate degree in his specialty leads his resume.

2 Professional certification follows.

3 **Overview** provides a focus in summary form and states the occupational objective.

4 The size facility is important for the position sought, so it is prominently mentioned.

5 **Capabilities** are shown in the terms recognized and valued by those who would review his resume.

6 A mix of technical and supervisory tasks supports aspiration to management. Showing he knows how to apply Internet technology to industry issues is worthwhile.

7 **Achievements** are phrased to show bottom-line consciousness.

8 They demonstrate effectiveness in hospital and HMO environments.

9 Employment is listed matter-of-factly after emphasis was placed earlier in the resume.

10 Range of experience from insurance company to hospital and HMO gives widest possible job market potential for his skills.

Kenneth N. Webb
78 Portsmouth Street
Manchester, NH 03103
603-222-9900 (Office)
603-333-9075 (Residence)

EDUCATION

① → Associate in Applied Science
Medical Records Technology
New Hampshire Community College, 1993

② → Accredited Records Technician (ART)
American Medical Record Association

③ **OVERVIEW:** Six years of increasingly responsible positions in the medical records field with in-depth exposure to hospital, insurance, and health management organization systems. Seek a supervisory medical records administrator position in a 500 bed or larger care facility. **④**

CAPABILITIES

⑤
- Code and record diseases, operations, and therapeutic procedures according to standard classification systems.
- Oversee the accurate transcription of medical records by clerks.
- Conduct analyses of patient medical records for reporting and statistical purposes.
- Quality control of medical records for completeness, consistency, and accuracy.
- Access insurance company Web sites to facilitate the filing of complex medical claims and the interactive resolution of conflicts.
⑥

ACHIEVEMENTS

⑦
- Completed the conversion of 35 years accumulated insurance medical records to modern computer coding and microform.
- Devised major hospital governmental reporting procedures that satisfied regulatory requirements and reduced staff time involved by 31 percent.
- Implemented a records clerk training program at the HMO that speeded entry by 48 percent and reduced errors by 82 percent.
⑧

EMPLOYMENT

⑨ June 1997 - Present: Medical Records Technician, Old New Hampshire Life and Casualty Company, Manchester, NH.

December 1995 - May 1997: Medical Records Technician, Boston Health Management Organization, Boston, MA. **⑩**

June 1993 - November 1995: Coding and Recording Technician, Northeastern Community Hospital, Bayside, NH.

Minister

FOCUSED RESUME

General Strategy

Mr. Chapman is a minister and the expectation is that one position will look pretty much like the last. He needs a device for bringing out the special strengths that he has developed in this series of similar positions—the **Focused Resume** is the preferred format to accomplish his goal.

The minister's resume will assist him in:

- demonstrating such things as his affinity for working with the business community;

- showing his expertise in church physical plant management; and

- making the point that he is effective in setting and achieving major goals.

Specific Points

❶ **Strengths** show a series of special skills that might be lost or stated repetitiously in a more traditional resume format.

❷ Since businesspersons often sit on church boards and selection committees, his mention of being able to work with them successfully is germane.

❸ An ability to communicate effectively beyond the pulpit is cited here.

❹ **Achievements** as a topic gives him a forum for mentioning goals set and met.

❺ The results of his businesslike approach are given in human terms meaningful to the congregation.

❻ Leadership and the ability to take initiatives that work and are worthy of replication by others is shown in this point.

❼ Specific, tangible achievements are noted.

❽ A proper career progression stands alone, with the exceptional aspects already noted.

❾ A respectable undergraduate degree is confirmed.

❿ Ordination is also shown, since it is the ultimate arbiter of his eligibility.

Harold J. Chapman
89 Atlantic Drive
Omaha, NE 68102
402-222-9988 (Office)
402-333-9075 (Residence)

Goal: To lead the congregation of a new church in a growing suburban setting.

Strengths

- Heavily involved in regional activities with particular attention to involving the secular business community in positive social commitments.
- Particularly knowledgeable of church physical plant management.
- Committed to staff development, especially involving clergy-in-training and the church youth activities systems.
- Popular articles published in religious and secular journals.

Achievements

- Increased business community giving by 67 percent over a two year period in current assignment.
- Lowered operating costs by 23 percent by implementing a physical plant modernization campaign that involved contributed labor and materials.
- Initiated the House The Poor Foundation in 1984 that has grown to a system now used throughout the Western Region.
- Encouraged a parishioner-based fund drive that yielded core investment for sanctuary elevator and air-conditioning that resulted in improved retention of active elderly members.

Experience

<u>June 1997 - Present</u>: Minister, Main Street Methodist Church, Omaha, NE.

<u>June 1993 - May 1997</u>: Minister, Asbury Methodist Church, Pueblo, CO.

<u>July 1989 - May 1993</u>: Associate Minister, First Street United Methodist Church, Las Vegas, NV.

Education

Bachelor of Arts
English Literature
Nevada University
1987

Ordination
Methodist Minister
Columbia Southern Seminary
1989

Network Administrator

FOCUSED RESUME

General Strategy

Ms. McDwyer's IT resume addresses a specific job and specialized kind of work so it is best structured as a **Focused Resume** which helps to:

- highlight specific kinds of technical skills;
- concentrate on building a logically ordered resume containing appropriate keywords since information technology (IT) resumes are generally sent by e–mail in an unembellished text format; and
- still create a strong core resume that is easy to adapt should aesthetics become important.

Specific Points

❶ If a resume was not sent by e–mail, a printed e-mail address may be key to acknowledging receipt when the resume is scanned into an automated personal system.

❷ The overview immediately flags her specialization, telecommunications.

❸ Shows her technical experience first using keywords recognizable to both programs that evaluate resumes electronically and people who read them.

❹ Experience section is focused on the job announcement and how she meets the employer's requirements.

❺ Work History substantiates her claims of experience and documents her progress through greater levels of responsibility.

❻ Work History accounts for continuous employment from graduation through her current position.

❼ Work History also communicates the scope of her responsibilities and is the place to convey additional keywords that respond to employer requirements.

❽ Showing work experience in her area of professional certification is valuable.

❾ Paints a word picture of her work environment to indicate the scope of her responsibilities.

❿ Professional certification is often on a par with college training in the IT field.

KAY MCDWYER

1309 West 22nd Street
Austin, TX 78705
512-744-9955 • FAX 512-744-3457
km@texnet.com

❶

OBJECTIVE

Network Administrator overseeing the operation and maintenance of a sophisticated network telecommunications configuration.

❷

❸ TECHNICAL EXPERIENCE

- Telecommunications competencies include TCP/IP, Netview, VTAM and WAN connectivity
❹
- Configured and managed connectivity extending devices from mainframes
- MVS/OS390 host experience
- Mainframe SMP/E product installation experience

WORK HISTORY ❺

1996-1999—<u>Information Systems Engineer</u>. Lake Country Systems, Inc., Austin, TX. Installed, maintained, and customized CONTROL-T, CONTROL-M/R, CONTROL-V, and CONTROL-O. Used AMP/E, ISPF, TSO, and JCL. Provided maintenance to products using SMP/E without IOAICE. Troubleshooting with Silo and Magstar Exits, Media DataBase, CTDTREE, Control-D Missions, and New Day Processing.
❻ ❼

1994-96—<u>LAN Administrator</u>. University Associates, Ltd., Denton, TX. Worked with NT Server Technology, Windows 95, and MS Office 95 applications software. Provided user support and implemented Novell NetWare and Windows NT network standards in multi-protocol and multi-server environments.
❽

❾

EDUCATION AND CERTIFICATION

University of Texas, Austin, TX
Bachelor of Science in Information Systems, 1994
Novell Certified NetWare Engineer (CNE)

Newspaper Reporter

COMPETENCY CLUSTER RESUME

General Strategy

Ms. O'Hare is in a field that lends itself well to identifying specific, valuable groups of professional skills. While they are not totally lost in a traditional job listing resume, they can be emphasized quite effectively in a **Competency Cluster Resume.**
   Her resume is crafted to show:

- four very specific areas of competency;
- enough detail to give them meaning; and
- confirmation of a suitable career path for the position sought.

Specific Points

❶ A journalism degree is central to a reporter's career, so it is the lead item.

❷ Four skill areas form the most obvious heart of her resume and communicate a great deal even without the associated elaboration.

❸ Emphasis is placed on the skill most relevant to her career aspiration.

❹ The numbers show a potential syndicator that she has serious potential.

❺ Nuts and bolts reporting skills are confirmed here.

❻ Evidence of initiative and courage that could spark a winning column.

❼ Four years in the big time add credibility to her desire to address national issues.

❽ **Employment** record shows a plausible rise through the ranks.

❾ Affiliations add to professional image.

❿ Comments indicate what she seeks—expanded on in her cover letter.

Susan T. O'Hare

5 North Harvey Street
Great Falls, MT 59405
406-232-9988 (Office)
406-323-9075 (Residence)

Education

(1) Bachelor of Science
Journalism
Southern Montana University, 1991

Competencies

(2)

FEATURE WRITING

(3) Writer of a regionally syndicated feature on
environmental and sport fishing concerns. **(4)**
Readership estimated at 350,000;
subscribers increasing 22 percent annually.

CITY REPORTING

(5) → Two years as a city desk reporter covering
court, jail, and community activities for an
urban population of 140,000.

INVESTIGATIVE REPORTING

Developed sources and published stories
that led to the indictment of the mayor on **(6)**
drug charges.

CORRESPONDENT REPORTING

Four years representing second largest
paper in the state in Washington, DC. **(7)**

Employment

(8)

June 1997 - Present: Feature Writer, Great Falls Courier, Great Falls, MT.

January 1993 - May 1997: Correspondent, The Minnesota Times Service,
Washington, DC.

July 1991 - December 1993: City Reporter, Minnesota Evening Times, Duluth, MN.

(9) Professional Affiliations

Women in Communications
North Central Print Journalists' Guild

Comments: Seeking an upper Mid-West newspaper affiliation from which to develop
a syndicated column.
(10)

Nurse

COMPETENCY CLUSTER RESUME

General Strategy

Ms. Purcell is a nurse with special skills to emphasize. She will use the **Competency Cluster Resume** in order to make her point.

Her resume is designed in such a manner as to:

• highlight her three strongest areas of competency;

• reinforce the skill areas by providing meaningful specifics; and

• show her educational progression and the goal it is intended to achieve.

Specific Points

❶ Overview makes the major point of the resume—experienced associate degree nurse about to become bachelor's degree nurse and assume greater responsibility.

❷ Competencies make the case for her comprehensive experience—keywords known in the profession take on an almost graphic quality in this format.

❸ Types the hospital and kinds of services in a way that will be understood.

❹ Places herself within a nationally known rating scheme.

❺ Specialized experience is emphasized here.

❻ Supervision experience is noted—relevant to aspirations.

❼ Another care dimension added with part-time experience.

❽ Employment History backs what she has claimed elsewhere in the resume.

❾ Her basic associate degree in nursing is noted.

❿ The expected completion date is listed as a proper qualifier on the bachelor's degree.

Delores K. Purcell, R.N.
3 Cook Avenue, Apartment 172
Columbia, MO 65203
573-222-9988 (Office)
573-333-9075 (Residence)

Overview: Associate degree registered nurse with 6 years of full-time professional experience nearing completion of bachelor's degree seeking supervisory or nurse practitioner opportunity.

Competencies

- GENERAL NURSING—Floor nurse in two major hospitals (500 bed facilities) with comprehensive care responsibilities including assisting physicians, providing treatment, and the administration of medications, physical examinations, and inoculations. Have attained level 4 on the 5-level career-ladder of experienced professional nurses.

- POSTOPERATIVE CARE—Implement physician prescribed treatment regimens for patients recovering from surgery. Special training in resuscitation assistance for cardiac patients. Experienced in the supervision of L.P.N. services in the postoperative-care environment.

- CONVALESCENT CARE—Weekend duty at a convalescent home caring for 274 elderly convalescents provided experience in this sector. Familiar with the treatment regimens and recurring problems found in this population.

Employment History

September 1995 - Present: Postoperative-Care Nurse, Our Lady of Hope Hospital, Columbia, MO.

May 1993 - August 1995: Staff Nurse, Central Memorial Hospital, Springfield, MO.

Education

Associate of Science	Bachelor of Science
Nursing	Clinical Nursing
Central Community College, MO	North Central Missouri University
1993	(June graduation anticipated)

149

Personnel Specialist

COMPETENCY CLUSTER RESUME

General Strategy

Ms. Stuart wants to structure her resume in such a way as to place an emphasis on the competencies most highly valued in her profession. She has a long work history that relates well to her career objectives, but the position-by-position style resume tends to obscure the points she wants to make. The solution is the **Competency Cluster Resume** that will allow her to:

- showcase her special groups of skills;
- provide the specifics needed to make them meaningful; and
- back it all with a logical progression of positions held.

Specific Points

❶ With a private office, a discreet call to her business phone presents no problem, so it can be listed along with the home phone.

❷ The outline arrangement of special skills offers an apparent central theme to the resume that makes an introduction or summary less essential.

❸ Recruitment skills are of great importance in a dynamic organization and her background as an executive recruiter is valuable in the several respects mentioned. She can also demonstrate successful use of the Internet for hiring purposes.

❹ Standard employee job training skills are among her talents.

❺ A more specialized training capability that relates to government regulations is also worth stressing.

❻ Ability to function in a collective bargaining environment adds a whole new dimension to her qualifications.

❼ A full range of regulatory compliance work from planning, to court cases, to complex reporting adds to her versatility and attractiveness as a candidate.

❽ **Positions Held** supplies the specifics expected, but requires no elaboration.

❾ Three working environments and orientations are apparent and valued.

❿ An appropriate degree is listed matter-of-factly.

Rosemary P. Stuart

56 Meridian Avenue
Columbus, MS 39702
601-473-8976 (Office) ← **❶**
601-234-5565 (Residence)

Specialized Abilities

RECRUITMENT   **❸**
- Experienced in defining hiring official needs both as an in-house personnel officer and as an executive recruiter.
- Capable of dealing effectively with executive search firms due to prior experience in that sector.
- Successfully exploited both resume and job posting Internet sites to fill key vacancies.

TRAINING   **❹**
- Conducted new employee orientation and task training in financial, consulting, and retail settings.
- Trained managers on compliance with their obligations under EEO and other regulations affecting their departments. **❺**

LABOR RELATIONS
- Company representative during NLRB conducted vote on union representation for major retail chain. ← **❻**
- Benefits negotiator for bank holding company.

AFFIRMATIVE ACTION
- Designed and implemented EEO/AA programs at two large firms.
- Party to suits at the district court level. **❼**
- Coordinated state and federal reporting.

❷

Positions Held

❽
June 1997 - Present: Personnel Officer, Center Bank and Trust Company, New Orleans, LA.

January 1993 - May 1997: Recruiter, Dunhill Executive Search, Inc., Marysville, MS. **❾**

July 1990 - December 1993: Training Specialist, Bloomington Department Stores, Ltd., Canton, LA.

Education

Bachelor of Science
Business Administration
Pearl University, Arkansas, 1990

 ❿

Pharmacist

FOCUSED RESUME

General Strategy

Ms. Brookings has a long history of steady, career-relevant employment, but wants to focus attention on her aggregate capabilities and achievements. This is best done by using the **Focused Resume** format.

This resume is designed to:

- pinpoint a discrete set of capabilities that she holds within her profession; and

- show a selected set of achievements that highlight her effectiveness.

Specific Points

❶ **Overview** spells out the broad outline of her experience and states a general goal.

❷ **Capabilities** provides a format in which highlighted skills are briefly outlined.

❸ Within the profession, this is sufficient to relate the basic competencies.

❹ Major retail management experience is unique and warrants mentioning.

❺ Computer literacy as applied to the industry and buyer experience are also specialized skills not expected in the average pharmacist.

❻ Consulting shows broader role and some authority professionally.

❼ Achievements verify in tangible terms how effective she has been.

❽ The range of accomplishments would be attractive to a major chain seeking a professional manager.

❾ Employment shows the positions in which her achievements were made.

❿ The appropriate degree underwrites her professional legitimacy.

Joyce C. Brookings
3098 Birch Lane
Bemidji, MN 56601
218-664-8957 (Office)
218-392-6032 (Residence)

① **Overview:** Fourteen year pharmacist with institutional and retail experience seeks management position in the pharmaceutical industry.

② Capabilities

④

• Licensed, degreed, board certified pharmacist.

• Retail manager with successful supervision of multi-store operation.

③ • Literate in the application of computers to the pharmaceutical trade.

• Extensive buying experience in both medications and sundries. **⑤**

• Consultant to hospitals and medical staffs on drug selection.

⑥

Achievements

• National Retail Pharmacist of Year runner-up 1987.

⑦ • Increased total prescription sales by 200 percent in three years. **⑧**

• Devised and implemented Cross-Check computerized prescription comparison system credited with identifying dozens of potentially serious medication conflicts monthly.

Employment

March 1995 - Present: Managing Pharmacist, MedPharm Drug Centers, Bemidji, MN.

⑨ June 1990 - February 1995: Retail Pharmacist, Start Drugs, Washington, DC.

July 1986 - May 1990: Pharmacy Officer, Army Medical Corps, Devens Army Hospital, MA.

Education

Bachelor of Pharmacy
Brainerd University, MN
⑩ 1986

Physician Assistant

WORK HISTORY RESUME

General Strategy

Ms. Reginald has a logical pattern of employment that is uncomplicated and career-supporting. Her choice of the **Work History Resume** is an appropriate one since it will allow her to:

- present her several credentials in the context of relevant work; and
- thoroughly describe the duties performed by health provider setting.

Specific Points

❶ **Overview** sets the tone for her work history, which is more PA than RN—an important distinction to establish for her objective.

❷ States her goal of entering a practice where her compensation will be more than a salary.

❸ Education is dual-track—degree plus important certification.

❹ Associate degree nurse status established—basis for achieving RN status.

❺ MEDEX Certificate that qualifies her as a PA needs no further explanation within the community that will examine her credentials—it has the status of an additional degree.

❻ **Employment** accounts for chronological continuity and describes duties in two settings.

❼ PA and HMO points are made in this job description.

❽ Actual tasks performed as a PA are outlined here.

❾ Accounts for the time period and shows that PA training was full time.

❿ Traditional nursing background is reaffirmed.

Cynthia L. Reginald, RN, PA
8 Rutherford Street
Boston, MA 02129
617-394-0038 (Office)
617-894-2934 (Residence)

❶ Overview

Experienced health care professional with formal RN and MEDEX/PA credentials, a year of nursing and 4 years as a PA. Seeking to enter a private practice situation as a financially participating physician associate. ❷

Education

❸

Associate in Science	MEDEX Certificate
Nursing	Physician Assistant
Greenfield Junior College, 1993	South Boston College, 1996

❹   ❺

Employment

June 1996 - Present: Physician Assistant, Boston Area Health Management Association. One of 4 P.A.s assigned to Team 1 of the HMO for the purpose of screening patients for primary physician care. Conduct physical examinations and consult on the results ❼ with the patients and, as appropriate, physicians. Other duties include ordering lab tests, diagnosing common maladies, and prescribing routine treatments.

❽

❻ September 1994 - May 1996: Full-time MEDEX/PA training. ❾

July 1993 - August 1994: Hospital Nurse, Greater Boston Presbyterian Hospital. General duty nurse responsible for attending patients on the postoperative care ward. Administered medication and therapeutic regimens prescribed by physicians. Typical shift involved managing the care for approximately 23 patients with the assistance of LPNs, orderlies, and other floor staff.

❿

155

Private Investigator

COMPETENCY CLUSTER RESUME

General Strategy

Ms. King is a law enforcement professional with several periods of traditional employment, but her most current one is in a self-employed capacity. She is more interested in showing what she can do than explaining why her business is not something she wants to continue. The most desirable way to combine her assets for an employer's evaluation is the **Competency Cluster Resume.**

The **resume** will be used primarily to:

- show that she can function as a law enforcement insider; and
- demonstrate that she can do the things that investigators are paid to do.

Specific Points

1 **Overview** instantly establishes her as qualified in both public and private sectors.

2 It also says what situation she seeks and where.

3 **Capabilities** highlight the three areas of primary competency.

4 Ties with the law enforcement establishment are established here.

5 Familiarity with the law on a practical level is confirmed.

6 Evidence that she is capable of gathering information from the standard sources.

7 Important capabilities in the domestic investigations field are noted.

8 Ability to use photo and video equipment to document observations for possible use in court or in out-of-court settlements based on convincing evidence.

9 Employment history verifies claims to various kinds of experience.

10 An associate degree in criminology adds credibility.

Ida J. King

8 Wilson Lane
Laurel, MD 20707
240-723-8677 (Office)
240-889-2349 (Residence)

Overview: Experienced law enforcement and security officer with police and licensed private investigator experience seeks affiliation with an established investigative firm in the Baltimore/Washington area.

Capabilities

INSTITUTIONAL

- Urban police officer in the capacities of patrolman and detective.
- Knowledge of enforcement and judicial bureaucracies.
- Acquainted with and respected by principals and functionaries throughout the regional law enforcement establishment.
- Working knowledge of civil and criminal statutes.

RESEARCH

- Government agency files.
- Telephone investigation.
- Personal interviewing.

SURVEILLANCE

- Domestic evidence gathering.
- Video and photographic techniques.
- Pursuit and documentation of movements.

Experience

<u>June 1997 - Present</u>: Security Consultant, Self-employed.

<u>April 1991 - May 1997</u>: Detective, Baltimore Municipal Police Department, Baltimore, MD

<u>June 1988 - March 1991</u>: Patrolman, Columbia Police Department, Columbia, MD.

Education

Associate in Applied Science
Criminology
Hamilton Community College, MD, 1988

Product Manager

WORK HISTORY RESUME

General Strategy

Mr. Akrin is using the **Work History Resume** to portray his series of career-related professional positions. This approach is desirable in his case because the terminology, position titles, company names, etc. are all readily conceptualized by the potential reviewers of his resume.

This resume is designed to:

- state his overall qualifications and next career objective;

- detail each position held and describe the duties related to each; and

- demonstrate that he has the academic credentials on which to base his career.

Specific Points

❶ **Overview** briefly states his three areas of specialization and market segment.

❷ Next, it says that he is after more of the same on a higher level.

❸ **Experience** is a straightforward listing of career positions held and verifies that employment has been continuous.

❹ A significant position coupled with a successful initiative makes for a powerful introduction to his work history.

❺ Dollar volume is needed to portray the scope of his effort and responsibilities.

❻ Results are clearly demonstrated—verifiable by references.

❼ Position is enhanced by noting the industry position of his company.

❽ Numbers and kinds of people on his staff show the magnitude of the effort.

❾ Served his time on the road selling the products he now manages.

❿ An ideal combination of degrees to back his career.

William K. Akrin

56 Tura Road
Bennington, CT 48009
860-222-9988 (Office)
860-333-9075 (Residence)

Overview: Seven years of sales, market research, and product management experience in the consumer products retail segment. Seeking expanded opportunities as a product manager in a related industry.

Experience

November 1997 - Present: *Product Manager-Consumer Health Remedies, Milken & Trosper Pharmaceuticals, Inc., Bennington, CT.*

Led Milken back into the forefront of the analgesic market by generating contemporary health benefits strategies for existing products. Directed an $11 million campaign that included the design and implementation of test-marketing procedures, product packaging redesign, direct-mail sample delivery to selected target groups, and national advertising keyed to life-extension health philosophy. Resounding success confirmed by three-fold increase of market share that has been sustained for two years.

May 1994 - October 1997: *Market Research Analyst, Tifton-Williams Company, Trewsberry, CT*

Analyzed the market potential for dozens of retail consumables for the country's 3rd largest producer of personal care items. Directed a team of 2 statisticians, 2 clerical, and 4 area specialists in the evaluation and statistical testing of product receptivity in pre-defined markets. Credited with co-developing the targeted marketing scheme rapidly being viewed as the coming standard of the industry.

July 1992 - April 1994: *Sales Representative, National Home Products, Ltd., Stillwell, CT.*

One of 12 representatives selling consumer home cleaning and personal care products to retail outlets in the Southern New England region. In 18 months rose to the 2nd highest volume in the region and received the Outstanding New Salesman Award for 1994 for the Eastern Division.

Education

Bachelor of Science
Marketing
Smith University, 1990

Master of Business Administration
Marketing Concentration
Drexton University, 1992

Public Relations Specialist

FOCUSED RESUME

General Strategy

Mr. Bellman can do the job of a public relations person and he has the job success to prove it. What he wants to do is avoid repeating essentially the same job description three times in a standard resume. The answer to his dilemma is the **Focused Resume.** Using its format, he will be able to:

• graphically list the skills he has;

• back them with solid accomplishments that demonstrate their application; and

• underwrite it all with the right work history and college degree.

Specific Points

❶ He opens the resume by targeting the precise position and level of authority he seeks.

❷ Next the institution is classified as one that will provide a growth environment in which he can ply his trade.

❸ **Skills** are those expected for the position and they are put forward without unnecessary elaboration—leave that for the interview.

❹ **Accomplishments** are general as well, but do focus on things with which a college president—the person hiring him—will easily identify.

❺ He can keep the alumni happy and contributing.

❻ Was the best in the state at conceiving an effective promotion for his college.

❼ Knows how to get the president visibility in popular academic media.

❽ **Employment** shows continuity and progression.

❾ The position he is coming from is a logical stepping stone to the kind for which he is making application.

❿ An acceptable undergraduate degree is in evidence.

Rodney H. Bellman

98 Fairway Circle
Presque Isle, ME 04769
207-564-2323 (Office)
207-895-0267 (Residence)

Target Position

 Managing the public relations staff of a major university with full decision making responsibility. Institution should be rapidly growing or already established as a leader in its sector.

Skills

- Speech preparation
- News release writing
- Media event coordination
- Publications creation
- Articulation of institutional image

Accomplishments

- Increased alumni participation by 23 percent during two year directorship.
- Won the State Education Associations' Promotion of the Year Award for 1995.
- Collection of President's speeches drafted by me published as a nationally distributed monograph.

Employment

June 1997 - Present: Public Relations Officer, Montpelier University.

February 1994 - May 1996: Director of Public Information, New England Association of Colleges and Schools. Freeburg, ME.

September 1992 - January 1994: Alumni Director, Lourdsburg College, Lourdsburg, ME.

Education

Bachelor of Science
Journalism
Smith University, 1992

Purchasing Agent

COMPETENCY CLUSTER RESUME

General Strategy

Ms. Johns has held two professional positions since graduating from college, but neither was for a very long period of time. She has good references, has learned important job-related skills, and wants to move on again. What is needed is the format of the **Competency Cluster Resume,** which can draw the reviewer's attention first to what she has to offer and, secondarily, to the brief tenure in her jobs.

The objective of this resume is to:

- present a capable person who knows what she wants and can demonstrate her ability to handle the task;

- graphically dominate the resume with desirable skills, highlighted and backed immediately with limited, supporting facts; and

- confirm work experience, proper college degree, and positions held.

Specific Points

❶ **Position Sought** says what she is after—including level of authority.

❷ Desired characteristics of the company are also noted.

❸ **Competencies** form the heart of the resume—no need to hunt them from within several job descriptions.

❹ Knows how to deal with suppliers in two primary situations.

❺ Level of responsibility best shown by dollar value of transactions managed.

❻ Important evidence that she can bargain and achieve savings.

❼ Without great detail, this says she can buy for heavy industry—details can be provided upon request and would be the subject of discussion anyway.

❽ Positions held tend to type her as what she claims to be.

❾ Degree held is appropriate and also needs to be mentioned.

❿ Key affiliation is an expectation in her field.

Mary Elizabeth Johns
42 Woodyard Drive
New Orleans, LA 70186
504-843-7886 (Office)
504-763-2133 (Residence)

➊

Position Sought: Group Purchasing Manager for commodities group in manufacturing environment with supervisory and purchase authorization responsibilities. Company should be currently profitable and growing.

➋

Competencies

➌

Supplier Relations

- Attend national trade shows to develop contacts and current market knowledge.
- Receive visiting sales representatives and evaluate offerings. **➍**

Bid Acquisition

- Prepared $300,000 to $2 million commodity bidding events and managed the outcomes. **➎**

Negotiation

- Achieved savings averaging 18 percent over industry tender prices for 3 commodity groups, 13 percent overall. **➏**

Commodities

- Active in raw materials acquisition for heavy industrial components. **➐**

Experience

➑

June 1997 - Present: General Purchasing Agent, Jones and Likeland Fabricators, Ltd. Gulf Coast City, LA.

July 1996 - May 1997: Commodities Buyer, Witson Manufacturing Company, Inc., New Carrolton, LA.

Education

➒

Bachelor of Science
Business Administration
Holy Saints University, 1996

Professional Affiliations

Member: National Association of Purchasing Managers

➓

163

Real Estate Broker

FOCUSED RESUME

General Strategy

Ms. Garrett is in a very performance-oriented field—real estate sales. Less emphasis will be placed on a perfect chain of positions held and degrees earned than on what she has done and how well. The correct vehicle for highlighting her strengths as a sales person and sales manager is the **Focused Resume.**

This resume will accomplish the following:

- demonstrate in not too many words the fact that she is a sales producer; and

- show that she has the professional licenses, affiliations, and experience needed to do her job.

Specific Points

❶ **Overview** is used to headline what she is, has done, and is after.

❷ The position sought is qualified—has to be a national franchise affiliate.

❸ **Capabilities** bullet her functional areas of expertise in the industry.

❹ In a few phrases she ticks off the essentials for the position to which she aspires—elaboration will be left for the interview.

❺ **Achievements** show how her basic skills have been applied successfully.

❻ Lead item is personal productivity as a salesperson—over time, not just one good year.

❼ Respectability, stature, and character reflected by state board appointment.

❽ Quantified success in performance that relates directly to the task proposed.

❾ **Experience** backs her claim to such levels of functioning in the business.

❿ Mention of a degree cannot hurt, even if unrelated and nonessential.

Joan F. Garrett

21 Pine Lane
Bowling Green, KY 42101
502-834-9879 (Office)
502-547-8210 (Residence)

①

Overview: Proven residential real estate sales producer and manager with eleven years of combined sales and brokerage experience seeks affiliation with major national franchise in a senior sales management capacity.

②

Capabilities

③

- Licensed Real Estate Broker
- Eleven years of successful, full-time, residential real estate sales **④**
- Certified real estate appraiser
- Rental management experience
- Training of sales personnel

⑥

Achievements

⑤

- Annual sales in excess of $1.5 million for the past 5 years
- Elected professional representative to Kentucky Board of Realtors **⑦**
- Managed nationally franchised office that led Central Region in sales volume growth in 1998. **⑧**
- Sponsored and trained 94 of the Million Dollar Residential Round Table salesmen recognized in the Central Region in the last year.

Experience

⑨

<u>June 1995 - Present</u>: Residential Broker, Stallings Better Homes and Farms Realty, Inc., Bowling Green, KY.

<u>June 1988 - May 1995</u>: Real Estate Agent, Norwood Realty, Staunton, KY.

<u>July 1984 - May 1988</u>: English Teacher, Lexington Junior College, KY.

Education

Bachelor of Arts **⑩**
English Literature
Western Kentucky University, 1984

Receptionist

COMPETENCY CLUSTER RESUME

General Strategy

Ms. Kyle is returning home with valuable experiences learned while spending a few years working in a large city. Neither her education nor job descriptions are anything noteworthy, so she wisely opts to feature her strengths in a **Competency Cluster Resume.**

The object of her resume is to:

- show that she can handle receptionist duties in a demanding setting; and

- affirm that she has already done so successfully and developed supporting skills in the course of gaining that experience.

Specific Points

❶ Since she has already left her last position, she lists only her home telephone number.

❷ **Overview** tells her situation and leads into her qualifications.

❸ **Competencies** highlight the kinds of things for which the employer will be looking.

❹ Telephone skills are absolutely essential—she establishes both technical competency and a measure of how trusted she has been (initial point of contact).

❺ Without saying more than would be proper, she volunteers that she is indeed attractive and good with people—something the employer would want to know, but could otherwise not determine until the interview.

❻ The ability to do more than answer phones is noted.

❼ Some of these skills could promise upward mobility from the receptionist position.

❽ **Experience** gives chronology and the employers suggest quality situations.

❾ References could be noted, but she elects to hold them until interviewed.

❿ Diploma is a desirable credential and subtle verification of regional linkage—they're not dealing with an uncomfortable outsider.

Carol H. Kyle
422 Haverhill Drive
Hutchinson, KS 67501
316-767-2843 (Residence)

Overview: Organizational receptionist returning to Kansas after five years of work experience in Washington seeks opportunity to apply skills locally.

Competencies

TELEPHONE SKILLS

Five years of PBX and key system experience in professional organizations of more than 50 people. Answered and referred calls as the initial point of contact.

PERSONAL QUALITIES

Well groomed, attractive woman with an excellent professional manner and an interest in people.

CLERICAL SKILLS

Type 60 WPM on conventional or word processing equipment. Filing, basic bookkeeping, and other general office skills.

Experience

June 1998 - Present: Receptionist, American Association of Insurance Adjusters, Washington, DC.

April 1995 - May 1998: Receptionist, Criminal Investigations Division, U. S. Department of Justice, Washington, DC.

Education

Diploma
Office Management
Fort Hays Business School, 1995

167

Retail Buyer

FOCUSED RESUME

General Strategy

Ms. Napier is an accomplished buyer who is seeking another position because a merger is about to eliminate hers. She has spent her entire career with two firms and she would like to distance herself from that limited background. The best approach is for her to relegate the job history to the end of her resume and amplify her special abilities and accomplishments directly and early in a **Focused Resume.**

Her resume will achieve:

- an honest statement of her situation and desire to continue in her career elsewhere;

- a clear demonstration that she has the skills needed to do the job; and

- evidence that she can apply her talents successfully and profitably.

Specific Points

❶ Office phone listing is fine since her employer is assisting in her effort to relocate.

❷ **Overview** says what she seeks and what motivates her to change positions.

❸ **Capabilities** make clear the fact that she has specific skills to offer.

❹ Dollar values make it possible for a reviewer to place her on a scale of responsibility held.

❺ Implications of national networking serve her purpose of breaking local image.

❻ Foundation of retail experience is established.

❼ **Achievements** show she is a rated performer nationally in her class store.

❽ Regional recognition and successful major deal add to her stature.

❾ **Experience** shows a chronology of work that backs her prior claims.

❿ Marketing degree further confirms the appropriateness of her career preparation.

Janice W. Napier

398 South Akin Boulevard
Cedar Rapids, IA 52407
319-823-7690 (Office) ← **1**
319-334-3254 (Residence)

2 **Overview:** Experienced retail department store clothing and accessories buyer seeks comparable position. Current firm recently acquired in national merger resulting in staff consolidations.

3 **Capabilities**

- Clothing and accessories buying experience for a three store, family owned department store chain with annual sales of $20 million. **4**
5 - Experienced participant in major trade shows presenting goods for the industry.
- Budget management for the $12 million clothing segment of the firm's annual sales.
- Proven observer of consumer buying trends.
- Extensive national contacts in the industry.
6 - Ten years of retail sales and sales management experience before becoming a buyer.

Achievements

7 - Top quartile performance in acquisitions/returns ratios for buyers in the $5-25 million departmental budget category nationally.
- Responsible for firm's successful adaptation to outlet pricing standards in the coat and outerwear garments segment.
- Twice selected Retail Buyer of the Year by the Iowa Retail Merchants' Association.
8 - Acquired price commitments on the Potter-Green jeans line before it achieved national status with resultant savings of $2.3 million.

Experience

June 1994 - Date: Clothing Buyer, Miller & Leget Department Stores, Cedar Rapids, IA.

9 June 1993 - May 1994: Clothing Sales Manager, Miller & Leget Department Stores, Cedar Rapids, IA.

July 1984 - May 1993: Women's Department Manager, Neeman's Fashions, Des Moines, IA

Education

Bachelor of Science (BS) **10**
Business Administration (Marketing)
Des Moines University, 1984

Retail Salesperson

COMPETENCY CLUSTER RESUME

General Strategy

Ms. St. Clair is a top-level retail salesperson whose productivity would be overshadowed by an ordinary resume. It is important for her to distinguish herself from the image of a passive retail clerk and establish herself as an effective sales professional with her own particular strengths and methods. She is advised to do this in the format of the **Competency Cluster Resume** since it allows her to:

- graphically portray herself as someone special in retail selling;
- note the special situation to which she aspires; and
- drop the shop names necessary to affirm her elegant image.

Specific Points

❶ **Overview** says tersely what she is and precisely what she wants to become.

❷ **Particular Abilities** was chosen to complement the phrasing popular in the advertising images of the kinds of places she works—and to which her resume is appealing.

❸ Marketing shows that she knows how to develop clients actively in the expensive goods segment.

❹ Volume demonstrates that she can become a one-person profit center.

❺ Presentation indicates basic retail skills cast in a special light.

❻ Individualized marketing is again stressed.

❼ Present position establishes the level of her sales practice.

❽ Respectable tenure shows reliability in this less-than-stable class of worker.

❾ Major national department store background provided excellent entry-level experience.

❿ Formal training at a respected institution adds to professional image.

Ruth V. St. Clair

875 Washington Avenue
Muncie, IN 47305
765-585-9367 (Office)
765-585-7657 (Residence)

①

Overview: Top retail saleswoman specializing in exclusive women's wear seeks participating interest in established boutique in winter resort area.

② **Particular Abilities**

MARKETING
③
- Client base of 587 in exclusive women's store located in suburban mall.
- Developed by direct mail and personal contact.
- Files maintained on tastes, interests, sizes, etc.

VOLUME
④
- Average annual sales of $367,000 over the past five years.
- Client pattern established at tri-seasonal average of approximately $2,500 each.

PRESENTATION
⑤
- Experienced in window and store presentation of elegant merchandise.
- Specialty is individual presentation to top clients on an appointment basis.
⑥

⑦ **Experience**

<u>June 1997 - Present</u>: Senior Sales Associate, Elegant Shops, Ltd., Muncie, IN.

<u>June 1993 - May 1997</u>: Retail Sales Consultant, Exclusive Clothing Boutique, Chicago, IL.

⑧

<u>December 1989 - May 1993</u>: Retail Clerk, Women's Fashions, Bloomingdales Department Store, Washington, DC.

⑨

⑩ **Education**

Certificate
Merchandising
Indiana Fashion Institute, 1989

Robotic Engineer

WORK HISTORY RESUME

General Strategy

Mr. Wright has followed the expected career ladder within his profession and it is proper and effective for him to rely on the **Work History Resume** to display his abilities and accomplishments.

His resume is designed specifically to:

- show a chain of responsible employment in his technical specialty;

- indicate the caliber of companies with which he has been associated; and

- highlight his special skills and contributions.

Specific Points

1 **Overview** authoritatively states his position in the industry and the fact that he is looking for an opportunity.

2 **Experience** is formatted to emphasize the position held, employer, and duties.

3 Level of responsibility is made clear with title and place in organization.

4 Measures are given of how well his efforts have served the company.

5 Scope of effort and responsibility are again shown with specific examples and numbers.

6 Cites a key talent—ability to gain government contracts.

7 Quantifies the magnitude of business generated so it can be easily appreciated.

8 Makes the link to his junior officer days that laid the groundwork for present-day understanding of the industry and business processes.

9 Specific value of time spent on the approval side of bid process is illustrated.

10 Powerful combination of technical degrees is self-explanatory.

Ned V. Wright
387 Streamside Lane
Twin Falls, ID 83303
208-977-6634 (Office)
208-788-3844 (Residence)

① **Overview:** Defense industry automation engineer with successful government and private sector experience in aviation-related robotics seeks growth opportunity in the applications area.

② **Experience**

<u>June 1997 - Present</u>: *Robotic Applications Engineer, Huge Aerospace,* Idaho City, ID

③ Chief engineering interface between the production and computer programming segments of the fixed wing avionics robotic production division. Responsible for coordinating and directing the resolution of technical challenges inherent in adapting production line electronics to automated control. Achieved successful **④** implementation on 37 percent of the line within two years. Production increased 23 percent and defects dropped 74 percent during the final quarter of evaluation.

<u>June 1993 - May 1997</u>: *Mechanical Automation Engineer, Nanonectics, Ltd.,* Valley of the Angeles Industrial Complex, Los Angeles, CA.

⑤ Project leader for a 5 member team consisting of 2 engineers, 1 technician, and 2 clerical assistants tasked with preparing bids for federal government requests for proposals. Team generated and managed an average of 14 major proposals **⑥** annually, assisted production department with staffing for contracts acquired, and **⑦** served as project monitor in-house. Yielded an average of 5 successful bids annually resulting in aggregate contracts of $45 million dollars per year.

<u>July 1989 - May 1993</u>: *Engineering Officer, United States Air Force Systems Command,* Andrews Air Force Base, MD.

⑧ Staff technical expert leading a team of 6 engineering evaluators appraising the potential of automated weapons systems proposed for USAF consideration. Served as intermediate screening authority after conceptual interest had been **⑨** established by senior managers. Feasibility of robotic applications to USAF mission requirements was the focus of the effort that yielded a 19 percent development approval rate over the three year life of the project.

Education

Associate in Science (AS)	Bachelor of Science (BS)
Computer Science	Industrial Engineering
Boise Junior College, ID, 1986 **⑩**	Idaho State College, ID, 1989

School Administrator

COMPETENCY CLUSTER RESUME

General Strategy

Mr. Varney has held a series of jobs as an educator that have prepared him for a senior administrative position. Rather than list the jobs and duties, he prefers to pull together what it all means in terms of being able to handle the job he is pursuing. His choice to do this is the **Competency Cluster Resume.**

The objective of his resume is to:

- telegraph the fact that he has the specific skills necessary—without the detail that might obscure their collective importance; and

- back his claim with enough brief specifics to illustrate that he can make his case.

Specific Points

❶ **Executive Summary** is used to say: "I have what you need—here it is point by point."

❷ He uses its headline format to convey both longevity and specific skills.

❸ **Competencies** outlines the very things that concern the people who will evaluate him for the position—shows he knows what their priorities are.

❹ Each point is made as a topic and then by specific, quantified example.

❺ Both business and educational skills are addressed in a result-oriented format.

❻ Awareness and involvement in the operational use of technology in learning is established.

❼ Underlying teaching skills are reaffirmed—did his time in the classroom.

❽ Respect for the importance of community relations and the ability to exploit cutting–edge technology are illustrated.

❾ Collective bargaining experience may well be essential and a basis for eliminating unsuccessful candidates early in the screening process—make the point, however briefly.

❿ Experience and degrees are essential, but matter-of-fact.

Dennis S. Varney
795 Carlyle Street
Kewanee, IL 61443
309-499-0988 (Office)
309-877-2132 (Residence)

(1) Executive Summary

(2)
- Public school administrator with 10 years of administrative and 5 years of teaching experience.
- Significant budget, community relations, and unionized teacher management experience.

Competencies

(3) ADMINISTRATION

(5)
- Principal of a 2000 student, 100 faculty public secondary school in a suburban environment. **(4)**
- Vice Principal of a 1500 student, 70 faculty rural intermediate school.

BUDGET
- Responsible for the preparation and management of a $5 million school budget.
- Planned and implemented a $1.7 million school renovation.
- Fiscal oversight for community generated non-taxpayer $980 million fund for school improvements.

CURRICULUM
- Implemented computer assisted math and reading instruction in a 500 teacher urban system. **(6)**

TEACHING
- High school mathematics teacher in urban and suburban settings for 5 years before entering administration. **(7)**

COMMUNITY RELATIONS
- Used a popular Internet Web page to ensure a successful bond drive by illustrating desirable outcomes and providing e–mail links stimulating community feedback. **(8)**

LABOR RELATIONS
- Senior district representative for 2 suburban systems with successful no strike negotiations concluded in both instances. **(9)**

Experience

(10)
September 1995 - Present: Principal, Suburban High School, Canton, IL.
June 1990 - August 1995: Vice Principal, Macon County High School, New Bedford, IL.
June 1989 - May 1990: Consulting Curriculum Leader, Intercity School System, Wilmington, IL.
June 1988 - May 1989: Mathematics Teacher, Millmount High School, East Millmount, IL.
August 1985 - May 1988: Mathematics Teacher, Southside Intermediate School, Westwood, IL.

Education

Bachelor of Science (BS)   Master of Science (MS)
Math Education   Public School Administration
Central Illinois University, 1985 Central Illinois University, 1998

School Guidance Counselor

FOCUSED RESUME

General Strategy

Mr. Sandsome wants to present his credentials as an established educator with a clear focus on his guidance counselor attributes. Rather than list jobs and follow with the usual paragraph of duties, he has selected the **Focused Resume** as the vehicle for communicating a more directed message.

The goal of this resume is to:

- focus the reviewer's attention on the specific qualities associated with the counselor's role in a school;

- substantiate claims to effectiveness with examples of specific achievements; and

- underline the presentation with solid experience and training credentials.

Specific Points

❶ A specific position is being sought, so it is designated at the head of the resume.

❷ **Abilities** is used to tick off the expected and insert some special talents related to the job in question.

❸ Substance abuse in schools is a major concern and he has experience dealing with it.

❹ Initiative shown in going beyond government sources of financial aid.

❺ Practical outreach to the community is a valuable asset.

❻ Results are available to back claims of effectiveness in all areas.

❼ Ideas have been good enough to institutionalize—projects he started now have a life of their own and reach beyond his area of influence.

❽ Evidence of stature given by involvement with a national organization.

❾ The right working experiences for the role he seeks.

❿ Degrees appropriate to his aspirations.

Wadsworth T. Sandsome
35 North Island Drive
Haleiwa, HI 96740
808-675-8345 (Office)
808-776-9078 (Residence)

Position Sought

Director of Counseling Services

Abilities

- State Certified School Guidance Counselor.
- Specialized training in the recognition and treatment of adolescent substance abuse.
- In-depth familiarity with the use of computer databases designed to aid students in the selection of appropriate colleges and majors.
- Experienced group counseling leader.
- Knowledge of private as well as public sources of college bound student financial aid.
- Extensive work with private sector community work-study arrangements.

Achievements

- 80 percent of counselees admitted to college of their choice for the past five years.
- Awarded Parents' Club Award for Excellence 1998 in appreciation for efforts to establish private sector linkage between North Shore School and the burgeoning hospitality industry.
- Founder of Island Helpers Teen Substance Abuse Hotline that serves 3500 callers weekly.
- Summer Consulting Fellow to College Boardroom, a non-profit organization that designs career planning software for students.

Experience

<u>June 1997 - Present</u>: Guidance Counselor, North Shore High School, Kawela Bay, HI.

<u>June 1993 - May 1997</u>: Counselor, Kanehoe Intermediate School, Kanehoe, HI.

<u>July 1989 - May 1993</u>: History Teacher, Pearl Harbor High, Pearl City, HI.

Education

Bachelor of Science (BS)
Social Studies Education
University of Maryland, 1987

Master of Education (MEd)
Guidance and Counseling
University of Hawaii, 1993

Secretary

COMPETENCY CLUSTER RESUME

General Strategy

Ms. Andersen's two periods of employment have given her more than a simple listing of duties and dates would indicate. When combined with her education, they provide the basis for describing a very attractive array of skills. In order to bring this to the immediate attention of potential employers, she has selected the **Competency Cluster Resume** to showcase her assets.

Her resume is specifically designed to:

- portray the professionalism with which she views herself;
- list the specific skills and traits that give her claim substance; and
- define the career path she hopes to pursue.

Specific Points

❶ **Overview and Objective** set her resume above the average for such applicants by classifying her interests as professional and executive—only appropriate because she can substantiate the claim.

❷ Clear implication that she is looking for an opportunity to do more than be a secretary—administrative management is her goal and that will appeal to an employer seeking to develop such a person.

❸ Her degree is specific and valuable—it gets prominent placement.

❹ **Professional Skills** is the wording chosen to highlight her talents and cast them in a more important light.

❺ The outline of skill topics tells a potential employer that she has the kind of comprehensive talent that can be considered for serious responsibility.

❻ It is made clear that she is in command of modern office technology.

❼ Knowledge of hiring procedures and regulatory requirements are apt to be valued by the executive she would support.

❽ Ability to make business arrangements is a vital skill worth featuring.

❾ **Experience** shows continuity of employment.

❿ Current position verifies executive secretary stature.

Lynn J. Andersen
973 Albacort Circle
Savannah, GA 31407
912-929-6479 (Office)
912-938-7783 (Residence)

① **Overview and Objective**

Professional Secretary with six years of advanced office services experience seeks Executive Secretary position with potential for assuming an administrative management role. **②**

Education

③ Associate in Science (AS)
Secretarial Science
Metropolitan Community College, GA, 1993

Professional Skills **④**

OFFICE MANAGEMENT
- Coordination of office clerical routine.
- Schedule management.
- Vendor liaison with suppliers of services.

DOCUMENT PREPARATION
- 60 WPM using electric typewriter or word processing equipment.
- Advanced user of principal word processing software packages.

EQUIPMENT OPERATION
- Personal computers and associated peripheral equipment. **⑥**
- Fax and modems.

⑤ DICTATION/TRANSCRIPTION
- 60 WPM vocal dictation.
- Accomplished transcriber.

PERSONNEL
- Preparation and placement of advertising.
- **⑦** Applicant response, appointment arrangements, EEO record keeping.

EXECUTIVE ASSISTING
- Planning of meetings and conferences, locally and at remote sites.
- **⑧** Arranging business travel.
- Screening and appointment management.

Experience **⑩**

November 1997 - Present: Secretary to the Director of Marketing, Rockaway Manufacturing Company, Ltd., Savannah, GA.

⑨ May 1993 - October 1997: Secretary, Jensen & Jensen Management Consultants, Tyron, GA.

Securities Broker

COMPETENCY CLUSTER RESUME

General Strategy

Ms. Proper has an employment history that shows only one relevant position, although her skills are really very well developed. She has decided that a **Competency Cluster Resume** will do a far more graphic job of displaying her strengths than would a bland position listing and description.

Her resume is intended to:

- show that she is an established and successful salesperson in the financial products field;
- prove that she has the professional attributes to practice her trade; and
- show that she has obtained the education to support her career change.

Specific Points

❶ **Executive Summary** establishes what she has done and in what market segment.

❷ It further states her goal to become a partner in a securities firm.

❸ Professional certification is immediately verified—no one needs to train her.

❹ She brings with her a specialty in the broad field of investment products.

❺ A base of buying clients is already established and likely to follow.

❻ She can demonstrate serious levels of productivity.

❼ Proof is offered that she can generate new business as well.

❽ Brokerage experience is anchored in a respected firm.

❾ Prior teaching experience is noted matter-of-factly.

❿ Education shows commitment to the business career.

Sandra K. Proper
1987 Clearpond Way
Miami Shores, FL 33138
305-966-0980 (Office)
305-877-2167 (Residence)

 Executive Summary

Proven exceptional productivity in the retail marketing of investment products to young professionals with performance sustained over a six year period. Objective is to attain participating partner status in a compatible firm.

Professional Abilities

LICENSURE
 • Securities and Exchange Commission licensed retail broker

PRODUCT SPECIALIZATION
• No Load Mutual Funds
• Emerging Growth Stocks
• College Tuition Fund Plans

CLIENTS
• Young professionals

PRODUCTION
• Achieved $2 million in annual sales in third year; sustained through sixth year.
• Business development activities yielded 54 purchasing clients last quarter.

Experience

June 1993 - Present: Retail Stock Broker, Blackmund Investing Associates, Ltd., Miami, FL.

August 1991 - May 1993: Teacher, Kevinville Schools, Kevinville, CA.

Education

Bachelor of Arts (BA)
Art History
Smith University, AL 1991

Master of Science (MS)
Business Administration
University of West Florida, 1998

Security Manager

FOCUSED RESUME

General Strategy

Mr. Cooper has had a long and complete work history, but he feels his attributes will be better shown if pulled from the individual job descriptions where they are to be found. He selected the **Focused Resume** because it lets him place the attention wanted on certain skills and traits that are the selling points of his profession.

This resume is designed to:

• paint an overall picture of an experienced professional whose talents stem from a number of work experiences;

• show achievements that demonstrate excellence in his field; and

• back it with responsible experience and relevant educational achievement.

Specific Points

❶ **Overview** sketches the experienced security practitioner and the goal he seeks.

❷ **Capabilities** lists specific assets that should be valued by private security firms.

❸ Basic qualifying items are affirmed.

❹ Special skills are identified.

❺ Public relations and management experience is noted.

❻ **Achievements** are the kind apt to be appreciated in his trade.

❼ Character reference items are also included.

❽ Ability to generate business is important to note.

❾ Experience validates claims made earlier in resume.

❿ Education is a nice concluding touch of professionalism—not a mandatory degree.

John V. Cooper
3976 98th Street, SW
Washington, DC 20098
202-992-7845 (Office)
202-765-2116 (Residence)

❶ Overview

Successful security officer and manager with experience in military, municipal, and private security settings seeks senior management position with private firm.

❷ Capabilities

- Licensed private investigator
- Military security police training and experience
- ❸ Advanced martial arts training ← ❹
- 5 years experience as a municipal police officer
- 6 years as a private investigator
- Expert firearms instructor ←
- ❺ Experienced speaker before community groups
- Proven security organization manager

Achievements

- Regional NRA pistol champion
- Appointed to state licensing board for private investigators ❼
- Deacon of the Midlands Methodist Church
- ❻ 4 time regional Karate champion
- Security consultant to industry and government
- Increased account dollar volume 45 percent in current position ← ❽

Experience

❾ <u>June 1997 - Present</u>: Director of Domestic Investigations, Blue Diamond Detective Agency, Inc., Washington, DC.

<u>June 1993 - May 1997</u>: Self-Employed Private Investigator, Bethesda, MD.

<u>July 1988 - May 1993</u>: Patrolman, Alexandria Police Department, Alexandria, VA.

<u>May 1985 - June 1988</u>: Army Military Police, California and Germany.

Education

Associate in Applied Science (AAS)
Law Enforcement Technology
Washington Area Technical College, DC, 1994

Supervisory Systems Analyst

FOCUSED RESUME

General Strategy

Ms. Goodwin's IT resume addresses a specific job and specialized kind of work so it is best structured as a **Focused Resume** which helps to:

- highlight specific kinds of technical skills;

- concentrate on building a logically ordered resume containing appropriate key words since information technology (IT) resumes are generally sent by e–mail in an unembellished text format; and

- still create a strong core resume that is easy to adapt should aesthetics become important.

Specific Points

❶ If a resume was not sent by e–mail, a printed e–mail address may be key to receiving acknowledgment after a resume is scanned into an automated personal system.

❷ The overview quickly indicates the level of responsibility she seeks; supervisory, in this instance.

❸ Information technology resumes show technical experience first using keywords recognizable both to programs that evaluate resumes electronically and people who read them.

❹ Experience section is focused on the job announcement and how she meets the employer's requirements.

❺ Work History substantiates her claims of experience and documents her progress through greater levels of responsibility.

❻ Work History accounts for her continuous employment from graduation through your current position.

❼ Work History also communicates the scope of her responsibilities and includes additional key words that respond to employer requirements.

❽ A mix of public and private sector employment is desirable in some positions.

❾ Shows that she has occupied the kinds of positions she will be supervising.

❿ Professional certification is often on a par with college training in the IT field.

THERESA P. GOODWIN
4303 Fernlake Drive
Carrolton, TX 75006
972-562-6403 • FAX 972-835-9027
tgoodwin@compuserv.com

OBJECTIVE

A Supervisory Systems Analyst position in which to take a leading role in the design and development of custom applications.

TECHNICAL STRENGTHS

Possess extensive knowledge and experience in managing systems analysis, design, construction, and implementation projects to include:

- Development of shared applications
- GUI and CASE technology
- Implementation using Mainframe, Client/Server, and LAN configurations
- Knowledgeable of UNIX, NetWare, TCP/IP, and Windows 95
- Database competencies include DB2, Oracle, Paradox, and Powerbuilder
- Background in recovery/restart, input/output control, and file backup
- SDLC documentation

WORK HISTORY

1997-1999—<u>Lead System Analyst</u>. Healthcare Cooperative Corporation, Lucerne, PA. Managed all aspects of systems design and development of custom applications. Supervised six programmer analysts using UNIX, Netware, TCP/IP, and Windows 95 technologies. Multiple database competencies used on Mainframe, Client/Server, and LAN configurations.

1994-97—<u>Programmer Analyst</u>. Co-Orbital Systems, Duke Research Park, SC. Worked on Year 2000 tasks for data collection systems using COBOL, IDMS, and JCL. ADS/O implementation and system enhancement.

1990-94—<u>Computer Systems Analyst</u> I. Clark County Government Center, Wilburn, NC. Provided technical and operational support to users countywide. Assisted in developing and distributing system and user documentation. Assisted in PC installation, maintenance, and troubleshooting.

1988-90—<u>JCL programmer</u>. Valley Healthcare Systems, Los Angeles, CA. Setting up systems to run and recover batch processing.

EDUCATION AND CERTIFICATION

- Austin Peay University, TN—Bachelor of Science in Computer Studies, 1988
- Oracle Certified Database Administrator (DBA)
- Microsoft Certified Systems Engineer (MCSE)

Teacher Aide

COMPETENCY CLUSTER RESUME

General Strategy

Ms. Sherington is a teacher aide without a particularly impressive list of jobs held. What she does have is a composite set of experiences that will be viewed with respect by someone looking for a competent assistant in the classroom. To present her skills more attractively, she has decided to use the **Competency Cluster Resume.**

The tasks to be accomplished by this resume are to:

- show a combination of life experiences and training that qualify her to serve as a paraprofessional teacher; and

- back the claims with character, educational, and working experiences that will give her claims substance.

Specific Points

❶ Present position is part-time and rather informal so she elects to be called at home, rather than at an office where the response might be uncertain.

❷ **Summary and Objective** states what she wants to do and qualifications.

❸ Skills are grouped in such a manner as to address the main concerns of the potential hiring official.

❹ Where possible, institutional experience is shown first and then further supported by less formal, in-the-home experience.

❺ Specific classroom assisting tasks are listed and can be verified.

❻ Classroom management assistance is probably what is needed most in the setting to which she aspires.

❼ Supporting skills: first aid and awareness of childhood health concerns.

❽ Personal character is important and must be established.

❾ **Experience** frames the chronology of her adult life and lists relevant, if less than full-time experience.

❿ The college certificate will strengthen her claim to competency and appeal to those who work in a highly credential-oriented field like teaching.

Helen M. Sherington

104 Sandstone Road
Wilmington, DE 19802
302-977-9887 (Residence) ← **1**

2 Summary and Objective

Experienced, formally trained paraprofessional with young children in pre-school educational settings seeks full-time public school position as a teacher's aide at the kindergarten or grades 1-3 level.

Relevant Skills

3

CHILD-CARE

4
- Assisted in the operation of a 23 child church day-care center for 2 years
- Privately cared for 4 pre-school children at my residence for 3 years

CLASSROOM MANAGEMENT

5
- Prepared art project materials
- Assisted with math and reading drills
- Arranged rest areas
- Led game activities
- Typed and reproduced materials

6

HEALTH CARE

7
- Certified in Red Cross First Aid
- Trained in early childhood health

PERSONAL CHARACTER

8
- Married mother of two teenagers
- 10 year resident of this community
- Active in community affairs
- Extensive references available

Experience

9
<u>June 1997 - Present</u>: Day-care Center Assistant, United Lutheran Church, Beltsville, DE.

<u>June 1995 - May 1997</u>: Private day-care provider at my residence.

<u>July 1985 - May 1995</u>: Housewife and mother.

Education

Certificate
Child-Care
Beacon Junior College, DE 1996

10

Technical Writer

WORK HISTORY RESUME

General Strategy

Mr. Akrin has several positions that constitute the sum total of his working experience and they are the context of his achievements. He decided that the best approach for him was to present a simple, but thorough, **Work History Resume** that would do a good job of:

- showing that he is a competent technical writer with the background to function at a computer user-oriented magazine; and

- detailing the kinds of training and experience that show technical preparation for this kind of writing.

Specific Points

❶ **Overview** frames the experience, training, and aspirations of the applicant.

❷ **Experience** is arrayed in such a manner as to break out the two positions, separate them by full-time study, and provide continuity to the brief section.

❸ The Brainware position establishes him as a technical writer in the industry.

❹ It also notes experience that would parallel the kinds of areas covered by a user-magazine writer—national workshops, instructions for laymen, etc.

❺ The study break should be shown—keeps the chronology unbroken.

❻ The Matson position shows that he has the technical expertise for his writing.

❼ Worked directly with users—indicative of sensitivity to their interests.

❽ User magazines really serve as a link between users and manufacturers, so these experiences are probably going to be attractive to the person hiring.

❾ The technical expertise is well addressed educationally by his associate degree.

❿ The bachelor's degree in technical writing completes the ideal credentials.

William K. Akrin
56 Tura Road
Bennington, CT 48009
860-222-9988 (Office)
860-333-9075 (Residence)

① ## Overview

Technical Writer with formal training and experience in computer technology and technical writing seeks editorial opportunity with mass market user's magazine.

② ## Experience

January 1995 - Present: Technical Writer
Brainware Computer Products, Inc., Bennington, CT.

③ Assist in the preparation of technical manuals that support the use of software products created at Brainware. Experience includes interviewing programmers and systems engineers to identify program features. Convey features and step-by-step instructions for use in lay language. Attend national workshops to receive feedback **④** on manuals and products. Full range of mass market software including desktop publishing, graphic arts, and business packages featuring word processing, data bases, spread sheets, etc.

⑤ September 1992 - December 1995

Full-time study for Bachelor's degree.

⑥ June 1990 - August 1992: Customer Service Technician
Matson Software, Ltd., Norwich, CT.

Telephone contact for users of Matson Software products including their complete line of word processing, spread sheet, graphic presentation, and data base programs. **⑧** **⑦** Assisted users in isolating their problems and guiding them to solutions. Maintained records on nature of questions addressed and assisted technical writing staff in the revision of manuals.

Education

Associate in Arts (AA)   Bachelor of Technology (BT)
Computer Studies   Technical Writing
Asnutuck Junior College, CT, 1990   West Connecticut College, CT, 1997
⑨   **⑩**

Telecommunications Specialist

COMPETENCY CLUSTER RESUME

General Strategy

Mr. Goodwell feels that his worth exceeds the sum total of the two job descriptions that he would be presenting with a standard resume. With his technical orientation and the specific nature of his services, he chose to portray himself in the aggregate using a **Competency Cluster Resume.**

The objective of his resume is to:

- place in bold relief the several highly marketable things that he can do; and

- back it up with job settings and strong educational credentials that imply that he has the substance to deliver.

Specific Points

❶ **Overview** is used to sketch experience, indicate goal, and show confidence in his ability to thrive in a performance-based pay environment.

❷ **Areas of Competency** as a topic group draws the reviewer immediately to the productive substance of what he can do, not a mere job description.

❸ Examples briefly show levels of technology and markets where they are used.

❹ Not tied to a single vendor—broader, more independent status established.

❺ Demonstrates hands-on field service experience useful in his proposed role.

❻ Ability to implement and manage user services is evidenced here.

❼ Consulting experience is verified.

❽ Sales experience is noted as well as implied knowledge of the major provider's products and operation.

❾ An applied associate degree is presented.

❿ A specialized technical bachelor's degree caps his formal credentials.

Bernard K. Goodwell
76 La Junta Drive
Colorado Springs, CO 80908
719-332-0983 (Office)
719-776-8955 (Residence)

❶ Overview: Six years of designing and marketing commercial telecommunications services. Seeking growth opportunity in the western United States. Receptive to performance-based compensation arrangement in consulting or end-user applications.

Areas of Competency

❷ NEEDS EVALUATION
- Assessment of voice, fax, data, and video requirements in banking, insurance, manufacturing and government environments. **❸**
- Appraisal of volume, costs, and best use of technology.

EQUIPMENT SELECTION
- Independent perspective based on solid technical education and international industry familiarity. **❹**
- Established contacts with major vendors.

SERVICES SELECTION
- Knowledgeable in the available contractible services sectors, both majors and independents.

INSTALLATION **❺**
- Supervised the installation of 25 to 500 set, multifunction telecommunications systems.

OPERATION **❻**
- Managed the user training programs of all installations sold.

Experience

❼ June 1997 - Present: Telecommunications Consultant, Buena Vista Technical Consulting, Ltd., Boulder, CO.

❽ July 1993 - May 1997: Commercial Services Sales Representative, Mountain States Telephone, Denver, CO.

Education

Associate in Science (AS)
Digital Electronics
Mead Community College, AZ 1990
❾

Bachelor of Science (BS)
Telecommunications
State University of Colorado 1993
❿

Television Support Technician

FOCUSED RESUME

General Strategy

Ms. Arnold is seeking recognition in a combination technical and artistic specialty where specific abilities and experience are more important than job listings and duties performed. In order to make the most of her attributes, she has elected to present her record in the **Focused Resume** format.

The tasks to be accomplished by the resume are to:

- show an aggregate of skills gained in several settings that, together, have a greater value than their individual parts; and

- provide the concrete employment and training structure to show that she has been consistently productive within the industry.

Specific Points

❶ **Overview** begins with award-winning status and moves on to touch segments of the industry worked.

❷ Her objective is also presented in the opening statement.

❸ **Professional Abilities** outlines the categories of technical and artistic skill that the reviewer would be laboring to pick from a less pointed resume.

❹ The kinds of productions supported must be made clear.

❺ Status on the production team speaks to authority and role.

❻ Industry-recognized awards cast their glow on those who worked on their more mundane production aspects as well as the stars and producers—claim credit when due.

❼ **Achievements** is the section that tangibly confirms excellence.

❽ Union cards are so important that they legitimately constitute an achievement.

❾ A team player on award-winning productions.

❿ Employment record and the education credential round out her picture of overall competence.

Margaret A. Arnold

89 University Drive
Santa Marina, CA 93455
310-886-1903 (Office)
310-876-3921 (Residence)

Overview

❶

Award-winning Television Support Technician with national experience in multiple aspects of professional news, talk show, and drama productions seeks network or national cable opportunity.

❷

Professional Abilities

❸

- SET MANAGEMENT — 6 years of experience in the management of set activities supporting news, talk show, and dramatic television productions. **← ❹**
- LIGHTING — 4 years as associate lighting director for a producer of nationally syndicated television musical productions. Accomplished user of Kludge and special effects lighting in television applications. **← ❺**
- SET DESIGN — 3 years professional and 5 years amateur set design. Professional years included assistant background construction director for the Emmy Award winning docudrama *War and Space*

❻

❼ Achievements

❽
- Union cards held in the areas of television stage management, lighting, and set design.
❾
- On the staff of 7 production companies that received national industry recognition for excellence during my tenure.
- 1988 Audience Appreciation Award winner for set design in the live audience participation Minnie Walker Talk Show series.

Experience

June 1993 - Present: Set Manager, Gordon Boxwood Studios, Hollywood, CA.
June 1992 - May 1993: Set Design Specialist, KNBB, Santa Clarita, CA.
July 1989 - May 1992: Lighting Technician, Samuel Whitworth Production Company, Los Angeles, CA.

❿

Education

Associate in Science (AS)
Electronics Technology
Allan Whetstone Junior College, CA 1989

Training-and-Development Specialist

WORK HISTORY RESUME

General Strategy

Dr. Burnside has a unique situation that can be strongly presented in a traditional format—his special talent has been the direct outgrowth of a specific series of occupational experiences that describe him well. He has chosen the **Work History Resume** to paint a well-ordered picture of his somewhat unusual situation.

The objective of his resume is to establish that:

- he has a successful consulting practice that would be an attractive affiliation for an established training organization; and

- it all stems from a totally verifiable and respectable rise through traditional professional positions.

Specific Points

❶ Affirms his status, specialty, and what he is seeking in a brief **Overview.**

❷ **Experience** section is used to show how he put his consulting practice together while pursuing a traditional career.

❸ It begins with a description of his current practice.

❹ Evidence is presented of the growing demand and established reputation. His attractiveness is enhanced by illustrating the successful use of a personally created Web page to expand his business.

❺ Shows how he remained in the mainstream while completing his doctorate and establishing a consulting business.

❻ A solid base of traditional experience and the source of inspiration for his consulting orientation.

❼ His publications would be important to those considering adding him to their stable of authoritative presenters.

❽ His basic degrees are now important background for his consulting field.

❾ The doctor's degree lends authority to his presentations and writing.

❿ Comments explain that he is offering a share of his proven product if an established organization will free him to pursue his specialty.

Robert J. Burnside, Ph.D.
233 Eastwood Street
Beebe, AR 72012
501-883-7913 (Office)
501-989-2244 (Residence)

① **Overview:** Established national sales and motivation trainer seeks affiliation with a major consulting firm based in the Southeastern United States.

② Experience

③ June 1997 - Present: **Independent Training Consultant, Robert J. Burnside, Ph.D., Inc.,** Beebe, AR. Published "The Burnside System for Sales and Motivation" and toured nationally promoting its use in the selling industry. A 2-day seminar was structured and presented at 62 companies and 6 national sales meetings during the past two years. Future schedule includes 37 commitments with deposits. Strong interest expressed in follow-on presentations at **④** advanced level. Used Claris Home Page software to create a personal business Web page that attracts inquiries from markets not previously reached.

⑤ June 1989 - November 1997: **Adjunct Faculty Member, Beebe Area Community College.** Taught adult evening courses in career decision making and small business start-up skills while completing dissertation, writing, and establishing independent consulting firm in industrial training.

⑥ July 1980 - May 1989: **Industrial Arts Teacher, Thurmont High School,** Casey, AR. Taught shop courses to high school students seeking positions in industry. Earned masters degree part time during this period, then began evening employment as a trainer in local industries. Developed insights regarding motivation and success and began doctoral studies in counseling.

⑦ National Publications

The Burnside System, 1997
Selling in the Professional Market, 1998

Education

Bachelor of Arts (B.A.)	**⑧**	Master of Education (M.Ed.)
Teacher Education		Industrial Arts
Smith University, TX, 1980		Arkansas State University, 1983

Doctor of Philosophy (Ph.D.)
⑨ Counseling
Florida University, 1990

Comments

The reason for seeking affiliation is that the growth in demand for my services precludes the timely development of follow-on products that have great potential. Willing to exchange partial rights for business management of my seminar business. **⑩**

Travel Agent

FOCUSED RESUME

General Strategy

Ms. Winters is a very productive travel agent with a special set of skills that she wants to present very clearly. The prospect of listing jobs and duties is not appealing and would not do her justice. She is advised to use a **Focused Resume** to make the most of her brief but appealing presentation.

The objective of her resume is to:

- describe a geographic travel specialty that she has developed into an attractive and profitable niche; and

- verify that her claim is substantive—complete with productivity figures.

Specific Points

1 Her **Objective** states what she is trying to achieve in terms interesting to the potential recipients of her resume.

2 It also identifies the specialty that she is promoting—Alaskan group travel.

3 **Capabilities** tells just exactly what she can deliver—and does so briefly.

4 Ability to take her presentations to her potential customers is noted.

5 Experienced tour leader adds to the appeal.

6 Willing and able to handle the essential routine.

7 Experienced in coordinating with other travel professionals using the cutting–edge technology of the Internet.

8 **Accomplishments** proves she can deliver—meaningful specifics given.

9 Yeoman experience in the industry is a matter of verifiable record.

10 Possesses some formal training in the business.

Suzanne V. Winters
4111 Providence Avenue
Fairbanks, AK 99702
907-747-9002 (Office)
907-776-7566 (Residence)

❶

Objective — Affiliation with a major mainland chain or franchise as a specialist in the promotion of Alaskan group travel.

❷

Capabilities

❹

- Lower-48-states sales presentations to promote Alaska agency sponsored activities

- Group presentations to civic and business groups

❸

- Group tour leadership **❺**

- Associated travel office routine and clerical responsibilities **❻**

- Liaison with specialized agencies and tour providers internationally using the Internet. Skilled in using search engine capabilities to research client special requests. **❼**

Accomplishments

- Personally responsible for the sale of $278,000 in group travel from mainland and Hawaii affiliates in 1998.

❽

- Initiated program of cooperative promotion with State Tourism Agency that has yielded 1823 referrals in the first 8 months of operation.

- Designed custom tour for environmental groups following oil spill that attracted an aggregate of 483 travelers in a 6 month period.

Experience

June 1997 - Present: *Travel Consultant,* Ask Mr. Williams Agency, Fairbanks, AK.

❾ June 1993 - May 1997: *Travel Agent,* Express Independent Travel, Ltd., Anchorage, AK.

Education

Certificate in Travel and Tourism
Anchorage Business College, AK 1993

Veterinary Technician

COMPETENCY CLUSTER RESUME

General Strategy

Mr. Kline is a specialized animal health paraprofessional whose talents lend themselves well to presentation under the format of the **Competency Cluster Resume.** While his attributes would be there to find in a more traditional resume, this approach brings them together for greater impact.

His resume is crafted specifically to:

- show a large-animal veterinarian that he has the groups of skills that can form clear profit centers in his practice; and

- substantiate the claim with specific examples, impressive experience, and legitimate professional credentials.

Specific Points

❶ **Overview and Objective** classify the candidate and say what he wants to do and where.

❷ AVMA certification of his program makes him instantly credible.

❸ Routine vet paraprofessional skills are recounted.

❹ Specialized skills like AI are added attractions.

❺ Emergency field treatment qualifications will appeal to his market—the large-animal vet.

❻ Working experience as a staff vet on a major ranch is of substantial value.

❼ Previous experience in private practice is desirable.

❽ Student experience was with the industry.

❾ The associate degree qualifies him for his specialty.

❿ The special quality of his degree is its AVMA certification—a point worth highlighting both here and under **Professional Abilities.**

Cary J. Kline, Jr.
788 Overpass Drive
Glendale, AZ 85301
602-345-9878 (Office)
602-667-6483 (Residence)

➊ Overview and Objective

Large animal veterinary technician with over 6 years experience in the treatment of commercial beef cattle seeks private practice affiliation in the Southwestern United States.

Professional Abilities ➋

➌
- Graduate of American Veterinary Medical Association (AVMA) program
- Trained in large animal care
- Experienced in the administration of medication and vaccinations
- Artificial insemination specialist ← ➍
- Surgical assisting
- Emergency field treatment of farm animals ➎
- X-Ray and laboratory procedures

Experience ➏

<u>June 1997 - Present</u>: *Veterinary Technician,* Queen Ranch, Glendale, AZ.

<u>June 1993 - May 1997</u>: *Veterinary Technician,* Davidson Large Animal Clinic, Glendale, AZ. ➐

➑ <u>July 1991 - May 1993</u>: *Seasonal employment* in the commercial cattle finishing industry of Northern Arizona as a work-study student in veterinary technology.

Education

➒ Associate in Applied Science (AAS)
Veterinary Technology
An AVMA Approved Program of Study
➓ Community College of Tucson, 1993

Web Developer

FOCUSED RESUME

General Strategy

Mr. Wohler's IT resume addresses a specific job and specialized kind of work so it is best structured as a **Focused Resume** which helps to:

- highlight specific kinds of technical skills;

- concentrate on building a logically ordered resume containing appropriate key words since information technology (IT) resumes are generally sent by e–mail in an unembellished text format, and

- still create a strong core resume that is easy to adapt should aesthetics become important.

Specific Points

❶ A complete address element for an IT resume should include e–mail. Use an office address if you are satisfied with the privacy aspect; when in doubt use private e–mail.

❷ The overview signals his area of specialization, financial in this case.

❸ Information technology resumes show technical experience first using keywords recognizable both to programs that evaluate them electronically and people who read them.

❹ Experience section focuses on the job announcement and how he meets the employer's requirements.

❺ Work History substantiates claims of experience and documents progress through greater levels of responsibility.

❻ Work History accounts for continuous employment from college graduation through his current position.

❼ Work History also communicates the scope of his responsibilities and is the place to convey additional key words that respond to employer requirements.

❽ Notes work experience in his area of professional certification.

❾ Paints a word picture of his work environment that communicates the scope of his responsibilities.

❿ Professional certification is often on a par with college training in the IT field.

① MUIR L. WOHLER
130 Matheson Street
Tucson, AZ 85732
520-397-8888 • FAX 520-397-8648
wohlerm@backroadsaz.com

OBJECTIVE

② Web Developer position providing support for both intra and extranet servers in a financial environment.

TECHNICAL EXPERIENCE ③

- Three years full-time line experience as a Web developer
- Development support expertise for both intra (IIS) and extranet (TBD) servers
- 4D and SQL Server relational database experience
- **④** Extensive use of HTML in Web page design
- Other programming and applications experience includes: MS Access, VB5, CGI, Cpp, ActiveX, and ASP

WORK HISTORY ⑤

1996-1999—<u>Manager of Online Services.</u> ABC Lending Technologies, Inc., Phoenix, AZ. Managed all aspects of identifying, implementing, and maintaining online services provided through the firm's site on the Internet. Used the Web site development and technologies described above to present online features to serve current and potential customer groups.

⑥ 1993-96—<u>Applications Engineer.</u> Dingwel Investment Information, Inc., **⑦** Flagstaff, AZ. Oracle Server 7 and MS SQL 6.5 server database administrator designing and implementing Internet strategies. Experience included Windows NT Server 4.0, MS Exchange Server 5.5, DNS, IIS 3.0, Proxy Server 2.0 and Sequel Technology, Inc. Net Access Manager 2.0. Responsible for second-level support enterprise applications and information production software.

⑧ **⑨**

EDUCATION AND CERTIFICATION

University of Arizona
Bachelor of Science in Computer Studies, 1993
Microsoft Certified Systems Engineer (MCSE), 1995

Word-Processing Operator

COMPETENCY CLUSTER RESUME

General Strategy

Ms. McDaniel has a narrow specialty and a specific goal in mind. Her strongest presentation format is the **Competency Cluster Resume** because it will allow her to:

- separate herself from the secretarial stereotype by graphically featuring her very specialized talents; and
- package it in such a manner as to convey both special skills and traditional preparation including clerical experience and formal training.

Specific Points

❶ Overview tells the reviewer that a very specific situation is being sought.

❷ The specialization involves both the word-processing product and the fact that the applicant aspires to a training role.

❸ Identifies the product and systems in order to allow effective employer screening and save the inconvenience of an interview by an inappropriate employer.

❹ Mentions the mail-merge and other tasks that can be efficiently done.

❺ Associate the capability with the most modern office technology—that based on telecommunications by fax and modem.

❻ Mentions the ability to support tabular and graphics applications.

❼ Speed in entering data remains an important attribute.

❽ Supporting software that enhances the final product is valuable to cite.

❾ Experience in the clerical environment is established.

❿ Formal training underwrites her practical skills.

Anna P. McDaniel
2909 Phoenix Avenue
Montgomery, AL 36196
334-727-5990 (Office)
334-884-1243 (Residence)

❶ Overview

Single product word-processing specialist with in-depth capabilities in the production and handling of business correspondence and documents in all formats. Seeking large office environment where production activities can be supplemented by the training and supervision of others. ❷

Word-Processing Capabilities

❸ • Expert user of Microsoft Word on Macintosh and IBM systems.

❹ • Mail-merge specialist experienced in the custom mailing of personalized correspondence.

❺ • Highly competent in the sending, receipt, and reformatting of electronically transmitted documents.

• Accomplished in the integration of tabular data and graphics into word-processing documents. ❻

❼ • 80 WPM for text entry.

• Thorough familiarity with the use of spell-check and other supporting software.

❽ • Extensive laser printer experience as well as tractor fed forms and label printers.

Experience

June 1997 - Present: Word-Processing Specialist
Alabama Northern Electrical Cooperative, Enterprise, AL.

June 1993 - May 1997: Secretary
❾ Alabama Association of Real Estate Appraisers, Montgomery, AL.

Education

Diploma in Secretarial Science
Enterprise Community College, AL 1993 ❿

4 COVER LETTERS AND INTERVIEWS

Preparation of the resume is only part of the process of getting hired. A poor resume can hurt you. A good one can help. But the end result depends on your ability to integrate the resume into an overall job search process that is well conceived and executed. This chapter will describe the necessary components associated with the practice of seeking a new position.

Presenting Your Credentials

The way you learn about the availability of a position determines how you apply for it. While the list is not exhaustive, here are some of the possibilities and recommended ways to respond.

In each of these instances, you need a current resume that has been written in a style most appropriate to the situation. The other thing that is essential in almost every case is a cover letter that personalizes the resume and conveys information not included in it.

Source	Response
Newspaper advertisement.	Send a resume and cover letter, then follow their instructions—possibly completing their formal application or adhering to strict e–mail resume submission guidelines.

Source	Response
Internet Web page announcement.	Follow the instructions given, probably for submitting an electronic resume. Depending on how rigid the requirements (i.e., some literally want only an unembellished text-file resume), you might include an electronic cover letter as well. In less limited situations you could provide a formatted e-mail enclosure of your resume and cover letter.
Unsolicited inquiry.	Send your resume and a cover letter explaining your interest in the company. The alternative letter discussed later in this chapter is also a possibility.
A recruiter contacted you.	Send your resume through the recruiter who has already developed contacts within the company. The recruiter will interview you and provide additional information focused on the position.
Posted announcement.	Follow the instructions and include a resume and cover letter.

Resume Cover Letters

The cover letter has a mission as important as the resume itself—to get it into the hands of the right person and to motivate that person to read it. Here are some points to consider as you prepare your cover letter.

Question	Answer
To whom should the cover letter be addressed?	The hiring official, if at all possible. There are times when you must respect the protocol of sending it through personnel, but the objective is to place it in the hands of the person to whom you would report if hired.

Question	Answer
How do I know who that is?	Inquire. Don't call and say you are an applicant. Do your homework and find out enough about the organization to identify the right person. Call the department and ask one of your potential co-workers. While you are at it, get the full name, spelling, and title correct.
How do I get their attention?	Make a statement or two that indicates you know something about the company and the position. Say you were impressed by their Web page. Say how you learned about the vacancy.
How do I learn how to get their attention?	Read newspapers, trade journals, business references in the library, call the public relations department of large firms for an annual report or recent news releases. Research the company on the Internet. Call the department and find a future peer willing to discuss the situation candidly. Call a competing firm and do the same.
What is your first priority for the cover letter?	To get your resume in the hands of the hiring official.
The next priority?	To get the hiring official's attention and impress him or her favorably enough to read your resume.
What would do that besides the company and position knowledge already mentioned?	Indicate how you can be of value to the company and the hiring official. How your skills and experience can solve a problem or contribute to company growth.
What is the ultimate objective of your cover letter?	To get an interview to state your case personally and have a chance at conveying the right chemistry, which only a personal interview can communicate.
What should the tone of the cover letter be?	Straightforward, positive, brief, in the language of the business in question—don't be overly obvious, but speak in terms meaningful to the hiring official.

Question	Answer
How should the cover letter end?	Asking for an interview. Suggest a time when you will be in the area and offer to stop by, if convenient.
What other issues might be addressed in the cover letter?	Suggested times and places to reach you by telephone—whether or not a call to your office is okay. Whether or not your current employer is aware of your inquiry, or if confidentiality is required. Current compensation might be volunteered—only if requested or if there is concern about the adequacy of pay for the new position.
What about dropping names?	If there is a relevant common acquaintance who has agreed to be used as such a link, it can strengthen your letter. Be sure the reference is freely given and positive—enthusiastic is better.
Should I mention my reason for leaving?	It is not essential, but can clear the air on a point that is likely to require explanation eventually. Make it brief, general, and positive. If there is a serious problem that must be disclosed, do so as benignly as possible at this point and offer to elaborate at the interview.

Model Cover Letter

Wilson W. Woodruff
399 Calumet Avenue, Apartment 130
Washington, DC 20017
202-283-0099

January 22, 1999
Carson A. Howard
Head, Trust Investment Division
Holiday National Bank & Trust Company
892 Brickyard Parkway
Williamsburg, VA 24891

Dear Mr. Howard:

I am responding to your announcement in the January 21, 1999 edition of *The Washington Post* in which you sought applications for the position of Corporate Trust Investment Officer. Please consider this letter and the accompanying resume to be my application for that position.

As my resume relates in more detail, I have five years of successful corporate trust experience in the $750 million dollar department of Jones Bank & Trust in Washington. Our institutions serve a similar middle market clientele and I believe my contributions to your corporate calling effort in the Washington market could be quite attractive. Last year I increased funds under management by 43 percent and am well on the way to substantially increasing that performance this year.

John Samuels of your institution and I attended evening classes together while pursuing our MBAs. I have discussed the position with him and he has agreed to respond to any questions that you might have concerning my personal or professional qualities. I would welcome your discreet inquires anywhere in the industry, but ask that you not contact my present employer until I am considered to be a serious candidate. At that point, I would make the appropriate announcement of my interest in your opportunity.

My tenure at Jones has been very positive and my goal in seeking this change is to achieve professional growth not available to me there. I hope that it will be possible for us to discuss our mutual interests personally in the near future. I will be in your area the week of February 7–10 and would be glad to stop by, if you would find that convenient. Please feel free to call me at the office or my residence if further information would be helpful.

Sincerely,

Wilson W. Woodruff

Sample Market Letter

Maria E. Forbes
3497 Grant Street
Pittsburgh, PA 15234
412-261-9987

January 25, 1999

Clyde J. Hoover
Dean of Alumni Affairs
University of Eastern California
700 Palm Drive
Eighty-Nine Palms, CA 00784

Dear Dean Hoover:

I enjoyed your presentation at the December meeting of the National Alumni Administrators' Association at Atlantic City. The insights you provided on the prospects for increasing alumni participation by the use of upscale travel and credit card programs were of particular interest to me.

In five years of service as Director of Alumni Membership at Concord College, I have increased participation by 120 percent. Much of that success accrues to smaller-scale versions of the kinds of promotional programs that you advocate.

Other professional accomplishments that might interest you are:

- Initiated the first statewide alumni rental car discount program in Pennsylvania;
- Successfully petitioned the state lottery for college alumni program development funding;
- Increased alumni volunteer participation by 200 percent.

I would welcome the opportunity to discuss the possibility of my joining your staff at the end of the current academic year. Since I will be in California on February 22nd, I will call your office to see if a brief personal visit might be possible on the morning of the 23rd.

Sincerely,

Maria E. Forbes

THE ALTERNATIVE LETTER

If you are sending out unsolicited resumes not directed toward a known vacancy, consider a combination letter and resume. These are one page long, addressed to a specific person with the potential to hire you, and contain enough information to highlight your accomplishments and tell why you would be qualified for a position in the organization. They have many of the characteristics of a Competency Cluster or Focused Resume.

Such letters are known variously as market letters, broadcast letters, confetti letters, and PAR (problem-action-result) letters, according to David Rottman, writing in a *National Business Employment Weekly* reprint (undated). The author says that a well-conceived letter of this type can draw a far higher response rate for unsolicited mailings than a traditional cover letter and resume. Twenty to thirty percent is possible for a good letter.

The objective is to get something brief and personally interesting into the hands of someone who can grant an interview if he or she likes the qualities you communicate in your one-pager. Rottman suggests that you begin with one of several lead-ins:

- Mention a mutual acquaintance who has the respect of the hiring official and would follow up with a strong reference if asked;

- Do some research and mention a quote or fact from a recent business publication that involves the target employer;

- List a personal accomplishment that has relevance for the person and company to whom you are writing; or

- Begin with something novel and creative—best left for those in creative career fields such as advertising.

After you have the person's attention, devote the core of your letter to establishing that you are qualified to do the job. Quantify what you have already done and then focus on what you would be doing for them. Close with a request for an interview, as in any cover letter.

Richard Davis, writing in *Continuing Education Today* (1989), describes a similar approach that he calls a Notice of Availability. Instead of a letter format, he suggests a one-page outline consisting of headings and information similar to these:

Letterhead

Date

Notice of Availability (Your job title)

Position Desired (Job title)

Salary Required (Negotiable)

Available (Date)

Qualifications (In summary form)

Current Position (Job title)

Special Skills

References/Resume Available Upon Request

Recommended Contact Request (Recipient provides this if he or she knows of someone looking for a person with the sender's qualifications)

Thank You

Davis suggests that response rates for mailings based on names and addresses taken from current professional directories have been in the fifteen percent range. He found that most resulted in leads for excellent positions not seen advertised elsewhere.

Sample Notice of Availability

Maria E. Forbes
3497 Grant Street
Pittsburgh, PA 15234
412-261-9987

January 25, 1999

ANNOUNCEMENT OF AVAILABILITY

Creative, Enthusiastic College Alumni Director

POSITION DESIRED: **Director or Assistant Director of Alumni Affairs**

SALARY REQUIRED: **Negotiable above mid-thirties**

AVAILABLE: **August 1999**

QUALIFICATIONS: **Master's Degree in Marketing**
Five years' experience as Alumni Membership Director
Two years as Alumni Publications Coordinator
Three years as Student Services Officer
Numerous professional publications
Alumni event planning
Alumni membership drive coordination
Secretary, National Alumni Professionals Association
Proposal writing
Private giving experience

CURRENT POSITION: **Associate Alumni Program Coordinator**
Concord College, PA

SPECIAL SKILLS: **Computer mailing list preparation and maintenance**

REFERENCES AND RESUME AVAILABLE UPON REQUEST

SUGGESTED CONTACT: If you have or know of a position available, please complete the information below and return it to me.

Position Available: _____

Contact Person: _____

Title: _____

Address: _____

Telephone: _____

THANK YOU

Interviewing

After the cover letter and resume have succeeded, it is time to go face to face—maybe voice to voice will come first, in the form of a telephone interview. Here are some considerations that will help you to make the most of this crucial opportunity.

- Know something about the company, the job, and the person doing the interviewing. You do not have to pretend to be an expert, just show awareness of at least the basics:

    What is the business of the company?

    Is it relatively new or long established?

    What kind of customers does it serve?

    What does it produce?

    What is your interviewer's position?

    Outstanding accomplishments, reputation, etc. for either the company or the interviewer?

- Dress for the occasion. Standard business wardrobe is easy to define and replicate. Unless you are absolutely certain that something less will do, dress as you would for a business meeting with a top client. Clothes clean and pressed, shoes shined—no rundown heels, etc.

- Be on time. Not very early—never late.

- Come alone. Let the emphasis properly be on you, not the spouse and kids or whoever might have made the trip.

- Make a dry run on the location, if practical, to know where to park and generally solve any problems that might make you late or flustered the day of the interview.

- No gum chewing, smoking, obvious perfume, aftershave, excesses of makeup, fashion, or anything else that might detract from your bearing.

- Have flexible arrangements—no parking meter to feed, no early flight that must be met, and never another interview that you must get to right after this one.

- Be relaxed, but not familiar. Let any informality be insisted upon by the interviewer—first names, removing jackets, etc.

- Respond freely, but do not volunteer information not requested if it has any potential for embarrassment.

- Be ready for the standard questions—Why do you want the job? Why do you feel qualified? Where do you see yourself professionally in five years? What can you do for the company? What do you think of our Web page? Are you willing to travel and relocate? What kinds of people do you get along with best? . . . least well? What do you like to read? Book last read? Your strong points and weaknesses? Your greatest accomplishments and failures? Tell me about your personality. How did you like your boss? Do you have any problems we should be aware of that would affect your performance in this position? Why should we hire you? When could you begin? Why are you leaving your present job? Why do you want to work for this company? What is your minimum acceptable salary? What would you like to ask me?

Internet Tip

Use this URL to locate the Web page for the company . . .
http://pic2.infospace.com/__1__244791928__info.jbank/bizweb.htm
. . . or enter the keywords "company web pages" or "job bank" in your favorite search engine.

- Stay honest in answering these and other questions, but understand that you are being tested. Do not close doors with absolute responses. Try to put a positive spin on anything you can and suggest that there is room to negotiate almost anything. Salary questions should wait until an offer is made other than to say what you presently earn, that you expect to make more, and that the advertised range would appear to accommodate that need. Do not get put into a position of being negative or getting mad. How you respond may be as important as what you say.

- Watch for clues that it is time to end the session. Do not persist with questions or explanations beyond the point indicated by the interviewer's body language and other signs that enough has been said.

- Have a neatly typed list of your references' names, addresses, and telephone numbers in case they are requested. It is assumed that you have informed them of the interview and the possibility that they will be contacted.

FOLLOW-THROUGH

When the interview ends, be ready with a comfortable handshake, a smile, and an expression of appreciation for the opportunity to discuss the position. You should also say that you have continuing interest in the position. After you have returned home, send a brief letter of thanks for the courtesies extended by the employer during the interview, include any additional information that you may have agreed to send, and, again, express your interest in being the person hired. Offer to clarify questions that may arise, provide further references that might be required, and furnish any other information that would be helpful.

With those things done, there is nothing to be gained by making further inquiries about the status of your application. After the interview and the follow-up courtesies, be responsive to any contact that might be made. If something materially changes in your situation, make the employer aware of it. Otherwise, the ball is in his court and you can only diminish your stature by seeming overly anxious. That does not preclude a businesslike check of your status if it has been an unduly long time or if you must decide on accepting another offer. My companion volume to this book, *Job Interviews That Mean Business, Second Edition* (Random House, 1999), contains a more detailed treatment of the follow-through process.

The Hiring Process

You need to understand the hiring process in order to participate in it most effectively. By knowing what to expect and having a realistic perspective, you will be spared some potential frustration and improve the odds of ending up with the position you want.

THE HIRING CYCLE

After your initial application, your resume and supporting materials are screened along with others and, if interest persists, you are called for a telephone interview. If that goes well, a personal interview is arranged. Depending on the firm, you may speak initially with a human resources specialist (personnel officer) who will confirm that you meet the major job qualifications, appear genuinely interested in the position, and seem to have the standards of warmth, personality, and professional image that the company seeks.

A word about salary. The company will want to confirm that it can afford your services. This is an initial, general inquiry and not a negotiation of salary. Unless you are clearly out of range, the hiring process will go forward. Do your best to leave the salary question open until late in the game when the employer has developed a strong interest in you. An appropriate response early in the screening is that you are presently making $—— and that you would be expecting a reasonable incentive above that to justify the move. Leave it at that, if you can. A realistic expectation for a salary increase when changing jobs is the ten to fifteen percent range—sometimes fifteen to twenty percent, rarely more. If that is inconsistent with what you feel you must have, you need to review the entire situation. While you might enjoy some unique status that commands more, serious differences in expectations should be resolved early. Use your grapevine or, if necessary, directly determine early on that your goal is achievable. Unless realistic compromise is potentially possible, the prospects of your ultimately being hired become small.

This may take awhile. Timing between the cycles of the hiring process can vary widely and you must be prepared for some emotional ups and downs. Rarely is your application followed immediately by the employer's call, a personal interview, and an offer. It more often goes like this—

- You get reasonably enthusiastic about the prospect of something new and better. If you have been encouraged to apply, it is a compliment—your value in the marketplace is reaffirmed.

- A week or more goes by and no call—due to a number of good reasons that usually have nothing to do with how the employer feels about you. A key person got sick, had to take a trip, or had to deal with an unexpected development. Someone decided that they must all await the results of another ad. A decision was made to interview several local candidates first . . . and so on.

- Such delays can work on your morale and attitude. Initial enthusiasm can turn to posturing to avoid rejection—"I didn't really want it anyway. . . ."

- That kind of thinking is usually unfounded and unnecessary. Rarely is the delay anything more than a large organization trying to fit something that it doesn't do everyday—hiring—into what it must do every day—deal with the business at hand and unexpected problems totally unrelated to your hiring.

- Be patient. Everything that was true on your most enthusiastic day probably still is. Well-founded personal and professional reasons attracted you to the position in the first place. Chances are they included a mix of opportunity, geography, and compensation. That is all still true and you have nothing to lose by seeing it through—possibly much to gain.

217

Your attitude means a lot. Whether you are competing for a CEO's position or something less, the company is trying to select the very best and will make the effort necessary to have an outstanding group from which to choose. You are well prepared or you would not have reached the point of serious consideration.

After the objective criteria have been satisfied, the selection process narrows to more subjective things. It is very important that you be yourself and do not attempt to play a role that you think will be popular. You have to come up with and maintain an honest, positive attitude that conveys something like this:

"Yes, this sounds like an opportunity that could really be of interest to me—I want to learn more about it and help you understand just how I could become a very fine addition to your organization."

You will experience ups and downs in your enthusiasm for the position. Ask the necessary questions to resolve your concerns, but keep your positive interest apparent throughout. You are always in a position to say no to an offer. You are rarely able to revive interest once you have turned interviewers off with an attitude with which they are not prepared to deal. Keep it positive and keep their interest growing. Final negotiations are best handled at the end when you are in the strongest position—they have selected you and made an offer. They want to see it work at that point and will be more apt to satisfy some concerns that you might have—assuming there are no big surprises that alter basic expectations that have been building from the beginning.

Impressions matter. When all is said and done and the final selection is made, you will have left impressions with a number of people. Good impressions can make you the winner in a group of relative equals. Consider how the following impressions can work for you:

- Quiet confidence and a good-natured interest in the company and future co-workers, consistently and naturally displayed with more than one person in a variety of settings.

- A general tone of openness and warmth. Say a genuine thank you to the person who helped arrange your visit, send brief, positive letters of appreciation following interviews. Express your continuing interest. Employers want to feel comfortable with you and expect that their clients will feel the same.

- Display of poise and equanimity, not overwhelmed by a single disappointment. Issues calmly resolved in a mutually satisfactory way.

- No up-front demands. Made sure that differences were potentially resolvable, but left their resolution for the proper point in the hiring process—at the offer stage.

- Had some things to offer for the good of the organization with an honest interest in accomplishing them.

- Positive attitude. Made no negative comments about past associations—even if warranted.

- Clean, crisp, well-groomed business image—traditional business wardrobe, obviously cleaned and pressed—the kind of person employers want representing their firm.

Employer fears. There is considerable risk, expense, and trauma for a hiring organization. It would like to avoid going through the same hiring demands again in the near future. You must be honest and genuine, but do not go in saying that you plan on leaving in two years. Before your interview, formulate a solid and positive career plan that shows your commitment to the organization will be long-term in nature—more than five years. Reality may dictate otherwise, but your incoming goal should be one with which the employer can be comfortable.

Finally, the counteroffer/buy-back. The hiring cycle has been completed successfully, an offer has been made and accepted. Is it over? Maybe not. What remains is for you to tell your present employer. It is not uncommon for employers to make an unexpectedly good offer in order to retain you. Such counteroffers are usually for the purpose of buying them time to replace you. Why did it take your resignation to make you so valuable to the company? Were you only leaving because of a change in pay or some alteration of your duties—or were there larger reasons? If so, it is doubtful that the counteroffer will change your mind about leaving. Think this all through and have your answer ready well before the emotional moment of actual resignation. Buy-backs are seldom still in their jobs a year later. Decide whether or not you really want to move on. If the answer is yes and the opportunity presents itself, be prepared to follow through without anguishing over the final step.

5 COMPUTERS, FAX, AND VIDEOTAPE

Technology can enhance your resume and support your job-seeking efforts. Nothing is a substitute for valid resume content and a well-executed job search, but modern electronic enhancements could conceivably provide you with the winning edge when the competition gets tight. What follows is new thinking in the field of resume crafting and presentation. It represents the exception and not the rule. Spend your primary effort on the preparation of the finest resume and cover letter possible—but be aware of the potential of computers, fax, and videotape.

Computers

Computers are at the heart of modern resume preparation and job search. Typewriters have been replaced by personal computers with word processing software and high-resolution printers that can create formidable resumes. Connect to the Internet and your computer lets you search job listings, submit instant e-mail resumes, research companies, find your way to interviews, and price homes in distant cities.

COMPUTERS AND RESUMES IN GENERAL

The computer gives you more than just a fancy final product. It is crucial to keeping your information current and accurate. By altering several elements of your basic resume, you can produce an endless variety of truly personalized editions. The need for printing a quantity of soon obsolete resumes ends with the ability to print an up-to-the minute one instantly.

If you neither own a personal computer with the qualities described nor have access to one at work, consider the rental option. Most cities now have walk-in shops where you pay an hourly rate for the use of a thoroughly modern computer system fully capable of producing a great resume. They will show you how to use it and sell you a disk on which to keep your resume and supporting correspondence for future use.

It is really quite simple to master a few techniques such as centering, bold-facing, italicizing, and selecting interesting type faces that will add immeasurably to the professional appearance of your resume. Printing it on a laser printer is no challenge whatsoever. The whole exercise will cost you far less than you imagine and it gets cheaper after you learn how to use the equipment efficiently.

All of the advantages just described for resume preparation apply to the support areas surrounding your job search as well. Correspondence is easily prepared and stored for later modification and use in future efforts. Lists of references can be maintained efficiently and customized lists put together to suit changing requirements. A record of your job search activities, company points of contact, and names, addresses, and telephone numbers are readily kept in the computer.

Your ability to use a computer is an invaluable skill. Rarely is a job interview conducted today that does not raise the question of computer literacy. It is not difficult to be able to answer with a confident "yes," and the preparation of your own resume is a great way to begin gaining the necessary skills. Friends and acquaintances who have conquered the basics of using a computer will fall all over themselves to show you how—let them. It is a great convenience and a real business necessity in the modern office.

SPECIFIC COMPUTER TECHNIQUES FOR RESUME WRITERS

- **Typing:** With the computer you gain complete flexibility to let your ideas flow, knowing you can alter, delete, cut and paste, and change things endlessly until you get it right—and right can vary with the recipient.

- **Proofing:** Most word-processing programs have spell checkers that will save you the embarrassment of most typos as well as misspelled words. Some programs will even suggest things that you might reconsider grammatically.

- **Aesthetics:** When you get beyond the fundamentals of saying the right thing with the correctly chosen and spelled words, much of the impact of your resume will depend on how it is arranged and presented. The computer extends the flexibility you enjoy in typing to viewing your resume as a whole.

Depending on your equipment and software, that might mean printing copies and revising them several times, or just summoning the preview feature of your system to see if you find it pleasing before going to the printer.

While computers and printers vary in their capabilities, it does not require desktop publishing skills or software to use the following techniques:

TYPE STYLE AND LAYOUT

Variety and emphasis can be added by changing the size and characteristics of what you type. Here are some examples of how you can add interest and direct the reader's attention by altering type style and its arrangement.

Plain left-justified courier type is clean and okay.

```
Kent L. Schwartz
3595 Congress Avenue, NW
Washington, DC 20033
202-991-0245
```

Centering it makes it a little more interesting.

```
            Kent L. Schwartz
        3595 Congress Avenue, NW
          Washington, DC 20033
             202-991-0245
```

You can stress the most important part by making it larger and reducing the size of a minor item like the telephone number.

```
         Kent L. Schwartz
        3595 Congress Avenue, NW
          Washington, DC 20033
             202-991-0245
```

Boldfacing can add even more emphasis.

```
         Kent L. Schwartz
        3595 Congress Avenue, NW
          Washington, DC 20033
             202-991-0245
```

The final touch might be the selection of a typeface that suits your image. (These are just a few examples—what is actually available will vary depending on your computer and supporting software.)

Kent L. Schwartz
3595 Congress Avenue, NW
Washington, DC 20033
202-991-0245

Kent L. Schwartz
3595 Congress Avenue, NW
Washington, DC 20033
202-991-0245

Kent L. Schwartz
3595 Congress Avenue, NW
Washington, DC 20033
202-991-0245

Kent L. Schwartz
3595 Congress Avenue, NW
Washington, DC 20033
202-991-0245

Kent L. Schwartz
3595 Congress Avenue, NW
Washington, DC 20033
202-991-0245

Kent L. Schwartz
3595 Congress Avenue, NW
Washington, DC 20033
202-991-0245

Even more variety is possible on systems that also let you italicize, outline, shadow, and underline (clockwise, beginning upper left)—capabilities that are not at all uncommon on today's personal computers.

Kent L. Schwartz
3595 Congress Avenue, NW
Washington, DC 20033
202-991-0245

Kent L. Schwartz
3595 Congress Avenue, NW
Washington, DC 20033
202-991-0245

<u>**Kent L. Schwartz**</u>
3595 Congress Avenue, NW
Washington, DC 20033
202-991-0245

Kent L. Schwartz
3595 Congress Avenue, NW
Washington, DC 20033
202-991-0245

The use of all of these variations is dictated by good taste and aesthetic balance, and the practical consideration of how they might affect your resume's readability by electronic processing equipment if you are applying to a large company or sending your resume by e–mail. (See Chapter 6, Electronic Resumes.) A traditional business resume would probably not get into the use of outline or shadow type. Boldfacing would have a place, as would underlining and italicizing. The latter might be more appropriate in the body of the resume where you strive to distinguish between job title and employer, for example. When in doubt, simplify. Do not succumb to the rapture of your computer and produce a resume that is so dominated by style variations that the reader is drawn away from the points you want to emphasize. If there is no item of information worthy of emphasis—or if the technique you have chosen fails to impart that emphasis pleasantly—forget it.

Typeface variations are not the only consideration in preparing a resume on your computer. Many popular word-processing software packages give you the means to arrange side-by-side paragraphs. They can be very useful in placing eye-catching headers with elaborating details next to them. Here is an example:

Skills	• Speech preparation • News release writing • Media event coordination • Publication creation • Articulation of institutional image
Accomplishments	• Increased alumni participation by 23 percent during two year directorship. • Won the State Education Associations' Promotion of the Year Award for 1985. • Collection of my drafted speeches published as a nationally distributed monograph.

Remember that many computers provide bullets (•) or check marks (✓) to add clarity to your lists of attributes. There are trademark (™), copyright (©) and registered (®) symbols that could add professionalism to a specialized resume. The same is true of scientific and language symbols. Avoid the contrived use of any of these techniques, but be aware of their potential when the situation calls for them.

Another advantage of computerized resumes is the option of reducing the size of the final version. If you have everything perfectly expressed and arranged, but find that it overflows to the next page by several lines, it is easy to reduce the type size by one setting and make it fit. Another approach is to print with a percentage reduction (e.g., when you select the print option you can elect to make it ninety percent of the actual size, etc.) that places your full resume on a page neatly without noticeable loss.

Cutting and pasting is computer terminology for electronically selecting and removing certain passages and inserting them somewhere else. On a lesser scale, inserting and spreading text is another means of flexibility not found on typewriters. With it you enter a word, sentence, paragraph, or document at any point and add text—the computer pushes the rest of the text forward and accommodates your changes. The reverse is true for deleting material.

Paragraphs can be treated with the balance and style previously only available from a print shop. Here are a few things that you can do conveniently on a personal computer.

> Preparing an electronic resume or one that might be scanned into a large company's database? See Chapter 6 for special tips on formatting.

Centering

BEFORE

Strong organizational and people skills. Proven leader with over 6 years of progressively successful experience in personnel, management, and sales. Seek to combine talents at senior management level as administrative assistant with potential for assuming broader responsibilities.

AFTER

Strong organizational and people skills. Proven leader with over 6 years of progressively successful experience in personnel, management, and sales. Seek to combine talents at senior management level as administrative assistant with potential for assuming broader responsibilities.

Justified Type

BEFORE

Strong organizational and people skills. Proven leader with over 6 years of progressively successful experience in personnel, management, and sales. Seek to combine talents at senior management level as administrative assistant with potential for assuming broader responsibilities.

AFTER

Strong organizational and people skills. Proven leader with over 6 years of progressively successful experience in personnel, management, and sales. Seek to combine talents at senior management level as administrative assistant with potential for assuming broader responsibilities.

Inset Margins

BEFORE

Strong organizational and people skills. Proven leader with over 6 years of progressively successful experience in personnel, management, and sales. Seek to combine talents at senior management level as administrative assistant with potential for assuming broader responsibilities.

AFTER

Strong organizational and people skills. Proven leader with over 6 years of progressively successful experience in personnel, management, and sales. Seek to combine talents at senior management level as administrative assistant with potential for assuming broader responsibilities.

Hanging Indents

BEFORE

• Strong organizational and people skills. Proven leader with over 6 years of progressively successful experience in personnel, management, and sales. Seek to combine talents at senior management level as administrative assistant with potential for assuming broader responsibilities.

AFTER

• Strong organizational and people skills. Proven leader with over 6 years of progressively successful experience in personnel, management, and sales. Seek to
   combine talents at senior management level as administrative assistant with potential for assuming broader responsibilities.

BOILERPLATE

Personalization is one of the computer's strongest capabilities for the resume writer. While it can be a disaster if you leave John Jones's personal data in the resume that you are sending to Frank Smith, the advantages are worth the extra diligence required to get it right.

If you are a person whose talents might be applied in several contexts, you can have a basic resume in which you insert special paragraphs denoting the emphasis appropriate for each. One may stress your portfolio management skills for job-seeking as an in-house money manager. Another might put the emphasis on your business development accomplishments, if the position calls for someone with strong marketing skills. Customized clauses and paragraphs, carefully used, can accomplish this degree of personalization.

Resumes can effortlessly be directed toward a specific person and position, if appropriate. Here is an example of how that might be done:

Marsha K. Grant
21 South Market Place
North Laguna, CA 96731
714-223-0977

Resume Prepared for the Consideration of:
Carlton M. Donnaly
Human Resources Manager
The Wilcoxon Companies

Director of Marketing Position

With such a beginning, a resume can be directed toward a succession of specific employers, each one giving the appearance of a customized document prepared for that person. Even for those jaded enough to know it is done with ease on a personal computer, this adds a nice touch and shows effort that speaks well for your interest, thoroughness, and initiative.

SOFTWARE AND INTERNET

Finally, the software itself (together with computer hardware that supports it) is what gives you the capabilities just discussed. There is a vast marketplace filled with products of varying costs and complexity that will work nicely in resume preparation. As you shop for a specific word-processing package, one thing you might consider is whether it has commercially prepared resume *templates* available. With templates you have an already formatted outline for various styles of resumes. You simply enter your own specific data. Depending on your level of interest and creativity, this may or may not be helpful. Such templates work in conjunction with specific word-processing programs. Local software or computer stores can assist you in putting together an effective combination of products. Computer magazines are filled with articles and advertising that discuss such things. They also contain advertising for firms that sell software by mail.

The Internet is also a source of resume templates and software, some of it useful, some less so. Enter "resume preparation" in your search engine to examine the latest fare, and also see Chapter 7, Using the Internet.

Internet Tip

To sample Internet resume advice try:
http://provenresumes.com/
. . . or enter the keyword "resumes" in your favorite search engine.

Fax

Facsimile transmission really is not anything new. News services have relied on it for decades. Today fax machines are commonplace in businesses and home offices. Small stand-alone units complete with a second telephone are priced at about $100, and they are easy to install and use. Inexpensive software can add the fax capability to your personal computer, although you might find it inconvenient leaving the computer always on to receive faxes. Fax services are also available for a fee at copy, mailbox, and business support centers.

What this means to the job applicant is a tremendous capacity for instant response to a hiring notice or a hiring official's request for additional information. A fax has the impact of a telegram. It certainly gets treated with more urgency than the incoming mail. Use that to your advantage both to meet urgent deadlines and as a device for standing out in the crowd of incoming resumes.

Since the quality of most fax machines leaves something to be desired, you should use a cover sheet indicating that a printed copy of your resume will follow in the mail. Properly done, the use of the fax to introduce yourself to an employer shows several desirable qualities:

- genuinely prompt reaction to deadlines or requests for information;
- familiarity with the latest in business technology; and
- a competitive quality translated into the business environment that precedes you and gives you a distinctiveness not shared by the average applicant.

It goes without saying that the fax will do nothing to enhance an otherwise unattractive resume. The advantage comes when you have something special to offer the employer and you add to that basic advantage by reacting with the speed and impact of a fax.

The same advantage can be used in all correspondence surrounding the hiring process. You can make an arrangement with a local fax service to call you when something is received in your name. They are happy to have you use their fax number as though it were your own. The charge is minimal for the impact of telling a hired official that they can fax the application or job description or company benefits brochure, or whatever, to you.

Another potential use is to provide immediate letters of reference. Most of your reference sources will have fax machines in their offices and would be glad to transmit their recommendations. It has the advantage of great promptness and says something about how you do business with others—if they care enough about you and you were sharp enough to arrange for a faxed reference, it cannot help but reflect favorably.

Anything can be overdone or done poorly. Be cautious about using the fax approach to resume delivery and support. Save it for when it might really have a place—a tight deadline, an urgent request for follow-up information, or a quick reference that might close a deal before the enthusiasm of the moment cools. If you add a commercial fax number to your resume for impact, be sure to check the service regularly and make certain that an important communication to you doesn't sit uncollected.

Of course, technology marches on. While it still has many appropriate uses, fax has been trumped in terms of immediacy and high–tech image by e–mail and Internet web pages. See Chapter 7, Using the Internet.

Videotape

The latest resume-service marketing device is adding a videotaped interview to basic resume preparation. The idea clearly has potential. One company claims to conduct a professional interview with the candidate and then make that tape available to employers seeking his or her skills. The advantages for both the employer and candidate are potentially great, if the process is handled well by all concerned.

The similarity of this approach to video dating services is apparent, as is the potential for abuse or costly ineffectiveness. If you find yourself in an area served by a video resume service, it may represent an interesting opportunity to present your talents in a uniquely effective way. You will have to judge the soundness of the particular company offering the service. References from both the candidate and the employer side of the hiring equation would be a reasonable place to begin in evaluating the potential effectiveness of such a firm. Readers should exercise the same level of consumer awareness that they would in selecting any important service.

In a totally independent vein, it would be entirely possible to arrange for the production of a short personal video with a professional studio. You could write the script for a video resume and distribute copies to selected employers around the country, perhaps after their favorable response to your printed resume or market letter. It might advance your prospects in a situation where your paper resume and telephone interview are sufficiently promising to warrant a look at you on the VCR, but not a trip across the country. If the tape conveys the qualities sought, the actual interview could follow.

A video tape definitely adds to the impression gained from the resume and a telephone conversation. Everyone has access to a VCR player, so there would be no difficulty reviewing your tape if the employer was interested. There is a good chance that the hiring official will be curious enough to ask for and look at the tape. You might even find that you have his or her personal attention at home after business hours. Hand-held home video cameras are not apt to convey the impression you want. Expect to spend some time and money on a quality studio production, if you decide to follow this approach.

As technology advances, look for adaptations of video interviewing that involve the Internet. Some companies are already using the technique.

Internet Tip

Try this URL to see an illustration of interviewing on the Internet:
http://iamag.com/infoage/virtual.htm
. . . or enter the keywords "job interview" in your favorite search engine.

6 | ELECTRONIC RESUMES

An engineering advertisement the Walt Disney World Company placed in *The Washington Post* ends like this:

> For consideration, please send a resume with salary history to the address below. Resumes must be formatted chronologically on white or light colored 8.5″ × 11″ paper in order to be entered into our resume tracking system. (6/25/95 page K25)

Newspaper classified advertisements now routinely end:

- "Please e–mail resume and salary history in .txt format for this position to: jobs@careers.whateverco.com" or

- "E–mail your resume in ASCII text to: resumes-us@xyz.com" or

- "E–mail resume with no enclosures to: hightech@wizard.org. Indicate 'programmer' in the subject line."

Don't discard your conventional resume, but there is a new technique in the job search business that is becoming an important supplement to the ordinary resume preparation and distribution process for many people. It is the *electronic resume*— a computer scan or e–mail transmission of your resume that ends up in someone's database. That someone might be a large company's *automated applicant tracking system* or a service bureau that makes your credentials available to potential employers—each with your permission, hopefully.

Internet Tip

Try this URL for more advice on electronic resumes:
http://www.eresumes.com/
. . . or enter the keywords "electronic resumes" in your favorite search engine.

Basically, a resume is still a resume, but there are special considerations to keep in mind if you want to benefit from the computer revolution. Successfully converting your credentials to a computer-friendly format gets you only so far. It won't compensate for your lacking the specific skills and experiences required for a position, but it may get you past the electronic gatekeeper and onto the to-be-considered-further list.

The electronic resume caters to the mass job market. If you have the wherewithal to market yourself directly to hiring officials who would welcome your credentials, you are a step ahead of these services and will find them to be unnecessary. On the other hand, if you need to cast your net broadly and see who expresses interest, post your credentials on an Internet resume service, e–mail text–formatted resumes, or mail optical character recognition–readable resumes to lots of companies.

The upside to posting your resume electronically is broad exposure and the chance to be plucked from the database on the merits of your key words. The downside is limiting your presentation to fit certain formatting conventions that are not terribly creative and the remote possibility that the wrong people will access your resume. The chance of your job market initiative coming to the attention of your own company is reduced by resume service procedures that allow you to authorize each release.

Scanner-Friendly Resume Formatting

The point of the electronic resume revolution is the efficient handling of massive amounts of information about job applicants and the positions they might fill. Whether you attribute the volume to a more educated society, equal opportunity and affirmative action hiring, or simply large numbers of applicants and positions, much paper gets processed.

It used to be that human beings scanned resumes and sorted them according to their desirability. That is the way hiring still works much of the time, and it is where even electronic job searches end. The difference is in how the sorting is done. People screening resumes with their eyes have been replaced in the initial stages by computers doing the same thing with electronic scanners.

Optical character recognition (OCR) is a two-part process: (1) a light source and an optical device that converts a paper image into an electronic one, and (2) computer software that sorts what the scanner sees into recognizable letters, words, and symbols. It is known as optical character recognition technology, and it runs the gamut from crude to highly sophisticated. To have your resume function well in the OCR environment, your presentation has to respect certain conventions:

- *Use a plain, popular font in your resume.* The best is a sans serif type like Helvetica or another in the family of typefaces that lack the fancy designer embellishments that could be confusing to OCR processes. If you must use serif type, stick to Times, Palatino, and others that the scanners would more likely recognize.

- *Use regular white paper and black ink.* The clear contrast improves recognition. Scanners are made to process paper of normal size and weight. The better the printer or reproduction process used, the better the scanner will perform. While you can get by with less, a good laser printer and a high-quality commercial copier are your best bets.

- *Mail a flat original or an excellent copy.* If you must fax a copy, use the fine setting.

- *Minimize the use of boldface and avoid italics.* Although both are readable by most OCR systems, use bold only in headings and skip the italic and script options.

- *Use a conventional type size, and don't reduce it.* Stay within the 10- to 14-point type range and avoid the temptation to reduce the final product to make it fit on a page or two.

- *Don't use shading, boxes, and horizontal or vertical lines.* These features tend to introduce errors by obscuring readable type and making the OCR software cope with characters it can't match.

- *Don't use multiple columns.* They require a special approach to scanning.

- *Use portrait, not landscape, page orientation.* Portrait is the traditional vertical page format; landscape is wider than it is tall.

- *Avoid folding or stapling your resume.* Anything you can do to present the scanner with clean, flat copy is to your advantage.

- *Use only one side of the paper.* It avoids the possibility of bleed-through and it eliminates the possibility that the page will not be turned over.

- *Limit your resume to two pages.* Longer resumes crowd databases and generally tell more than the evaluators want to know.

- *Place your name at the top.* The scanner should encounter your name, unencumbered by other information, on the first line of your resume.
- *Use white space.* Just as white space is pleasing to the eye and useful in distinguishing one part of a resume from another, scanners need it to make logical breaks in the information provided—both horizontally and vertically.

Here are some examples of how popular OCR systems read several fonts in the same format and with identical content:

HELVETICA ORIGINAL

EXPERIENCE

June 1987–Present: **Assistant Loan Officer,** **Southland Banks,** Columbia, SC. Commercial loan officer with extensive business development responsibilities in the Carolinas, Georgia, and North Florida. Manage a $35 million portfolio which includes $27 million outstanding and $8 million committed. Generated $11 million in new deposits and $19 million in new loans in 2.5 years—number 2 performer on a staff of 12 regional lenders.

HELVETICA SCAN

Experience

June 1987–Present: *Assistant Loan Officer,* Southland Banks, Columbia, SC. Commercial loan officer with extensive business development responsibilities in the Caro~inas, Georgia, and North Florida. Mana~e a $35 million portfolio which includes $27 million outstanding and $8 million committed. Generated $11 million in new deposits and $19 million in new loans in 2.5 years—number 2 performer on a staff of 12 regional lenders.

COMMENT

The scan of this common sans serif typeface is nearly perfect; underlining and italics were no problem, although the boldface, while read successfully, was not retained.

SCRIPT ORIGINAL

EXPERIENCE

June 1987–Present: Assistant Loan Officer, Southland Banks, Columbia, SC. Commercial loan officer with extensive business development responsibilities in the Carolinas, Georgia, and North Florida. Manage a $35 million portfolio which includes $27 million outstanding and $8 million committed. Generated $11 million in new deposits and $19 million in new loans in 2.5 years—number 2 performer on a staff of 12 regional lenders.

SCRIPT SCAN

~X-R£5t~Jlte£
7~c 1987~g.~a~aAt ~~,

5e~aJ *and JVJud~*   35
p~u~h~S27 n~n~

~nd S~9 m~ 1~ ~ toa~ ~n 2.5 y4w~—nu~2
pa~ on a da~ ~412 ~lon~ ~

COMMENT

While it makes a distinctive visual presentation, this script typeface resume was virtually unreadable by the OCR system.

TIMES ORIGINAL

EXPERIENCE

June 1987–Present: *Assistant Loan Officer,* **Southland Banks,** Columbia, SC. Commercial loan officer with extensive business development responsibilities in the Carolinas, Georgia, and North Florida. Manage a $35 million portfolio which includes $27 million outstanding and $8 million committed. Generated $11 million in new deposits and $19 million in new loans in 2.5 years—number 2 performer on a staff of 12 regional lenders.

TIMES SCAN

ExpERIENcE

June 1~7 - Pre~ent: *Assistant Loan Officer,* **Southland Banks,** Columbia, SC. Commercial loan officer with extensive business development responsibilities in the Carolinas. Georgia, and North Plorida, Manage a $35 million portfolio which includes $27 m~llion outstanding and $8 million commit~d. Gencrated $11 million in new deposits and $19 million in new loans in 2.5 years—number 2 performer on a staff of 12 regional lenders.

COMMENT

This well-known serif type, while not a first choice for electronic resume preparation, was largely readable by the OCR system. The results are inferior to the sans serif Helvetica type used in the first example, and they demonstrate how the decorative touches like the embellishments on the horizontal bars of the letter "F" in Florida read as the closed letter "P."

KEYWORDS

Just as the human mind is impressed or not impressed by what it sees in a resume, so, too, is the computer that scans your credentials for specific content. OCR is only the first step in handling electronic resumes. The next step is examining them for content. Since even impressive computer applications lack the flexibility and judgment of a brain, narrow search criteria are used. That is why you must craft your resume to show the job search computer what it wants to see—keywords.

Every occupation has its own jargon, acronyms, and buzzwords. To make a list for your specialty, examine the help wanted listings in the national employment publications that cater to your field. Also read current professional publications with the goal of identifying the terminology that is being used to define and communicate what a successful practitioner does in your job. They can be the belabored, lengthy terms of science and medicine or the crisp acronyms of computing, engineering, and government. It doesn't take a lot of imagination to find the keywords valued in your specialty—retailers might be looking for UPC scanner skills; a brokerage firm could be looking for an asset valuation analyst with NASDAQ experience. The terms and their variations are endless, and they have greatest value in their particular fields, so do your homework and define the keywords for the position you seek.

There are also general keywords that apply to such things as interpersonal skills. Depending on your field and level, the computer may be programmed to find people who express a willingness to travel, are team players, delegate responsibility, possess organizational skills, speak in public, are innovative, are oriented toward customer service—or any of dozens, if not hundreds, of terms used to describe your work style.

If you are responding to a specific job announcement, analyze it for keywords. Next, design your resume to display the keywords the employer is looking for—within the limits of honesty and not pandering so blatantly to the advertisement that it becomes a turnoff.

Take care to get the acronyms right. The same advice applies to making your college and field of study recognizable. Job titles also need to contain terms that an automated sorting system will recognize and value—manager, trainee, supervisor, etc. Computers recognize and analyze numbers well, and they are often programmed to do so. Make your year of college graduation a single date that can be read, not a range. A range is fine for job experience that is expected to span a period of time and thus can yield meaningful results in the computer's evaluation of your work history.

If the concept of keywords and using them to search for information are alien to you, help is readily available. One approach is to sign on to any online service with a computer and modem. You won't get far without applying the concepts of keywords and searches. If you don't subscribe to such a service, many libraries do and you can introduce yourself to keyword searching with the help of the librarian. It isn't necessary to go online—any library with a computerized card catalog can provide you with a worthwhile experience in keyword searching. Books, after all, have had indexes based on keywords for a long time—it is the same idea applied to computers and databases.

ELECTRONIC RESUME TEMPLATE

Bringing keywords clearly to the attention of the automated applicant evaluation system is a matter of formatting, after you have satisfied the content criterion by determining the keywords. The advice from those who run job database services is to have a plan or theme for your electronic resume. Rough out the essential content, and arrange it from top to bottom in categories and in order of importance. Within those categories, make your presentation concise and direct, respecting the need to communicate the keywords valued by employers.

On the following page is a recommended design for a successful electronic resume.

Sample Electronic Resumes

Full name
Street address
City, state, Zip Code
Telephone number (residence if you don't want to be called at work)

KEYWORD OVERVIEW

Begin with two or three sentences that telegraph exactly who you are professionally and what you want for your next job. Include the keywords that make you recognizable to the electronic evaluator.

EXPERIENCE

Start with your current or last job and work back using this format . . .

Employer   Dates of employment

Title of position

Include several sentences that describe your job knowledge, skills, and experience followed by some accomplishments in a bulleted format. Include keywords.

Repeat the format for each significantly different position held with each employer. Limit the list to relevant experiences, but account for all periods of time. If you traveled for a year after college, explain briefly—post-college travel abroad, dates.

EDUCATION

Name the degree and college, and state the year of graduation. Follow with other training valued in your industry—name the course of study, where it was taken, and the year. List professional licenses and certificates, including a license number that can be verified and the date awarded.

AFFILIATIONS AND ACCOMPLISHMENTS

List your professional memberships and dates joined. List significant awards and publications briefly—not everything you ever did or received. Use good judgment in separating entries of professional and personal value—omit the purely personal. Use keywords that denote leadership, such as chairman.

Don't waste space indicating that references are available upon request, that you are married, belong to certain nonprofessional organizations, have excellent health, are of a certain age, have a certain number of children, enjoy certain sports or activities, etc.—the computer doesn't care.

SALLY N. ANSON
8567 South Murray Lane
Columbia, SC 29208
803-222-9988 Office
803-333-9075 Residence

OVERVIEW

Commercial lender with four years of successful experience in regional bank lending to middle market accounts as a credit analyst and corporate calling officer.

EXPERIENCE

Southland Banks   **Columbia, SC**
Assistant Loan Officer   6/1997–Present

Commercial loan officer with extensive business development responsibilities in the Carolinas, Georgia, and North Florida. Manage a $35 million portfolio, which includes $27 million outstanding and $8 million committed.

- Generated $11 million in new deposits and $19 million in new loans in 2.5 years.
- Number 2 performer on a staff of 12 regional lenders.
- Developed an on-line loan application on the bank's Web page that pre-qualifies candidates. Significantly reduced lending officer calls on unqualified prospects.

Coastal National Bank   **Sea Pines, GA**
Credit Analyst   6/1995–5/1997

Entry position upon college graduation. Credit review and analysis for middle market companies. Rapidly assumed full supporting activities for lenders prior to leaving to accept an officer position in the interest of professional growth.

Part-time college jobs   7/1991–5/1995
Various part-time positions while attending college, including seasonal retail sales, clerical positions, and summer employment as a bank teller.

EDUCATION

University of West Georgia   **State College, GA**
Bachelor of Business Administration,   June 1995
Banking and Finance

PROFESSIONAL AFFILIATIONS & TRAINING

- Professional Member, Robert Morris Associates, Secretary of Carolinas Chapter.
- Currently pursuing National Commercial Loan School, Norman, Oklahoma.

[Contrast this presentation with Sally N. Anson's conventional resume in Chapter 3.]

ROBERT P. VANGOGH
284 Chanute Lake Drive
Bellevue, WA 98009
425-222-9988 Office
425-333-9075 Residence

OVERVIEW

Senior electrical engineer with extensive avionics experience in civilian and military environments seeking a civilian aviation position. Familiarity with FAA protocols and specialist in EWSD crossover and SeepTAC-4 applications in multi-engine jet aircraft.

EMPLOYMENT

Wilson & Bell Avionics Corporations   **Bellevue, WA**
Senior Engineer   November 1998–Present

Electronic Warfare Systems Division, Elliot Systems   **Los Angeles, CA**
Project Engineer   June 1996–October 1998

Full-time graduate study   **September 1995–May 1996**

United States Air Force   **Nellis AFB, NV**
1Lt, Electronics Warfare Officer, F–15 Eagle, ACC   June 1990–August 1995

APPLICATIONS EXPERIENCE

- Used night flying and terrain avoidance radar systems as an operational crew member flying F-15s in all-weather simulated combat environments.
- Revised Huguenot calibration procedures for standardization of LanSat-based night navigation equipment on transport aircraft.
- Implemented total auto-pilot integration subsets for all J-79 systems in use, military and civilian, during the mid-1990s.

MANAGERIAL EXPERIENCE

- Led a team of 4 engineers and 5 technicians supervising the installation of retrofit SatSys decoders on the commercial passenger fleet of Divided Airlines, Inc., over a period of 17 months.
- Quality assurance engineer in charge of 35 technical inspectors in the Final Phase Division of Wilson & Bell Avionics responsible for satisfying FAA mandates on all KeyStat installations.

RESEARCH AND DEVELOPMENT EXPERIENCE

- Flew debugging missions as an EWO in F-15 aircraft for the operational testing and calibration of BV-3 Birdseye radar systems during their first all-weather night tests.
- Master's thesis focus was an unclassified cross-talk translation of military to civilian night wind shear avoidance systems.
- Developed first solid-state blind-flight ergometer with sufficient deviation tolerance to satisfy FAA and military STANBOARDS.

ACHIEVEMENTS

- Twice received the USAF Commendation medal for contributions to night flying safety, first as an active-duty aviator, then as a contract engineer.
- Reduced material costs 86 percent on EWSD's crossover shear detection night goggles by implementing first industry use of SeepTAC-4 in such applications.
- Secured 14 contracts with a total value of $83 million during 6 years as a contractor's engineer.

EDUCATION

University of Seattle   Seattle, WA
Bachelor of Science, Electrical Engineering   1990

University of Seattle   Seattle, WA
Master of Science, Electronic Systems Engineering   1996

[Contrast this presentation with Robert P. VanGogh's conventional resume in Chapter 3.]

DISTRIBUTION OPTIONS

There are several options for making your electronic resume available. One is to send it directly to employers who scan your paper resume into their electronic databases with OCR equipment and search for keywords that interest them. A broader approach is to submit your resume to professional associations that maintain electronic databases containing members' resumes. The placement departments of colleges offer similar services. And executive recruiting firms often use electronic applicant tracking systems.

Internet Tip
See URLs mentioned in this section for illustrations of career sites, career experts, and resume posting services on the Internet.

If you are looking for the latest in electronic resume distribution, go to the Internet. One place to start is your favorite search engine using the keyword "resumes" or variations thereof. Find your way to the career section of something like www.yahoo.com and begin clicking topics that seem to meet your needs. On the hyperlinked Web, one thing leads to another in the constantly changing universe of Internet-based information. If you want help, let career gurus like *What Color is Your Parachute*'s Richard Nelson Bolles guide you to favorite sites from his Web page at www.washingtonpost.com/parachute.

Another approach to finding the right spot to post your resume on the Internet is the print advertising pages of *The Wall Street Journal's National Business Employment Weekly* or its Web site, www.nbew.com. The possibilities are endless—current estimates run from between 1,300 and 100,000 job-related sites on the Internet, depending on the breadth of your definition. Chapter 7, "Using the Internet," follows with more suggestions.

7 USING THE INTERNET

Looking for a job today without reasonable awareness of the Internet is like showing up for work not wearing a significant article of clothing. You simply aren't complete without it, and it could prove to be embarrassing.

That varies, of course, with the job you seek and the market in which you are competing. Provincial jobs and companies still exist, but they grow fewer by the day. Web commerce, information, and communications make the Internet relevant to almost everyone, everywhere.

If the Internet is relevant to companies who hire, it is relevant to the people who want to work for them. As a resume writer and job seeker, the Internet can help you:

- Learn more about resume and letter writing
- Look up zip codes and telephone numbers
- Get career advice
- Find employers interested in hiring you
- Present your resume to the world (or selected parts of it) at little or no cost
- Communicate instantly by e-mail with employers and others who can help
- Research career opportunities, salaries, and working conditions
- Train for a new job or specialty
- Stay current in your field
- Learn more about the company to which you are applying

- Examine the cost of living and view homes where you consider moving
- Map your way to an interview and make travel arrangements
- Have an initial interview

At a minimum, even if you do not have access to the Internet personally, find an acquaintance who does or go to a library where it is available to familiarize yourself with it. In a short time you can remove the mystery that separates you from those who have experienced the web. It isn't necessary to spend much time or become an Internet enthusiast to grasp how it works and get a feel for its key features.

Looking over someone's shoulder, you can take a tour that leaves you comfortably aware of what a "search engine" is and what it can do, and that is half the battle. Enter a few topics and appreciate the shear volume of information presented. Click some hyperlinks and see how one thing leads to another on the Internet. Armed with that brief experience you become a different person, better prepared to take your place in the new world of high-tech job hunting and employment.

If the only use you make of even superficial Internet exposure is in an interview saying, yes, you know what it is, your time was well spent. But there is so much more you can do to facilitate your job search.

This chapter is filled with illustrations, but a word of caution before you begin. Internet references are perishable: Internet addresses (URLs or Universal Resource Locators) change. Like telephone numbers and address changes in the non-cyber world, forwarding addresses (links, in the case of the Internet) are posted only for a limited time. However, when they expire, you can go to a search engine and enter keywords until you find the new address. If that fails, visit a site that logically might list the site you are looking for among its "suggested links." Web page sponsors pride themselves in referring visitors to their own favorites; the one you want or something better may be among the suggestions.

Illustrative Web Sites

What follows is a loose collection of useful information intended as starting points for what will quickly become your own original search. View these suggestions as a few places where you might first put your nose under the tent of Internet job search. Any one of them will start you on a journey that can easily last for hours, crisscrossing and interlacing the topics listed and unearthing others that may be even more relevant to your particular needs and interests. Should you find a URL expired or need a different emphasis, go to a search engine and begin entering keywords: "maps," "real estate," "travel reservations," "white pages," "yellow pages," "zip codes," or whatever you need—it is probably there for the asking.

Useful Job Search Internet Sites

Topic Keywords	URL	Comments
area codes	http://decoder.americom.com/	Returning a call to an unfamiliar area code? Identify the city entering the area code at this site.
business newspapers	http://www.amcity.com	Examine specialty business papers serving 40 leading cities for general information and networking contacts.
career advice	http://www.washingtonpost.com/parachute	*What Color is Your Parachute* author Richard Nelson Bolles's Web page is filled with recommended links.
	http://jobsmart.org/	Resumes and more, including salary surveys.
	http://stats.bls.gov/ocohome.htm	The Department of Labor's *Occupational Outlook Handbook* online describes nearly every job you can imagine and discusses pay, working conditions, the demand for workers, expected education, where to go for more information, etc.
	http://www.careerweb.com	Job search, career-management advice, and more.
	http://www.dbm.com/	Click "Site Map" and go to articles and a great guide to Web job hunting.

Topic Keywords	URL	Comments
careers	http://www.usnews.com/usnews/edu/beyond/bccguide.htm	*U.S. News & World Report*'s excellent collection of career articles, advice, hot jobs, and salary information for entry-level candidates.
	http://careers.wsj.com/	Salaries, advice, articles, and more. Also features *Korn/Ferry Futurestep*, an appraisal of your market value by a preeminent search firm.
college job placement	http://www.jobtrak.com	A site serving prospective college grads and alumni at more than 700 colleges. Professional advice.
company information	http://www.hoovers.com/	Research a company: Free capsule, financials, and news or you can enter the keyword "investing" in a search engine and find sites with links to other company research resources.
company search	http://pic2.infospace.com/__1__244791928__info.jbank/bizweb.htm	Find any company's Web page using this site.
dictionary and thesaurus	http://www.m-w.com/netdict.htm	Look it up in this giant online reference.
employment	http://www.nbew.com/	*National Business Employment Weekly*'s Web page includes the expected job search features plus an index of Web job listings.

Topic Keywords	URL	Comments
equal opportunity	http://www.eeoc.gov/	Everything you need to know about EEO rights.
foreign language translator	http://babelfish.altavista.digital.com/cgi-bin/translate	Enter a phrase and get a translation.
health care info	http://www.dol.gov/dol/pwba/public/health.htm	Department of Labor's consumer information on health care rights.
interviewing	http://iamag.com/infoage/virtual.htm	"CU-SeeMe" interviewing mainly for technology-related positions.
	http://www.golden.net/~archeus/intres.htm#articles2	Links to interview sites that are reviewed for value and relevance.
	http://www1.kaplan.com/view/article/0,1275,536,00.html	Advice on preparing for your interview.
IRS forms and instructions	http://www.irs.ustreas.gov/prod/forms__pubs/index.html	Download tax forms and instructions.
job listings	http://www.ajb.dni.us/	Department of Labor Public Employment Service job/resume posting site. National and regional job search capabilities the Web's version of the local employment office.
	http://headhunter.net/	An advertising-supported Web job and resume posting site.
	http://www.wm.edu/csrv/career/stualum/jregion.html	Links to listings by region of the country.
	http://www.washingtonpost.com/jobs	An example of a big city newspaper listing with extensive job search resources of its own.

Topic Keywords	URL	Comments
	http://www.jobbankusa.com/	Links to everywhere in the job search universe.
job market	http://stats.bls.gov/blshome.htm	The Bureau of Labor Statistics's latest numbers relating to status and trends in all sectors of the labor market.
	http://www.dol.gov/	Department of Labor laws, regulations, statistics, data, and news.
job search	http://www.jobweb.org/catapult/catapult.htm	National Association of Colleges and Employers links to useful job information.
	http://www.career.vt.edu/INTERNET/WEBHEAD.html	Virginia Tech's links to regions and occupational specialties. Other colleges have similar services—try your alma mater.
	http://www.job-hunt.org/	An extensive index of job search Web sites complete with evaluations of usefulness.
letters	http://www.careerlab.com/	General advice and over 200 model letters on nearly every topic.
maps	http://www.mapquest.com/	Maps and directions to your interview.
pension information	http://www.dol.gov/dol/pwba/public/pension.htm	Department of Labor's consumer information on pension rights.
pension guarantees	http://www.pbgc.gov/	Pension Benefit Guarantee Corporation information on pension rights.

Topic Keywords	URL	Comments
polygraph	http://www.dol.gov/dol/asp/public/programs/handbook/eppa.htm	Employee Polygraph Protection Act—your related rights.
resume advice	http://provenresumes.com/	Tips for various kinds of resumes including types of occupations and electronic formats.
	http://www.eresumes.com/	Electronic resumes are this page's specialty.
retirement benefits	http://www.dol.gov/dol/asp/public/programs/handbook/erisa.htm	ERISA and related laws to protect your pension.
salary information	http://www.dbm.com/jobguide/salary.html	Salary surveys, negotiation strategies, and more.
	http://jobsmart.org/tools/salary/sal-prof.htm/	Salary surveys by professional category.
search engines	http://www.metacrawler.com	Six search engines in one. Also try *Yahoo! HotBot, Infoseek, Exite, Lycos, Magellan,* etc. and examine their individual career sections that link you to many other sites.
	http://www.albany.net/allinone/all1www.html	A constantly updated index of specialized search engines—more than 100.
timezones	http://www.mich.com/~timezone/	Find the current time in a distant city before you call.
travel information	http://www.biztravel.com	Check flights, make reservations of all kinds, and optimize travel incentive programs.

If your appetite for job search information is not satisfied after exploring these links, try http://www.dog-ear.com where for a modest fee you can purchase several thousand bookmarks to job-hunting sites that can be downloaded and clicked without typing URLs. The list is updated regularly and you are alerted by e-mail when revisions are available.

Limitations

While the Internet is a wonderful source of career information, it has limitations. Use it with the same cautions you would apply outside cyberspace:

- If confidentiality is important to you, investigate and understand the safeguards job posting services employ before giving them your resume.

- Be sensible in offering personal information on the Internet. Employment listings are generally legitimate, but be skeptical enough to protect your privacy and personal safety. Verify with whom you are dealing before providing personal information or meeting a stranger for an interview. Don't become paranoid, but use common sense.

- Expect to be spammed (receive unsolicited commercial e–mail) if your e–mail address appears on the Internet. It is, unfortunately, the price you pay for using the Web.

- Understand that Internet job search works best for hard-to-find technical people. To judge how many responses your Internet resume is apt to attract, ask yourself how many calls you already receive from headhunters. Unless your telephone regularly rings and an executive recruiter is on the other end of the line, posting your credentials on the Internet may be disappointing. Employers seldom pay recruiters or search the web for vacancies they can fill from ordinary print advertising that is cheaper and documents fair hiring practices compliance.

- Anyone can represent him or herself as a career expert on the Internet. Evaluate them as you would any other service before following advice that may lead you where you don't want to go or before buying ineffective goods and services.

   With those few words of caution, by all means explore and make the most of the job search riches of the Internet. Remember, there is so much more than resume posting that might prove helpful in your job search.

8

SPECIAL SITUATIONS

A special resume may be called for to address the particular needs of job seekers who approach the world of work from nontraditional situations. The normal expectation of an employer advertising a vacancy is to attract people who are working full time in a job logically aligned with the position being offered. The person applying for a senior management position is usually someone doing well as a middle manager in roughly the same kind of setting as that of the prospective new employer.

When the expected pattern is broken, the approach to resume writing needs special attention. The final product is not that different, but negative things are anticipated and neutralized by properly drafting and presenting the resume. Strengths can be accentuated that actually make the nontraditional worker more attractive than those with patterns of ideal career progression.

Among those who will find this chapter particularly useful are individuals who are:

- *returning to the workplace following an absence* caused by family obligations, a small business venture, involuntary loss of employment, full-time study, or the end of a relationship in which a spouse's professional identity was that of an executive partner and not an employee;

- *making work-study arrangements* as a lead-in to a career position;

- *establishing a second career* following an early retirement;

- *looking for flexibility* in working hours or overall arrangements; or

- *coming from other countries and cultures* and struggling to articulate the value of their work and training in alien settings.

Returning to the Workplace

Stepping out of the lock-step career path is increasingly common. Many reasons account for breaks in the entry-level to mid-level to senior-level march through the ranks that is sometimes expected. A free society provides opportunities for uniquely personalized work lives and many Americans exercise the options. Another factor is that our rapidly evolving, competitive economy does not necessarily guarantee job continuity throughout a lifetime. Still another factor is the ending of relationships in which a spouse functioned on the executive level supporting the career of the other person whose departure, through death or divorce, forces an unexpected transition to formal employment—the executive partner syndrome.

While the possibilities go beyond the examples, here are some reasons why you might find yourself preparing a resume explaining why you are coming to the job market with a less than traditional work history:

- A period of unemployment, self-employment, or part-time employment for the purpose of raising a family;

- A small business or consulting venture of your own that is no longer as attractive as a traditional position;

- A merger or other organizational quirk that leaves you on the outside looking in;

- A period of full-time study that was necessary to change careers or achieve a desired level of employment;

- Ending a relationship in which you served as an executive partner (spouse of an executive) but not an employee.

RECOMMENDED APPROACH

In each of these instances the resume, cover letter, and your general approach to the potential employer is one of positive objectivity. You do not attempt to mask your true situation, neither do you apologize for it. Determine what your marketable strengths are and decide how to bring them to the attention of someone who can use them.

You are what you are—there is no need for, or anything to be gained by, posturing as something else. If you are a homemaker who only worked briefly as a management trainee before spending ten years outside the workplace, then you are an entry-level employee with some experience—PLUS a great deal of added maturity and motivation with which to make the best of your remaining career.

There are ways to deal with the apparent negatives of your situation. The following table lists a few of the things you might face (overtly or beneath the surface) and how to compensate:

Challenge	Response
Your experience is out of date.	I have remained active in the marketplace as a consumer of your services and can bring that valued perspective to the job.
You are too old for this level position.	Think, act, and look young—this is usually more a problem of perception than reality. Chronological age has little to do with working age in most contemporary, non-physically demanding jobs.
Your education is dated.	Take a refresher course or seminar. It will not only bring you up to date on terminology, but you stand a good chance of networking with people who can help you find employment.

RESUME TIPS

Since you lack the perfect continuity that looks best in a Work History Resume, opt for the Competency Cluster or Focused Resume that places the emphasis on what you can do, rather than where and for how long you have done it. Market yourself very deliberately. Do your homework on the company and the job being offered. Put yourself in the hiring official's shoes and make a case for why you should be an attractive hire.

Avoid gimmicks, but take advantage of couching your experience in terms and examples that relate to the situation. If you are listing experience as a telephone volunteer for your alumni association fund drive or the local public television station, speak in terms of telemarketing. Use the OVERVIEW part of the resume to portray yourself as someone

- aware of what the position entails;
- qualified to perform the duties; and
- motivated to assume a realistic role in the company.

Before the hiring official ever becomes embroiled in your precise experience and training, you want to have made the point that you know what she or he wants and can make a convincing case for being able to provide it.

Next comes the selection of competency clusters or qualifications and achievements that will substantiate your claim. This is where your homework pays off—by knowing what the situation actually entails, you have the advantage of being able to translate your attributes into those valued by the employer. The same experience can be stated in general terms or reasonably job-specific terms—the latter will tend to focus employer attention on exactly what you can do for him, rather than tasking him with reaching the same conclusion the hard way—by puzzling over a less deliberately arranged resume.

Question	Answer
Why did you leave your last job?	The company was recently bought by XYA Corporation and thirty accounting positions were consolidated into ten at XYA's West Coast offices.
Why did you close your business or consulting practice?	After five years of successfully building my company, it was acquired by the ABC Company. I am intrigued by the opportunity your vacancy represents.
With your background, what appreciation could you possibly have for our career development expectations?	I am currently enrolled in the CFA study group and plan to sit for the Series I examination in June.

Comments can be used as a closing reaffirmation that you understand the realities of the employer's needs and can meet them. You can tersely answer the obvious questions that might be associated with your situation and put them to rest—at least until the interview. Brief comments can become subtle building blocks of confidence between you and the reader of your resume. Throw out as many little lifelines as you can that will give them honest cause to reel you in for a closer look. The employer wants to sense that you understand his needs, can meet them, and have the potential for fitting in and growing. A traditional work history is not the only way to go about establishing such a link between applicant and employer—you just might have to work a little harder at the logic of the presentation if you lack the step-by-step progression of readily understood and expected jobs.

Chapter 1 includes a resume prepared by an executive partner seeking re-entry into the workplace after the relationship with her spouse ended. Refer again to the resume of Bernadette J. O'Conner and the point-by-point explanations of how her resume was strengthened by changing it.

Work-Study Arrangements

There is no more certain way to get the job you want after graduation than having an already established working relationship with the target company as a highly regarded student-worker. Summer and part-time jobs are the link to career positions for thousands of students every year. There are approaches to resume preparation that can help the aspirants achieve this goal.

RECOMMENDED APPROACH

As a student applying for a part-time position with an organization, the best way to make your resume and cover letter stand out is to show evidence of career thinking. Convey that you are highly interested in the seasonal position for which you are applying, but aware of the opportunity's implications for overall career development.

Desired Message	Method of Relating It
I want this seasonal job—it is important to me for several reasons.	I value the work ethic and financial responsibility—this job will help me gain valuable work experience and avoid building debt as a student.
My education can contribute to doing this job well.	As a student of (engineering, marketing, or whatever) I have seen a lot of theory and case study examples of what you do at XYZ Corporation. That would bring me to the job with a lot of orientation already in place, anxious to apply it as a worker.
I can see future possibilities with XYZ Corporation.	I have a lot of respect for the market position of XYZ, have heard positive things about it as a place to build a career, and would welcome the opportunity for us to learn to know each other better in a worker-employer relationship.

This has to be done without overkill. The desired tone is that of someone aware of his present place in the order of things, but equally cognizant of where the career path leads. That is done by expressing interest in both the position and the company. Your cover letter is a good place to communicate awareness of what the firm does and its position in the marketplace. Remember to use a moderate tone and not to phrase your letter like a report. It is easy enough to check the business reference section of your library and learn the basic demographics on the company with which you are communicating. Brief mention of a recent acquisition or new product is an appropriate way to note that you have some current awareness of the business world in general and your target company in particular.

RESUME TIPS

It is unlikely that you, as a student, have a chronology of employment that would warrant using the Work History Resume format. You are primarily interested in packaging your abilities, achievements, and strengths for the purpose of appealing to a certain kind of situation. The best resumes for that objective are the Competency Cluster and Focused Resume formats.

The OVERVIEW can be used to accomplish the following objectives:

- name the seasonal position you seek;
- qualify yourself for performing the required duties; and
- show possible career motivation.

All of this has to be done in several sentences. The statements merely need to convey that you know what the job entails, can (and, without saying so, are willing to) perform the work necessary, and that you have an interest that goes beyond this position after you finish your studies. Leave it to the body of the resume to actually develop and substantiate your OVERVIEW. It might read something like this:

> OVERVIEW: Third-year electrical engineering student applying for the summer position as Field Engineering Aide III. Studies and prior Army experience qualify me for the testing environment. Concurrent objective of exploring future professional affiliation with XYZ Corp.

If you find it desirable to tie your resume presentation together with a concluding statement, the COMMENTS section can be added for that purpose. It is not the place to relate what has already been established, but it can be useful to focus everything on the particular objective and dispel any anticipated problems.

Question	Answer
Why are you still a student at the age of twenty-eight?	Describe your military service as relevant to your career—possibly a year spent touring Europe after leaving the service and prior to returning to college.
Why would you within a year of being a graduate engineer want a job like this?	Amplify your respect for learning the business from the inside out—this position could give you that perspective before crossing over to the professional level.
What kind of career expectations do you have?	If your awareness is sufficiently specific, briefly conclude with an expression of interest in exploring future employment with them in fiber optics transmission or whatever.

Establishing Second Careers

Government and industry both use the practice of offering early retirement to reduce their work force in a nondestructive way. People leave careers still vigorous enough to want the continued ritual of the workplace—the reason for getting out of bed in the morning, socialization with coworkers, the satisfaction of accomplishing something, and—last, but not necessarily least—money. Whether you are a military officer retired with a substantial pension in your mid-forties, or an older clerical worker relieved with a modest income by a large corporation, you may find yourself attempting to market your employment skills with a resume.

RECOMMENDED APPROACH

As a person with one career behind you, your objective is to look ahead to the next with a combination of experiences past and challenges desired. You are making a transition and trying to make the case that you have something to offer in the world of the new employer. Here are some of the attitudes that you may want to anticipate addressing with some subtlety in your resume and cover letter.

Attitude	Response
You are retired—why would I want to hire you?	In the modern workplace careers are sometimes incremental—retirement is often a misnomer for a person successfully transiting to another career stage.
Your background is from an entirely different work environment—how will you adapt to our situation?	Work is far more appropriately categorized by task than employer—I have successfully managed people and resources for the last X years and I can do it for you.
What if you are looking to retire on the job?—my job!	The work ethic is very much a habit. My motivation for applying for this position is to continue deriving the satisfaction of a job well done—my references will vouch for my level of energy and commitment.

RESUME TIPS

The person pursuing a second career has a full choice of resume formats. If the position being sought is a logical extension of the career path that led to early retirement, the Work History Resume may very well be appropriate. If there is to be a substantial change of career direction, the better bet might be the Competency Cluster or Focused Resume format where prior experience can be translated into skills gained and achievements made.

Regardless of resume format, an appropriate OVERVIEW can be helpful in immediately establishing several basics:

- identify the position or category of position sought;
- mention your general qualifications for the job; and
- express some sincere motivation to pursue it.

While the points made will vary by job and background, here is an example of how you might begin:

OVERVIEW: Retired Navy senior enlisted woman with successful paramedical career seeks affiliation with a civilian health management organization. Fully certified professional anxious to continue rewarding health services career without interruption.

The body of the resume is then used to demonstrate that your claims to competency and experience are valid.

A concluding **COMMENTS** section can be helpful if you feel there is anything that would benefit from further interpretation. Although it must be kept brief, several sentences can tie together the several points that make your case for career continuity. Here are samples of issues that might be laid to rest with an appropriate comment:

Question	Answer
How do I as an employer in the X business compare the certification of a specialist who has spent an entire career working in Y?	Professional certification for paraprofessionals in military health care facilities is the same as for those in civilian hospitals.
How will a person accustomed to having military rank and authority function in the less structured civilian environment?	Express your authority and rank functionally with examples of responsibility, rather than power and rank—that will be more readily understood in the civilian sector.
You are still in Japan, how can I be assured you will be able to report for duty on the date you promise?	Mention that your retirement orders have been issued and that you will be separated from the service on a date comfortably in advance of your reporting date for the new position.

Chapter 1 includes a resume prepared by a senior military officer seeking reentry into the workplace after retirement. Refer again to the resume Thomas A. Woodland and the point-by-point explanations of how his resume was strengthened. A more direct transfer of military technical skills to the civilian sector is illustrated in the Electronic Engineer resume in Chapter 3. The Bank Collector resume offers another example.

Looking for Flexibility

People find themselves wanting to be employed in the regular work force, but with less than a full-time schedule and, perhaps, at irregular hours. To their surprise, the same requirement often exists on the hiring side of the equation—employers sometimes welcome the idea of having first-rate talent available to them on an as-needed basis, rather than as a full-time employee. The challenge for the job seeker is one of communication. The resume and cover letter can be crafted to convey both solid competencies and a rational desire to work a nontraditional schedule.

RECOMMENDED APPROACH

As a nontraditional worker you have to make your availability known as a practicing professional whose only difference is situational—fully qualified, but not wanting to work full time. There are advantages to the employer as well as the worker in such arrangements. All that is needed is a meeting of the minds and that begins with a proper presentation of your credentials. Here are a few examples of traditional thinking that you should be prepared to cope with:

Possible Concern	Your Response
How could less than a full-time person possibly plan the annual meeting?	The job is a series of tasks to be accomplished, not hours to be logged. Let's discuss what has to be done and I'll show you how it can be done.
You won't be able to get a feel for the working of our organization if you are only here part time.	Involvement and perceptiveness are not measured by hours in the presence of others. Has my reading of your requirements thus far been accurate?
How will we handle the question of taxes and benefits?	There are several approaches to that problem. If you want me to be an employee, then pay the taxes and provide partial benefits. If you prefer that I work as an independent contractor, a more arms-length relationship can be arranged.

These are just representative issues that might arise. If you have a particular orientation or want to steer the hiring in a certain direction, then things like the independent contractor vs. the part-time employee arrangements can be a part of your resume or cover letter.

RESUME TIPS

The question of resume model is an open one for the nontraditional worker. Basic qualities of the different resume formats become important, depending on your situation. If the proposed position flows logically from positions previously held, then the Work History Resume may be appropriate. Competency Cluster and Focused Resumes are better if you are selling the ability to perform tasks without regard to length of time or settings in which you have been doing them.

A well-phrased **OVERVIEW** is the starting point for stating your case, with the understanding that the body of the resume will substantiate what you propose. An example of how that might be done follows:

OVERVIEW: Paralegal with 6 years' experience in the preparation of corporate documents seeks part-time employment in that specialty. Prefer to operate as an independent contractor accomplishing the work in my own office. Professionalism and respect for confidentiality verifiable by prominent local references.

This is a case where the desired situation has been described, the terms under which the work would be accomplished stated, and an expected question answered. The groundwork has been laid for stating educational qualifications, specific abilities and achievements, and, possibly, concluding COMMENTS, such as:

COMMENTS: Following 6 years of successful full-time employment in law firms, I am continuing my professional pursuits privately to insure the flexibility desired in the raising of my children.

The COMMENTS section is optional and would be used if there are points of clarification that might improve the reader's perception of what you are trying to accomplish.

Coming from Other Countries and Cultures

The United States is still a melting pot rich in the contributions and special talents of people coming here from other countries. The challenge for these job-seekers is in translating their experiences into terms that can be readily understood by U.S. employers. This can be done with a resume and cover letter especially designed for this purpose.

RECOMMENDED APPROACH

If you fit into the category, you must begin your job search with a candid evaluation of what you have to offer. You probably have educational and work experiences that will be valued by American employers. Enlist the assistance of an American friend to help you. See if you can translate your skills and capabilities into those valued by employers in this economy.

Once your competencies have been identified, you can begin the job search. Determine where your talents can be applied and the employers who could use your skills. Decide where you are willing to relocate in order to accept a position. Speak to people and organizations who might be of assistance. Locate publications that can alert you to the firms that might employ you. Read about them and watch for positions advertised. Draft a resume and cover letter that will carry your message to potential employers.

RESUME TIPS

If your past field of employment has a direct crossover into an American position, use the Work History Resume in the job search. However, the resume formats that will probably help you best in your new workplace are the Competency Cluster and Focused Resumes.

Chapter 1 includes a resume prepared by a Chinese student seeking professional employment in this country. Refer again to the resume of Lan Wang and the point-by-point explanations of how her case was made more convincing by altering the style and content of her resume. Here are some concerns common to foreign workers seeking employment in the United States and suggestions on how to cope.

Concern	Possible Solution
From my resume, the employer may not know how to address me—gender may not be apparent.	If such things are of concern, put Mr. or Ms. before your name or include a reference to gender in the OVERVIEW or elsewhere in your resume.
My schooling was not in a system equivalent to American schools and colleges.	Do your best to sort your educational experiences into categories that do equate to American levels—high school, junior college, trade school, or college. If a sentence of explanation would make it clearer, use it.
I will need my employer's support with visa considerations—how do I treat that subject?	Be honest about your immigration status, but do not make an issue of it. Objectively state the category that you hold and that to which you aspire—other details can be discussed later in the hiring process.
I want to establish that I can function in the American culture, that I understand the language and customs.	Demonstrate what you have done—earned a degree attending an American college, held a job that clearly required English language proficiency, etc.

In the final analysis, foreign students or workers face the same problem as other job candidates—making the point as directly and convincingly as possible that they know what the job entails and that they can do it. Writing a great resume and cover letter is one way to demonstrate both.

9 | TRENDS IN THE WORK FORCE

Total employment will increase nearly 14 percent from 132 million jobs in 1996 to 151 million in 2006, according to the Bureau of Labor Statistics. That represents 19 million new jobs, but as you prepare your resume for the next step up the career ladder, do it with an awareness that the job market is changing. What follows are trends that could affect your career between now and the year 2006. They come from the latest studies of Department of Labor economists who constantly monitor the world of work.

> **Internet Tip**
>
> Update these estimates anytime or examine them in greater detail by visiting http://stats.bls.gov:80/0c0/0c0s179.htm. Should that URL expire, use your search engine and the keywords "Bureau of Labor Statistics."

While you cannot ensure success by choosing an expanding field or predict failure by entering a declining one, it pays to know the trends. The advice given by hiring authorities ten years ago Robert and Anne Snelling remains true:

> While two equally talented beginners may eventually reach comparable levels of career success, the job seeker who starts out in a promising field is almost surely destined to move farther faster than the one who aspires to work in a field that is experiencing little or no growth. Being aware of today's trends is one sure way of choosing a field that is destined to grow. (1989, p. 23)

So whether you are a beginner at the entry-level stage or an early retiree starting a second career, examine the list of trends that your government makes so readily available. If you have the choice, steer your career in the direction of growth where the opportunities will best accommodate your ambitions and abilities.

Where the Jobs Will Be, 1996–2006

- *Service-producing industries* will account for virtually all of the job growth.

- *Manufacturing's share* of total jobs is expected to decline.

- *Health services, business services, social services, and engineering, management, and related services* are expected to account for almost one of every two wage and salary worker jobs added to the economy during the 1996–2006 period. Of the 10 fastest growing industries, nine belong to one of these four industry groups.

- *Professional specialty occupations* are projected to increase the fastest and add the most jobs—4.8 million.

- *Executive, administrative, and managerial occupations; technicians and related support occupations; and marketing and sales occupations* are also expected to grow faster than average.

- *Administrative support and clerical occupations* are projected to grow much slower than average due to office automation.

- *Precision production, craft, and repair occupations and operators, fabricators, and laborers* are projected to grow much more slowly than average due to technology, changing production methods, and manufacturing's decline.

The following tables are adapted from Bureau of Labor Statistics's web site and the *Occupational Outlook Quarterly* and show where job growth is expected to be greatest. BLS says this about the first table:

Of all the occupations expected to have faster than average employment growth, above average earnings, and below average unemployment, the 25 shown have the largest number of projected openings. These 25 occupations will account for 5 million new jobs, or 27 percent of all job growth. Eighteen of the 25 require at least a bachelor's degree. The occupations are somewhat concentrated, with four each in the computer technology, health care, and education fields.

Occupations That Have It All: Fast Growth, High Earnings, and Low Unemployment, 1996–2006

Occupation	Projected Employment Growth
Systems analysts	519,600
General managers and top executives	467,000
Registered nurses	410,800
Teachers, secondary school	312,100
Clerical supervisors and managers	261,500
Database administrators, computer support specialists, and all other computer scientists	249,200
Maintenance repairers, general utility	245,800
Teachers, special education	240,700
Computer engineers	235,300
Social workers	187,600
Food service and lodging managers	167,700
College and university faculty	162,300
Engineering, mathematical and natural scientists	155,100
Licensed practical nurses	148,400
Financial managers	146,400
Marketing, advertising, and public relations managers	137,600
Computer programmers	129,200
Instructors and coaches, sports and physical education	123,400
Lawyers	118,400
Physicians	117,500
Electrical and electronics engineers	104,800
Correction officers	103,300
Securities and financial services sales workers	99,600
Physical therapists	81,100
Artists and commercial artists	78,200

Department of Labor, Bureau of Labor Statistics, *Occupational Outlook Quarterly*, Winter 1997–98, page 17.

Fastest Growing Occupations by Level of Education and Training, 1996–2006

Education/training	Fastest Growing Occupations	Largest Numerical Increases Occupations
First-professional degree	Chiropractors, veterinarians and veterinary inspectors, physicians, lawyers, clergy	Lawyers, physicians, clergy, veterinarians and veterinary inspectors, dentists
Doctoral degree	Biological scientists, medical scientists, college and university faculty, mathematicians and all other mathematical scientists	College and university faculty, biological scientists, medical scientists, mathematicians and all other mathematical scientists
Master's degree	Speech-language pathologists and audiologists; counselors; curators, archivists, museum technicians; psychologists; operations research analysts	Speech-language pathologists and audiologists; counselors; psychologists; librarians, professional; operations research analysts
Work experience plus bachelor's or higher degree	Engineering, science, and computer systems managers; marketing, advertising, and public relations managers; artists and commercial artists; management analysts; financial managers	General managers and top executives; engineering, science and computer systems managers; financial managers; marketing, advertising, and publish relations managers; artists and commercial artists
Bachelor's degree	Database administrators and computer support specialists; computer engineers, systems analysts; physical therapists; occupational therapists	Systems analysts; teachers, secondary school; database administrators and computer support specialists; teachers, special education; computer engineers
Associate degree	Paralegals, health information technicians, dental hygienists, respiratory therapists, cardiology technologists	Registered nurses, paralegals, dental hygienists, radiologic technologists and technicians, health information technicians

Education/training	Fastest Growing Occupations	Largest Numerical Increases Occupations
Postsecondary vocational training	Data processing equipment repairers, emergency medical technicians, manicurists, surgical technologists, medical secretaries	Licensed practical nurses, automotive mechanics, medical secretaries, emergency medical technicians, hairdressers, hairstylists, and cosmetologists
Work experience in a related occupation	Food service and lodging managers; teachers and instructors, vocational education and training; lawn service managers; instructors, adult education; nursery and greenhouse managers	Clerical supervisors and managers; marketing and sales worker supervisors; food service and lodging managers; teachers and instructors, vocational education and training; instructors, adult (non-vocational) education
Long-term training and experience (more than 12 months of on-the-job training)	Desktop publishing specialists; flight attendants; musicians; corrections officers; producers, directors, actors, and entertainers	Maintenance repairers, general utility; cooks, restaurant; corrections officers; musicians; police patrol officers
Moderate-term training and experience (1–12 months of on-the job training)	Physical and corrective therapy assistants and aides; medical assistants; occupational therapy assistants and aides; social and human services assistants; instructors and coaches, sports and physical training	Medical assistants; instructors and coaches, sports and physical training; social and human services assistants; dental assistants; physical and corrective therapy assistants
Short-term training and experience (up to 1 month of on-the-job training)	Personal and home care aides; home health aides; amusement and recreation attendants; adjustment clerks; bill and account collectors	Cashiers; salespersons, retail; truck drivers, light and heavy; home health aides

Source: http://stats.bls.gov/oco/ocotjt1.htm

Conclusion

Resumes play an increasingly important role as a large percentage of the labor force completes for new positions. The employer wants to know what you bring to the job in terms of training and work-related experience. More positions requir⌐ prospective employees to organize their thoughts and express them—the job resume is an early test of that ability.

Adapting successfully in a changing work force requires the skillful use of a resume as you articulate your abilities in response to a constantly evolving set of employer needs. A simple chronology, which generally does not focus your talents on the position in question, may place you at a disadvantage. As American work life becomes more a series of adaptations to changing opportunities, and less a cradle-to-grave endurance march, you must learn to be an advocate of your cumulative worth to the next in a succession of employers. Your resume will be the vehicle for accomplishing that goal—both in your mind (through planning and preparing) and in the eyes of those evaluating you for a situation that may be quite different from the one you are leaving (by reading a resume that communicates why you are the person for the job).

The coming years promise to be a challenging and—for those with the ability to work the system—a rewarding time. Displaying your education and experience will call for resume-writing abilities that do those talents justice in the exciting and lucrative job market that is materializing.

10 PROTECTING YOUR EMPLOYEE BENEFITS WHEN YOU CHANGE JOBS

Unless you are applying for your first job, you are a "job changer" and have important personal interests to protect while preparing a resume and finding another job. You need to be aware of your pension and medical coverage continuation rights as you move from one employer to the next. If you are leaving a position in a solvent, well-organized company, you should routinely receive statements describing your pension and medical coverage options. Employers are required by federal regulations to provide this information. But if you are involved in a takeover, merger, pension plan termination, or bankruptcy, or if your former employer fails to comply with the regulations, you need to know how to pursue your rights.

Your Pension Rights

If you work for a private company that "affects commerce"—which almost all of them do—and that company has a pension plan, it is protected by the Employee Retirement Income Security Act of 1974 (ERISA). So unless you work for the government or have an unusual employer like certain international or religious organizations, you are among the 54 million workers covered by ERISA.

WHAT ERISA ENSURES

- Age and service requirements for pension plan participation are reasonable.

- People who work for a specified minimum period under a plan will receive at least some pension at retirement.

- Money will be there to pay pension benefits when they are due.

- Plan funds are handled prudently.

- Employees and their beneficiaries are informed of their rights and entitlements.

- Spouses of pensioners are protected.

- The benefits of certain plans are protected in the event of a plan's termination.

- You can appeal if you are denied benefits.

- You will not be harassed or interfered with for exercising your pension rights.

- You can sue in federal court to recover your benefits.

WHAT ERISA DOES NOT DO

- Require any employer to establish a retirement plan.

- Deal with the amounts of money to be paid out or the adequacy of pensions.

- Provide termination insurance for all plans.

- Guarantee that an employee can automatically transfer pension credits or benefits when changing jobs.

HOW TO USE ERISA

Three agencies of the U.S. government administer your ERISA pension rights:

1. The *Pension and Welfare Benefits Administration of the U.S. Department of Labor* enforces the participants' rights provisions of the law and makes sure that pension plans operate according to ERISA requirements.

2. The *Internal Revenue Service of the U.S. Treasury Department* requires employers to report certain information about their pension plans and makes that information available to the participants. The IRS is also responsible for overseeing pension plan funding and vesting requirements and for insuring compliance with federal tax laws.

3. The *Pension Benefit Guaranty Corporation,* a government agency created by ERISA, oversees insurance programs that guarantee payment of retirement benefits to participants in private pension plans.

If you have trouble getting pension information from your company, these agencies can help you determine the status of your plan, its provisions, your entitlements, and the possibility of collecting insured payments. But you should start by reviewing the pension information already provided or by asking your employer. Proceed this way:

Step 1. Examine your personal records and check what you have against the entitlements listed in Step 3.

Step 2. Determine the name of the Plan Administrator either by looking for her or his name in the materials provided by your company or by asking your employer.

Step 3. Ask your Plan Administrator for anything missing from this list of items that he or she must provide:

- The *Summary Plan Description* tells you how your plan operates, when you are eligible to receive your pension, how to calculate the amount of your benefits, and how to file a claim. Your employer has to give you this information within ninety days of your becoming a participant, it must be understandable, and you are entitled to updates if the plan changes.

- The *Summary Annual Report* tells you the financial status of your plan and has to be provided every year.

- *Survivor Coverage Data* tell you what your survivor coverage is and how it affects you and your spouse. Your employer must provide these data when you have worked long enough to be eligible for pension benefits.

- Employers usually voluntarily provide the *Individual Benefit Statement.* If you have not received a copy and want one, you have to ask for it in writing from your Plan Administrator, who must provide it once a year upon request. The statement tells you the dollar amount of the benefits you have earned and whether you have a permanent right to receive them. Make sure you have received a copy of this information, and verify its correctness whenever you leave a company.

Step 4. Ask your Plan Administrator for any assistance you need in understanding the information.

Step 5. If you have not been able to learn the name of the Plan Administrator or get copies of the information, request them in writing from the personnel department.

Step 6. If a month or two passes and you do not get a satisfactory response, modify the following "last resort letter" to suit your circumstances. Send it to the head of human resources by certified mail, receipt requested. If you do not know the name and title of that official, go to the business reference section of your library and look it up. It may be easier to call the firm's receptionist and ask. Be sure to get the full name and title, spelled correctly.

Suggested Last Resort Letter

Your Name
Street Address
City, State, and Zip Code
Telephone Number

Date

Name of chief human resources officer
Correct title
Company name
Mailing address

Dear [correct name]:

My last date of employment with XYZ Corporation was March 31, 1995. In my termination package dated March 26, 1995, I was advised that as a vested member of the retirement plan I would be notified within sixty days regarding the various options by the Plan Administrator—ABC Holding Company, Inc.

The notification was not forthcoming, and I requested the information in a September 12, 1995, letter to Jane P. Doe, Human Resources Assistant, the person who signed my May 15, 1995, COBRA notification regarding healthcare coverage and my last point of contact in your company. Ms. Doe did not respond to my letter, so I called several times, the last time on December 8,

1995. She never provided the information promised in these conversations. Frustrated, I investigated my rights under the Employee Retirement Income Security Act of 1974 (ERISA). To judge from documents provided by the Pension and Welfare Benefits Administration, U.S. Department of Labor, and the Pension Benefit Guaranty Corporation, it appears that you have failed to fulfill your obligations under the law. As a vested member of an ERISA-covered plan I am entitled to know the status of my benefits.

I am providing the following information from my last individual benefit statement from XYZ Corporation, dated January 1, 1992. Name: Your Name; Social Security Number: 222-44-3456; Date of Birth: 11/19/50; Date of Plan Participation: 12/88; Normal Retirement Date: 12/20/2015; Status statement: "If you leave the company before retirement but after you are vested, you are entitled to plan payments starting at your normal retirement date. Your benefit will be based on your accrued benefit at termination. As of December 31, 1996, you are 100% vested in your accrued benefit."

Please consider this letter my final attempt to resolve the question outside regulatory channels. I will end my inquiry if you provide a thorough written statement explaining the status of my benefits and identifying the plan under which I am now covered. If I do not receive a satisfactory written response to this request within thirty days, I intend to exercise my full appellate rights under law.

Sincerely,

Step 7. If the information is still not forthcoming or the response is unsatisfactory, contact the Division of Technical Assistance and Inquiries, Pension and Welfare Benefits Administration, U.S. Department of Labor, 200 Constitution Avenue NW, Washington, D.C. 20210. It can advise you how to proceed. Your options include these:

- The Department of Labor has summary plan descriptions, annual financial reports, and other information on pension plans. You can have copies made for a small fee. Contact Public Disclosure Room, Room N-5707, Department of Labor, 200 Constitution Avenue NW, Washington, D.C. 20210 (or call 202-523-8771).

- The Internal Revenue Service collects information from pension plans and makes it available to employees participating in the plans. Submit your request to the Director, Disclosure and Security Division, Internal Revenue Service, P.O. Box 388, Ben Franklin Station, Washington, D.C. 20045, or examine this information in Room 1567 of the National Office of the Internal Revenue Service in Washington.

- The Internal Revenue Service informs the Social Security Administration when vested plan participants terminate their employment before they retire. The Social Security Administration provides that information to employees and their beneficiaries upon request and automatically when they apply for Social Security benefits. Ask your local Social Security office for assistance.

- The Pension Benefit Guaranty Corporation administers insurance programs for eligible terminated plans. If you find out that your plan has been terminated, contact the PBGC at this address: Technical Assistance (45400), Pension Benefit Guaranty Corporation, 1200 K Street NW, Washington, D.C. 20005 (or call 202-326-4000).

Step 8. Once you get the information necessary to determine your status, you have the right to appeal if your claim for benefits is denied or the amount is contested. Your Plan Administrator has to explain in writing why your claim was denied. If you do not agree, you can appeal and be informed of the decision, including the specific reasons for it. You also have the right to bring a lawsuit against your pension plan if your appeal is denied. Finally, you and your beneficiaries are protected from harassment as you appeal. Anyone who interferes with rights under a pension plan or ERISA is subject to up to one year in prison and/or a fine of up to $10,000.

WHAT YOU NEED TO KNOW ABOUT PENSIONS

- Two Basic Kinds of Pension Plans

□ *Defined benefit plans* promise a specified monthly benefit at retirement, either an exact dollar amount or a formula used to calculate the benefit based on such things as salary and service. These are the only benefit plans eligible for Pension Benefit Guaranty Corporation insurance; 40 million workers and retirees in about 85,000 private-sector pension plans are insured this way.

☐ *Defined contribution plans* do not promise a specific amount of benefits at retirement, but employers contribute to employees' pension accounts, and the actual amount of benefits is not predetermined. The benefit depends on the amounts contributed and investment returns. It is usually paid in lump sum and includes such arrangements as 401(k) savings plans, money purchase plans, deferred profit-sharing plans, and target benefit plans. Defined contribution plans are not eligible for Pension Benefit Guaranty Corporation insurance.

If you are unclear about which kind of plan you have, ask your Plan Administrator.

• Basic Pension Plan Provisions

☐ Since 1988 you cannot be excluded for being too old.

☐ You can usually participate if you are at least twenty-one and have one year of service.

☐ A year of service is generally a twelve-month period during which you work at least 1,000 hours, including paid vacation and sick leave.

• Vesting

☐ You become vested when you earn a permanent, legal right to receive all or part of your benefits at retirement age, even if you stop working for the employer.

☐ You are always entitled to receive any funds you contributed to a plan, plus interest, even if you are not vested.

☐ *Cliff vesting* requires that you be fully vested not later than after five years of service in a single-employer plan, after ten years in a multi-employer plan.

☐ *Graded vesting* requires that you must be at least 20 percent vested after three years, that an additional 20 percent must be vested for each of the next four years, and full vesting must occur by not later than the end of seven years.

☐ Since 1989 you must be vested at least as fast as one of these two vesting models provides, and you are automatically vested if you reach retirement age.

☐ *Breaks in service* occur when you work 500 hours or less in a year, and with certain exceptions like military service in war or a national emergency, and certain limitations related to having or adopting a child, they can have adverse effects on your pension benefits. Check with your Plan Administrator.

- Changing Jobs

☐ If you change employers before becoming vested, you will get back any contributions you made, but you will probably not be eligible for retirement benefits.

☐ Since 1989 if you left all your jobs in fewer than five years (or ten years before 1989), you may receive little or no private retirement pension.

☐ Exceptions include plans that continue when you move between employers and your vesting is maintained even when you work shorter periods of time with any one employer. Some trade unions have this benefit in their plans.

☐ Questions to Consider When Changing Jobs
How will your entitlement to an early retirement benefit change if you change plans?
How do the benefit levels and vesting provisions of the two plans compare?
Will the sum of the benefits you ultimately receive from the two plans be equal to what you would receive if you remained in the first plan? (The sum of the two could be less even if the plan provisions are identical.)
If you have the option of a lump-sum cash distribution from your current plan, is it to your advantage to take the funds or leave them in the plan?

- Survivor Benefits

☐ Annuity (monthly payment) pension plans have to provide survivor benefits, although you and your spouse can decline them.

☐ Benefits can be delayed until the date of the vested participant's earliest retirement eligibility.

☐ After retirement, benefits must be at least 50 percent of the benefits the retiree had been receiving and must continue for the life of the survivor.

☐ Exceptions: If you terminated your employment before 1985 (1987 for some collectively bargained plans), your spouse may not be eligible for survivor benefits. Check with your Plan Administrator.

☐ Divorce orders by a court can direct a pension plan to pay a share of your pension directly to your former spouse while you are alive and survivor benefits if you die.

- Payment of Benefits

☐ Most plans pay at normal retirement age of sixty-five; some offer early retirement after a certain number of years' service or at a younger age. Early retirement reduces your monthly benefit: Payments made beginning at age fifty-five are typically less than half of those beginning at age sixty-five.

☐ Lump-sum payments are often an alternative to annuity (periodic) payments. If you leave the company before retirement and are vested, you may be required to take your benefits as a lump sum if they total $3,500 or less. Some plans do not offer the lump-sum option at all; others let you choose regardless of the amount, whether or not you are retirement age. You have to determine the future value of your benefits and any early retirement options before deciding to take a lump-sum settlement.

☐ You can invest lump sums as you like, but they are immediately taxable, and you may have to pay a penalty unless you elect to roll them over into an individual retirement account (IRA) within sixty days. This approach lets you defer paying taxes on the benefits until you begin withdrawing them, which must be no later than in the calendar year following the year you turn seventy and a half. The other option is to use five-year forward income averaging if you are at least fifty-nine and a half years old when you get the lump-sum distribution. Ask your accountant for current and detailed information before electing any of these options.

• If Your Pension Plan Is Terminated

☐ Employers are not required to offer pension plans, and they can replace them with other plans or terminate them.

☐ *Standard termination* refers to a company's electing to pay all the benefits it owes the plan participants and ending the plan. The company has to notify the participants and buy an annuity from an insurance company to pay the promised benefits. Then it is free to use any excess funds as it sees fit; the term for this practice is "reversion."

☐ *Distress termination* occurs when an employer files for bankruptcy, is in such poor financial condition as to be unable to pay its debts, or has a work force decline that makes the costs of continuing pension funding "unreasonably burdensome." In these circumstances the Pension Benefit Guaranty Corporation intervenes, uses what private assets remain to fund the plan's obligations, and pays the rest with pension plan insurance funds.

☐ Notification is required when a plan is terminated. Your Plan Administrator has to notify you in writing at least sixty days before the proposed termination date. In the case of a standard termination, you must get a second notice in plain language that tells you the amount of your benefit, the form in which it has been valued, and the personal data and assumptions used in calculating it. If you receive an annuity rather than a lump-sum payment, be sure you get a certificate from the company issuing the annuity. If the termination was "distress," you will be notified by the PBGC, which becomes the trustee for your plan and oversees its administration.

ADDITIONAL INFORMATION ON PENSION RIGHTS

- *What You Should Know About the Pension Law* is a comprehensive sixty-page booklet; *How to File a Claim for Your Benefits* and *How to Obtain Employee Benefit Documents from the Labor Department* are brief pamphlets on specific topics. These publications are available from the Pension and Welfare Benefits Administration, U.S. Department of Labor, 200 Constitution Avenue NW, Washington, D.C. 20210 (202-219-8776), or the Superintendent of Documents, U.S. Government Printing Office, Washington, D.C. 20402.

- *Your Pension: Things You Should Know About Your Pension Plan* is a twenty-four-page booklet available from the Pension Benefit Guaranty Corporation, 1200 K Street NW, Washington, D.C. 20005 (202-326-4000), or the Superintendent of Documents, U.S. Government Printing Office, Washington, D.C. 20402.

- Publication 575, *Pension and Annuity Income,* is a thirty-two-page booklet that explains the tax ramifications of pension benefits, including lump-sum distributions, rollovers, etc. It is available at your local office of the Internal Revenue Service or by calling 800-829-3676.

Internet Tip

For the latest consumer information on pension plans visit http://www.dol.gov/dol/pwba/public/pension.htm. Should that URL expire, use your search engine and the keywords "Public Welfare and Benefits Administration."

Your Health Benefit Rights

In 1985 Congress passed the Consolidated Omnibus Budget Reconciliation Act, known as COBRA. It provides that terminated employees or those who lose group health coverage because of reduced work hours can buy group coverage for themselves and their families for limited periods of time.

WHAT YOU NEED TO KNOW ABOUT HEALTH BENEFIT RIGHTS

- COBRA covers group health plans of employers with twenty or more employees. It applies to plans in the private sector and to those sponsored by state and local governments.

- If you are entitled to COBRA benefits, your health plan has to notify you of your right to continue your benefits at your own expense. Plan Administrators have fourteen days after receiving notice of a "qualifying event" to notify employees and family members of their election rights. You then have sixty days to accept the coverage or lose all right to benefits. If the employer paid part of the premium while you are employed, COBRA coverage will probably be more expensive.

- Qualifying events for COBRA for employees:
  - □ Voluntary or involuntary termination of employment for reasons other than gross misconduct
  - □ Reduction in the number of hours of employment

- Qualifying events for COBRA for spouses:
  - □ Termination of the covered employee's employment for any reason other than gross misconduct
  - □ Reduction in the hours worked by the covered employee
  - □ Covered employee's becoming entitled to Medicare
  - □ Divorce or legal separation from the covered employee
  - □ Death of the covered employee

- Qualifying events for COBRA for dependent children:
  - □ Termination of the covered employee's employment for any reason other than gross misconduct
  - □ Reduction in the hours worked by the covered employee
  - □ Loss of dependent child status under the plan rules
  - □ Covered employee's becoming entitled to Medicare
  - □ Divorce or legal separation of the covered employee
  - □ Death of the covered employee

- You have rights of appeal if your claim is denied. In most cases you submit your claim in writing to your employer or Plan Administrator. If it is denied, you have to be told why in writing within ninety days and can then appeal in writing within sixty days and receive a decision within sixty days.

- Private-sector employees can get additional information by writing to Division of Technical Assistance and Inquiries, Room N-5658, Pension and Welfare Benefits Administration, U.S. Department of Labor, 200 Constitution Avenue NW, Washington, D.C. 20210. State and local government employees write: Grants Policy Branch (COBRA), Room 17A-45, Office of the Assistant Secretary for Health, U.S. Public Health Service, 5600 Fishers Lane, Rockville, Md. 20857. Federal employees should contact their agency personnel office.

Qualifying Events	Beneficiary	Coverage
Termination or reduced hours	Employee, spouse, or dependent child	18 months
Employee entitled to Medicare; divorce or legal separation; death of covered employee	Spouse or dependent child	36 months
Loss of dependent child status	Dependent child	36 months

ADDITIONAL INFORMATION ON HEALTH BENEFIT RIGHTS

- *Health Benefits Under the Consolidated Omnibus Budget Reconciliation Act (COBRA)* is an eighteen-page booklet available from the Pension and Welfare Benefits Administration, U.S. Department of Labor, 200 Constitution Avenue NW, Washington, D.C. 20210, or call 202-219-8776, or contact the Superintendent of Documents, U.S. Government Printing Office, Washington, D.C. 20402.

Internet Tip

For the latest consumer information on health plans visit http://www.dol.gov/dol/pwba/public/health.htm. Should that URL expire, use your search engine and the keywords "Public Welfare and Benefits Administration."

Note: Chapter 10 is based on information contained in the government publications cited under the Additional Information headings.

11 ACCOMMODATING FORCED CAREER CHANGES

You are doing nothing unusual if you are changing jobs. Americans do it often, according to the Bureau of Labor statistics. Recent figures show most people worked for their current employer for only about four years. At any given time, about one–fourth of wage and salary workers have been with their employers for twelve months or less. ("Job Tenure Summary," http://stats.bls.gov:80/newsrels.htm)

This suggests that several job and career changes may take place during your working life. It would be unusual for you to retire from the job in which you began your career. And while some job changes are voluntary, as workers move from one opportunity to the next, many people are forced to alter their plans. As technology and a changing global economy reshape the workplace, job changes can mean career changes, too, as specialties lose their attractiveness and lifelong career maps become obsolete. Cradle-to-grave jobs are a thing of the past.

You need a new approach to career planning to take advantage of opportunities in the changing workplace and not become its victim. The dangerous approach is to remain passively in your position, waiting to be uprooted in a predictable cycle of change, and relying on chance for your next job. A better alternative is to understand the trend, anticipate change, and prepare to make the most of it.

In this chapter you will learn to deal with jobs that may not last a lifetime. Specifically you will see: (1) how to deal with getting fired—or otherwise unexpectedly terminated, (2) how to plan your working life to avoid surprises, and (3) how to adjust to an irregular career path that includes reversals.

Worst Case: You're Fired

You may feel it coming, or it can be a surprise. You can have your options ready or be in disarray. You can get the news from a compassionate boss, or it can be a nasty experience. Any way you experience it, being fired is traumatic. But like any social ritual, knowing what is coming helps you protect your interests. Here are tips on what to expect and how to react, according to outplacements experts and professionals who deal with terminated employees (Pollan and Levin, 1992):

- If you sense the ax is about to fall, discreetly verify your suspicion with other employees, your supervisor, or someone in personnel. Once you have confirmed the likelihood of your dismissal and made what preparations you can, consider initiating preemptive negotiations that might result in a more generous severance package.

- Before your access is limited, copy things that could be helpful in your severance negotiations and finding another job: your address file, parts of the personnel manual, etc.

- Shore up your personal finances: Pay off bills, don't buy things that can wait, build a cash reserve, refinance your home, or establish a home equity credit line while you still have a job.

- See if you are protected by antidiscrimination laws—Title VII of the Civil Rights Act of 1964 (race, color, sex, religion, national origin) and the Age Discrimination in Employment Act (forty years and older)—and check your state laws. They probably will not stop your dismissal, but they may provide leverage in your negotiations. Consider retaining an employment lawyer.

- At meetings held to discuss your dismissal: (1) be professional but don't be intimidated; (2) take notes in case you have to prove things in the future; (3) convey awareness of your rights and a subtle willingness to act on them if necessary.

- Do not sign a waiver of your rights to future actions against the company until you have a satisfactory settlement signed and in your possession.

- Try to negotiate for more than the company offers: extended lump-sum severance, outplacement assistance, company-paid health insurance, your computer, continued office and clerical support while job hunting, etc.

- Apply immediately for unemployment benefits.

- Evaluate your situation realistically, and start your job search.

Controlling Future Job Changes

Once you are reinstated (or before you face dismissal), understand that you can control your fate in tomorrow's job market. Here are things you should be doing on your own behalf—before a forced change limits your options.

MANAGING YOUR CAREER

You deal with change better when you anticipate it. So use planning to keep unexpected circumstances from disrupting your career. The difference between being awkwardly thrown out of work and making a comfortable transition depends on personal initiative. So prepare for orderly change while you have a job, and make the next move on your terms.

You don't have to relocate every few years to revitalize your career. Change can occur in ways that are to your liking and advantage. That could mean anything from advancing in your present position to starting a business or beginning a new career. These are realistic goals if you appraise your situation objectively and prepare.

Managing your career to accommodate the inevitability of change involves different things in different situations: (1) If you have lost your job, you begin by reentering the world of work—preparing a resume, networking widely, identifying available positions, then polishing your job interview skills (my *Job Interviews That Mean Business* [Random House, 1999] can help). (2) If you are working, look ahead to what you would do if your position were eliminated. Don't become negative about your present job, but start planning for personal growth. Network and take the other necessary initiatives to position yourself well whether you choose to capitalize on an opportunity where you are or move elsewhere.

ADAPTING TO REALITY

Perform a reality check as if you were being forced to change jobs. Verify that you can do what is necessary to succeed in the working environment you've chosen. Are you willing and able to adapt to the demands of organizational life? Your plans should reflect an appreciation of several basic realities:

- There are fewer jobs at each step up the career ladder, and most people will reach their plateau short of the top.

- The good guys or gals don't automatically rise on their merits. The dynamics of success usually include more than competence (add "likability," "organizational fit," and other intangibles).

- Organizational gamesmanship is a necessary part of most careers. A good mentor, for example, speaks well of you behind closed doors and eases your entry into necessary professional relationships.

Decide whether you can correct the problem if you plateaued, failed the likability test, or were an unsuccessful gamesman. If not, consider consulting, a business of your own, or a performance-oriented specialty more immune to organizational pressures. If you are an individualist and choose to make it on the inside, select an organization in which you can partake of the necessary relationship building activities.

An attitude and organization mismatch can spell career disaster. Avoid being "selected out" because you don't fit the group dynamic—a common cause of job loss when critical skills are not at stake. As you choose current employment options or plan future career moves, select a comfortable setting. The way you feel about your working environment, your relationships with your colleagues, and the social and professional dynamics of the organization in which you work can affect your ability to succeed.

PURSUING TRAINING

One sure way to prosper in any employment climate is to have skills employers can't do without. Take additional training, and become an irresistible candidate; you have to stay on top in your field to remain competitive. Look for training opportunities that set you apart. Training is tangible; it can go on a resume and be discussed at a job interview. Earn your basic credentials; then seek out trade and professional opportunities that focus on skills of the future. You gain more than knowledge attending sessions with a leading-edge orientation; you learn new buzzwords and make contacts that open future career doors.

Find training opportunities that are relevant to your job *and* longer-term professional objectives. If your request exceeds what is routinely provided, barter with your company. Explain how what you learn will benefit your employer; then volunteer to pay for the course if the firm will allow you time to attend.

By participating in training sessions, you get an opportunity to meet people and hear of career leads you never would have in the formal job market. So whether you are out of work and looking or are comfortably employed and wise enough to know your circumstances could change, use training to enhance your employability. Earning a college degree, taking the right combination of courses, or attending a workshop to acquire special skills can enhance your value and ease your climb to the top.

NETWORKING

Stay connected to sources of influence and career information in your field. Begin networking in your own organization, and then cultivate contacts at other companies with which you do business or have colleague relationships. Use telephone networking to supplement the face-to-face variety, and establish even more professional linkages that can help your career grow. In the modern business environment there is no need to limit your contacts to people you meet. Executive recruiters, who use personal connections to build careers and make a living, meet only a small percentage of the people with whom they interact.

Being known, liked, and respected in your field is no accident. A few people accomplish it by the sheer weight of their talents and personalities, but most cultivate it. Watch your successful colleagues. The very activities they profess to dread—attending meetings, sitting behind closed doors with the boss, being on selection committees—are the ones they want to be part of because they represent vital connections.

That is how business is done, and you should participate in the process unless you consciously choose to spurn the organization and have the talent to succeed on the outside. Networking and mentoring are important in traditional jobs, and you have to initiate the necessary connections if they don't occur naturally. You can choose whether your network leads upward in your own organization or reaches across to another one, but you must network. Even starting your own business means cultivating contacts; the only difference is that you represent yourself.

So whether you are secure in a career or are on the street looking for a way back in, networking is an essential activity. You choose how and with whom to network, but to be effective, your relationships should be mutually advantageous and genuine.

CONTROLLING YOUR PERSONAL FINANCES

If your personal finances are in poor condition at job-changing time, they can limit your flexibility. The balance between your debts and your savings often determines whether you choose a real opportunity or rush into something less desirable. Personal finances also mirror how you manage your life. Credit checks are common in hiring, and a financial statement is sometimes required—always, if you start a business.

Your personal finances can also affect your confidence and poise. Strained personal finances show when you network with friends, interview for a job, or seek financial backing for a business venture. If you find yourself in financial difficulty, make the best of it, correct the problem, and then give personal finances the importance they deserve in your overall career plan.

Personal financial planners advise you to:

- Have at least six months' worth of bill-paying power in liquid assets to deal with the unexpected.

- Keep your credit obligations to a minimum.

- Build investments that can yield income if necessary—a growth mutual fund that you can convert into an income fund, for example.

You can find books and professional advisers to help you plan a sound personal financial situation. Do what is necessary to make the contingency of disrupted income a part of your lifetime career plan.

Taking One Step Back

In today's job market you cannot count on moving up (or even sideways) after losing a middle-management position. U.S. Department of Labor projections call for growth in management jobs, but you still might be affected by structural changes in the economy that ended the careers of many mid-level workers in the early 90s.

In the unusually strong economy of the late 1990s, it is not surprising that jobs are plentiful. Recruiters report energetic hiring to staff up new industries and to make up for heavy downsizing that took place earlier, according to the *National Business Employment Weekly* (Rurak, 1997).

The August, 1998, Bureau of Labor Statistics "Displaced Workers Summary" reported that fewer workers lost their jobs and more regained equivalent employment than earlier in the decade. More than one-half the workers' new jobs paid as much or more than their old ones, although one-fourth of them experienced earnings losses of twenty percent or more.

If you find yourself repositioning in the job market as the new millennium dawns, here is the environment you can expect:

- Skilled managers are in demand, but companies "are decidedly tougher about whom they'll hire these days." (Capell)

- While demand is high across most industries, the hottest ones include information technology, telecommunications, the Internet, and professional services like consulting firms dealing with utility deregulation, health-care, technological change, downsizing, re-engineering, and mergers. (Fox in Capell)

- The "perfect" candidate is the one "having similar industry or functional experience . . . someone who has been there and done that, rather than someone who will grow into it." (Allerton in Capell).

- Communication skills are essential, and some finalists are eliminated after performing poorly when asked to "briefly explain in writing how they might handle a problem." (Herndon in Capell)

- Managers are needed who can lead teams and oversee business operations. It is not good enough merely to have specialized skills or be a "supervisor"—the manager is expected to participate in the work of the group. (Rurak)

- Promotable management layers were cut severely so companies are looking outside to fill "gaps in the stream of talent" needed to oversee such new functions as outsourcing. (Rurak)

- Employed candidates can expect to receive significant increases; unemployed candidates can expect companies to match their most recent pay packages. (Hetzel in Capell)

In a climate like this many transitioning managers have excellent prospects; however, if you do not meet the high demand profile you may have to adjust your attitude and expectations to realistic levels and be ready for the questions of employers who may view you as overqualified for a one-step-back position. It is critical that you make three points:

- You really do want the job in spite of the fact that it appears to be a step backward on your career ladder.

- You can live with a fair compensation package for the position being offered and recognize the potential differential with what you had been making.

- You expect to prove yourself just like everyone else, and you won't be coming in wearing vestiges of your former "rank" on your sleeve.

When you exhaust your possibilities for a parallel or better move, you face reality, get back on the career ladder, and start moving up again. You will discover additional strategies for finding a first-step-back position in "Applying for a Less Prestigious Position" in the "Special Situations" chapter of my *Job Interviews That Mean Business, Third Edition* (Random House, 1999).

If you have prepared for the challenge, you face opportunities for renewal and growth that might never have been yours in a cradle-to-grave job. Your success depends on your being able to consider options ranging from an entrepreneurial solution to taking one step back to make future steps forward. When your employment situation stabilizes, be sure to use the five keys to having the luxury of choice in the future: (1) manage your career, (2) adapt to reality, (3) pursue training, (4) network, and (5) control your personal finances.

BIBLIOGRAPHY

Bolles, Richard N. *What Color Is Your Parachute?* Berkeley: Ten Speed Press, 1998.

Capell, Perri. "Demand Runs High For Senior Managers." Dow Jones: National Business Employment Weekly (October 11, 1997).

Carey, John. "The Changing Face of a Restless Nation." *Business Week,* Number 3125, 92–106 (September 25, 1989).

Davis, Richard S. "Have You Tried a Notice of Availability?" *Adult and Continuing Education,* XIX (17), 7 (September 11, 1989).

Eyler, David R. *Job Interviews That Mean Business.* New York: Random House, 1999.

Health Benefits Under the Consolidated Omnibus Budget Reconciliation Act. Washington: Pension and Welfare Benefits Administration, U.S. Department of Labor, 1990.

How to File a Claim for Your Benefits. Washington: Pension and Welfare Benefits Administration, U.S. Department of Labor, 1991.

How to Obtain Employee Benefit Documents from the Labor Department. Washington: Pension and Welfare Benefits Administration, U.S. Department of Labor, February 1990.

Occupational Outlook Quarterly. Washington: Bureau of Labor Statistics, U.S. Department of Labor, 17, Winter 1997–1998.

Pension and Annuity Income, Publication 575. Washington: Internal Revenue Service, 1991.

Pollan, Stephen M., and Mark Levin. "How to Survive Getting Fired." *New York,* 26–35 (September 7, 1992).

Richardson, Douglas B. "The Confessions of a Skeptical Resume Reader: What Happens When Your Resume Is 1 of 400." Dow Jones: *National Business Employment Weekly* reprint (undated).

Rottman, David. "How to Get Interviews Using Market Letters: A New, More Efficient Approach to Reaching Decision-Makers." Dow Jones: *National Business Employment Weekly* reprint (undated).

Rurak, Maura. "Need for Middle Managers is Growing, Recruiters Say." Dow Jones: National Business Employment Weekly (October 11, 1997).

Ryckman, W. G. "Seasoned Executives Emphasize Accomplishments: Alter Format of Resumes, Cover Letters." Dow Jones: *National Business Employment Weekly* reprint (undated).

Snelling, Robert O., and Anne M. Snelling. *Jobs! What They Are . . . Where They Are . . . What They Pay! The Seven Top Entry-Level Job Areas.* New York: Fireside/Simon & Schuster, 1989.

Washington, Tom. "Creating a Resume with Qualifications: Add Summary Statement for Emphasis." Dow Jones: *National Business Employment Weekly* reprint (undated).

What You Should Know About the Pension Law. Washington: Pension and Welfare Benefits Administration, U.S. Department of Labor, May 1988.

"Worker Displacement, 1995–97." *Displaced Workers Summary.* Washington: Bureau of Labor Statistics, U.S. Department of Labor, August 19, 1998.

Your Pension: Things You Should Know About Your Pension Plan. Washington: Pension Benefit Guaranty Corporation, undated.

INDEX

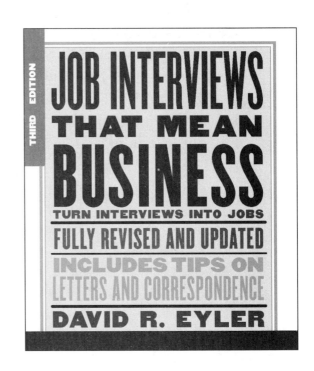